Studying Oscar Wilde: History, Criticism, and Myth

JOSEPHINE GUY & IAN SMALL

| ELT Press |
UNIVERSITY OF NORTH CAROLINA AT GREENSBORO

ELT Press English Department PO Box 26170
University of North Carolina   Greensboro, NC   27402–6170
e–mail: langenfeld@uncg.edu

NUMBER TWENTY–TWO : 1880–1920 BRITISH AUTHORS SERIES

ISBN 0–944318–22–3

Library of Congress Control Number: 2005938754

Front & Back Covers   *Oscar Wilde*

W. & D. Downey, London (1889)

TYPOGRAPHY & DESIGN

Display Type: Trump Medieval
Text Type: Bembo Standard & Optima

COVER & TEXT

Designed by Robert Langenfeld

Printer: Thomson–Shore, Inc.   Dexter, Michigan

CONTENTS

Prefatory Note   vi–viii

| I | Studying Wilde: Academic Scholarship
and the "General Reader"   1–12

| II | Lives of Wilde: Facts and Fictions   13–46

| III | *De Profundis*: Tragedy and the Art
of Self-Fashioning   47–76

| IV | *Intentions*: A Serious Writer for Trivial Readers;
Or, A Trivial Writer for Serious Readers?   77–113

| V | The Plays: The Public and Private Worlds
of Oscar Wilde   114–163

| VI | *Dorian Gray* and the Short Fiction: Choosing Between
"Sinburnianism" and Pleasing the British Public 164–195

Appendix: Wilde's Unfinished Plays and Scenarios   196–226

Index   227–232

Academic books on Wilde usually come in three forms. There is the academic bibliography, a work designed purely as a research tool for the academic community: bibliographies might tell us, for example, about the location of manuscript material. Such tools are essential for the scholar, but of little use for the general reader. Second, there is the traditional monograph, which is usually (although not always) based on new research, either the kind which displays new information about the work or the life, or which makes new interpretations of existing material. These works typically follow rigorously—or should do—an argument. Equally typically, that argument will be set out in relation to other scholarship or other interpretations—in relation to what, in academic jargon, is called the "field." It is usual for monographs to come laden with foot- or endnotes as their authors feel obliged to substantiate every critical assertion they make. Once again, however, for the general reader, a traditional scholarly apparatus can be just clutter. Equally off-putting can be the constant reference to other scholars' work, information which often seems an impenetrable mass; the language of some monographs, too, can be jargon-ridden and often seems specifically designed to exclude nonspecialists.

And then there are introductory or student books; these come in a number of forms. Some are simply anthologies of scholarly essays which give the reader a sample of current research. Others are designed to explain the career and *oeuvre* of Wilde; these may also include a general overview of critical readings or indicate current research trends. Their limitation, though, is that most of the information contained within them is secondhand, and few out of the critical books designed for students aim to develop original arguments. Others seek to explicate texts—to give readings of particular works. Very few student books actually give the reader a feel of how the researcher works and the kinds of materials he or she has to use.

The present book fits none of these categories very easily, but it tries to combine aspects of all of them, with the aim of providing an accessible but research-based study. One of the challenges facing academic critics is to persuade readers that what they do is relevant to a wide audience. In trying to face up to this challenge this book does not provide a survey or map of past and current research on Wilde; nor does it summarize or evaluate what the totality of academic research has had to say about any particular work by him. Both these tasks have already been undertaken in a number of specialist bibliographical studies, including two earlier ELT publications by Ian Small, *Oscar Wilde Revalued* (1993) and *Oscar Wilde: Recent Research* (2000). Rather, we are interested in providing readers with snapshots of how specific *kinds* of academic research—particularly those relating to information which they will not normally possess or have access to, such as details about how Wilde wrote or how he used his sources—can be brought to bear on their own reading experience.

Several decades ago some critics lamented how the popularity of Jane Austen's handful of novels had persuaded many readers that they "knew" her, her world, its values and its prejudices. As a consequence Jane Austen became a familiar figure in the lives of many readers. The whole cultural phenomenon acquired the label of "Janeism." Wilde has never made for such a comfortable companion, but nonetheless, as his biography has become increasingly well known, so a comparable phenomenon of "Oscarism" seems to be imminent. Oscar Wilde has become the "Oscar" of popular mythology, and our hope is that we allow some readers to see beyond this mythological icon. We are especially concerned with research which challenges or controverts the appealing but oversimplistic assumption that Wilde's writings, as one of his most recent biographers, Neil McKenna, put it, are "highly autobiographical, reflecting and revealing ... his secret life." By contrast it is the secrets of Wilde's texts, rather than those of his life, with which this book is concerned; and our main argument is that unlocking those textual secrets—understanding how and why his literary works were written—requires us to pay attention to elements in them above and beyond their biographical importance.

In order to make the research in this book accessible, we have kept referencing to a minimum. Uncontested facts and statements that are commonly repeated in any number of critical or biographical works have not been sourced. However, lists of works consulted, including those from which we quote, are given at the end of each chapter, thus enabling the interested reader to pursue the ideas rehearsed in individual chapters in more detail. In addition the reader will find distributed throughout the body of the main text a series of "capsules." These "capsules" contain discrete items of information, indicated by a brief title in a bold typeface, which are linked to the main narrative below which they appear, but which are also designed to be read independently. They cover a wide range of issues ranging from details about Wilde's habits of composition to often-asked questions of biography such as, why was Lord Alfred Douglas never tried for gross indecency or, did Wilde die from syphilis?

It will be obvious in the chapters which follow that we are not attempting a comprehensive re-reading of Wilde's *oeuvre*: we have, for example, little to say about either his poetry or his anonymous journalism, even though both forms of writing comprised a significant proportion of his creative output and occupied a great deal of his life in the late 1870s and 1880s. Nor, with the partial exception of some of Wilde's unfinished and little-known works, do we offer systematic readings of individual texts. Our concern with the relationship between popular and academic readings of Wilde's *oeuvre* has dictated that we focus our attention on the most widely read of his works, and these are, obviously, *De Profundis*, *Intentions*, the society comedies and *Dorian Gray*. Where we do examine less-well-known pieces, such as the unfinished plays and scenarios, or the fairy tales in *A House of Pomegranates*, it is largely with a view to expanding the general reader's sense of Wilde's creative interests, and this in turn, we hope, will help to illuminate those works which are most familiar.

| I | Studying Wilde:
Academic Scholarship
and the "General Reader"

IN THE LATE 1980s and 1990s the future of literary studies as a discipline of knowledge within universities was being assiduously debated by academics on both sides of the Atlantic. The issues involved in that debate were complex, but one salient topic concerned the relationship of literary studies to cultural studies, and thus the relationship of literary judgments to political and ideological issues. This in turn brought to light a further set of questions about what came to be known as the role of value within the academic study of literature and whether or not it was the responsibility of academics to identify a hierarchy of values by reference to which some literary works could be judged to be better than others—however the concept of "better" was to be defined. And lastly—and for our present purposes most importantly—there was a discussion of the relationship between the specialist knowledge produced by the academic study of literature and the "uses" which such academic knowledge had for the "general reader"; or, in the jargon of the discipline, the relationship between academic specialization and social utility.

The paradox at the heart of English or literary studies concerns this claim to social relevance. Do academic literary studies address "big" questions in a way that most individuals can understand? Any claim that they do so constantly runs the risk of being undermined by the increasing specialization of research taking place within an academic discipline. The British intellectual historian, Stefan Collini, usefully isolated this dilemma when he characterized the formal study of literature as possessing an inevitable Janus-like quality. The study, he suggested, exists in a "tension between, on the one hand, being simply one specialized activity alongside other specialisms ... and ... still carrying the burden of being a kind of residual cultural space within which general existential and ethical questions can be addressed."[1] Recent academic research into Oscar Wilde might stand as a textbook illustration of this tension: Wilde's literary works continue to live in the public imagination partly because they are so entertain-

1

ing and partly because they have become a focus for a widespread, lively, and easily accessible debate about gender, ethics, nationality, and politics. Yet at the same time those literary works have attracted an enormous body of specialist scholarship. In an ideal world, we could confidently anticipate a fruitful encounter between specialized academic knowledge and a writer's popular reputation: one would naturally feed into the other. Yet it is a moot point whether academic enquiry has had any sustained effect on Wilde's popular reputation, or on the ways in which his works are typically read, or—in the case of performances of his plays—seen.

Our own contribution to the debate about literary value and the status of the discipline was made in the early 1990s. It was to argue quite forcefully for the need for the discipline of literary studies to maintain its status: that is, not to allow itself to be collapsed into a minority concern of politics or sociology or philosophy, areas to which its function as Collini's "cultural space" for "general existential and ethical questions" so often seemed to propel it. Our suggestion was that the way for literature departments to achieve this end was to concentrate on defining what is unique to literary knowledge. That is, to identify the particular character and value that political or philosophical questions achieve by being posed in or articulated via literary works. Since that time we have, individually and collaboratively, been involved in detailed studies of Wilde's writing, using exactly the sorts of archival source materials—manuscripts, letters, book contracts, and so on—which are not easily available to the general reader. In so doing, however, we have become increasingly aware of a growing gap between the ways in which we, as academics, are attempting to understand Wilde and his reputation among general readers.

The size of this gap was demonstrated by the publication in 2003 of Neil McKenna's sensationalizing *The Secret Life of Oscar Wilde*, a work which, in its use of evidence, in its methodology, and in its basic assumptions about the relationship between authorship and literary expressivity, flew in the face of most academic opinion, but which nevertheless enjoyed a high profile because of its appeal to an enduring public interest in Wilde's sexual life. A dilemma which a decade earlier we had discussed in abstract terms had now taken on a painfully concrete form. The question which the reception of McKenna's book forced upon academic critics was, to whom is their specialized knowledge addressed? More pointedly, to whose reading of Wilde will it make any difference? And more pointedly still, what is the relationship between specialized academic knowledge of Wilde and his works and his reputation among the general reading public? The present book is an attempt to confront these uncomfortable questions, and to investigate in a practical way whether and how the demands of the academic community can be made more relevant to the interests of the general reader.

The Popularity of Wilde

As we have hinted, over a century after his death, the writings of Wilde are among the most popular of any British, Irish, or American author; this is certainly the case if we measure popularity in terms of recognition, quotability, and sales. All of Wilde's main (that is, his completed) works are still in print and continue to sell well; his four society comedies are regularly staged and have been adapted several times for film and television. His aphorisms, correctly or incorrectly attributed, are so frequently quoted that many (such as "to fall in love with oneself is the beginning of a lifelong romance" or "I have nothing to declare but my genius") have become part of a common language. Those enthusiastic amateur reviews of Wilde's works that Amazon.com frequently posts on its website touchingly, if perhaps naively, testify to his permanent appeal. Moreover, in crude terms, his financial stock, at least if it can be measured in terms of auction prices, has never been higher. For example, a work of negligible literary importance, a first edition of *Oscariana* (a collection of epigrams edited by Wilde's wife Constance in 1895), was recently valued by Sotheby's at £2,000–£3,000, while a single autograph sheet of six epigrams was valued between £6,000–£12,000. Even such ephemera as an (admittedly rare) copy of the sixteen-page Tite Street sale catalogue, a document of virtually no literary significance, was priced at £30,000–£40,000; and a faded print of Maurice Gilbert's photograph of Wilde on his deathbed in Paris in 1900 was offered at £7,000–£10,000.[2]

These prices certainly point to a continued public interest in Wilde, much of which centres on his personal life, even if an obsession with the life does not on its own account for the increasing regard for his literary output. One thing, however, is certain: members of the academic community—critics, editors, biographers, and bibliographers—have often claimed some agency in bringing about the change in Wilde's reputation, at least in part. Commentators invariably point to the availability of new research tools—for example, to Rupert Hart-Davis's 1962 edition of the *Letters*, to Richard Ellmann's 1987 biography, and to scholarly editions of Wilde's works (such as the New Mermaid editions of the society comedies produced in the early 1980s). It has been argued that, taken collectively, these provided the means to revalue Wilde's literary and cultural significance, and thus to rehabilitate him with the general reading public. However, as we hinted earlier, it is questionable whether academic interest in Wilde has been setting a fashion, or merely and perhaps slavishly following it. The relationship between the Wilde of popular myth—the homosexual martyr who wasted his life through a reckless love affair—and the politicized subject of so many academic studies might suggest, to the cynical mind, that the contribution of scholarship to Wilde's modern reputation is neither as original nor as influential as its advocates have claimed. By the same token, critical works which have diverged from these general academic trends by, say, documenting both a less glamorous career and the derivative qualities of the literary works have gone relatively unread, their influence often restricted to graduate essays and academic conferences; and even there the unpopularity of the image of Wilde they tend to exhibit has led them to be overlooked.

Of course, and as we noted above, there is nothing novel about pointing to the gap between academic research and the sorts of material of interest to the general reading public: over the past decade or so the increasing irrelevance of academic criticism to what nineteenth-century commentators used to call the "home reader," or to what Virginia Woolf rather later called the "common reader," has been frequently observed. The pressures of specialization have led to much modern academic literary writing becoming so complex and arcane, or so freighted with esoteric information, that it can only be understood by a few. Moreover, as the sales of academic publications continue to decline, so a number of well-known critics seek more popular outlets for their work, preferring newspapers and magazines, radio and television, to the traditional academic medium of the refereed journal or the monograph. Such distinguished scholars and critics of nineteenth-century literary history as David Lodge and John Sutherland prefer to write for "serious" British national newspapers like the *Independent*, the *Guardian*, and the *London Review of Books* than for academic journals. Ironically enough, the beginnings of this fundamental division between the professional critic and the general reader had been observed even when Wilde was alive, and when academic literary criticism had barely been established. As the novelist and man of letters Grant Allen observed as early as 1882: "there are … critics—ay, and good ones, too. But they cannot stem the tide of public taste: they find themselves slowly stranded and isolated on their own little critical islets. Their authority is only recognised within a small sphere of picked intellects, and does not affect the general current of the popular mind."[3] The uncomfortable truth of that observation is neatly substantiated by a confident observation made in 1900 by one of those "picked intellects," that "nothing that [Wilde] ever wrote had strength to endure"—a literary judgment which must count as one of the least accurate ever made.[4]

We ought to note that recent academic responses to Wilde's literary reputation have taken place in the context of a number of larger processes at work in academic culture in the twentieth century. The first was the propagandizing of the often difficult works of Anglo-American literary modernists, of grandees such as Ezra Pound, T. S. Eliot, and James Joyce. This occurred principally (and certainly initially) in higher education institutions and publishing houses within the United States. It was part of an attempt to mark out a role for professional criticism, particularly as a special kind of reading practice which, in the words of F. O. Matthiessen in a 1949 lecture entitled "The Responsibilities of the Critic," "aimed to give the closest possible attention to the text at hand, to both the structure and texture of the language."[5] In other words, there was a mutually reinforcing relationship between the celebration of technically or formally difficult texts and the promotion of a critical practice that required specialist reading techniques; the effect of that special relationship banished the "common reader." In such a climate a writer like Wilde seemed just too easy or too straightforward to require professional explication: his language did not apparently possess the levels of complexity and ambiguity that would repay "close reading." Nor did the repetitions, plagiarisms, and "loose" structure of many of his works answer to the definition of the literary text as "iconic" or "an example of ... complexity and individuality."[6] As importantly, the extremely close identification of Wilde's life with his work—then, as now, it was virtually impossible to "see" the text without first seeing the man standing in front of it—violated a basic modernist presumption of the autonomy of the text, of what T. S. Eliot had termed that quality of "depersonalisation" by which "art may be said to approach the condition of science,"[7] a concern which was translated by New Critics into a focus on the text as a purely linguistic object.

A second process, which was in part a reaction against the perceived exclusivity of the first, was most strongly felt in the United Kingdom, particularly (and ironically, as far as the present writers are concerned) in the universities of the English midlands. It centred on the new discipline of cultural studies which had developed out of strong traditions of working-class English Marxist and socialist thinking, reinforced by the socially engaged criticism of writers such as George Orwell. This was combined with the personal experiences of cultural studies' founding fathers, in particular Raymond Williams and Richard Hoggart. Predicated on a reassessment and a legitimization of the various forms of popular culture, cultural studies as a discipline emerged as a dynamic alternative to traditionally defined literary studies, whether that practised by the New Critics or that to be seen in F. R. Leavis's famous definition of literary value as a celebration of "life." Its initial impact on nineteenth-century scholarship was to shift critical attention away from works that were marked off by their textual difficulty to more popular and entertaining writers and to popular art forms, such as (in the nineteenth century) the music hall, the sensation novel, and detective fiction. Moreover, judgments about the literary or aesthetic value of such works tended to be set aside in favour of an emphasis on what might be termed sociological questions, such as a work's role in representing the values of hitherto marginalized or excluded communities (for example, the urban working classes or middle-class women). Ironically, although Wilde's works were certainly held to be entertaining, and although many used popular literary forms, the concern that most had in representing the upper strata of British society, and Wilde's frequently expressed disdain for "public opinion" and "lower-class" life, did not easily fit these political priorities. Put simply, the new discipline of cultural studies had virtually nothing to say about Wilde, and Wilde the writer continued to be a relatively marginal figure among academics.

As cultural criticism developed some more sophisticated methods of analysis (in large part through the influence of French critical theory and its renewed focus on textuality), academic reassessments of popular culture took a slightly different direction. Noting that contemporary reviewers had often disparaged popular cultural forms for a lack of sophistication, modern critics began to hypothesize "subtextual" or "against-the-grain" readings which apparently revealed layers of complexity that were analogous in value to the erudition or formal experimentation and complexity of "higher" literary culture, or the elitist works associated with early modernism. Here finally, then, was a critical practice which seemed entirely adequate to the challenge of revaluing Wilde as a writer. As a consequence, any number of "new" issues were found in his *oeuvre*, and works once dismissed as trivial or dilettante were revalued as subversive, as attacks on bourgeois culture or as anticipations of postmodernist views about linguistic instability. So, to use an obvious and possibly tired example, critics "rediscovered" the value of *The Importance of Being Earnest* not because it was (and remains) one of the wittiest plays in the language, but because careful analysis could reveal a complexly coded critique of late-Victorian sexual mores: or, as Christopher Craft put it, "in the revolving door of Wildean desire, the counters of comedic representation are disclosed as formal ciphers, the arbitrarily empowered terms whose distribution schedules and enforces heterosexual diegesis."[8] Of course nothing could be further from how most Amazon.com correspondents experience Wilde's work, and it is hard to think of very many readers (modern or late-nineteenth-century) who would be fully attuned to the allegedly "seven" gay meanings that Craft gives to the name Bunbury. It is thus somewhat ironic that the price of universities' belated embrace of Wilde's literary talents was to estrange the figure whom they wished to celebrate almost completely from the common reader.

As we have already observed, this tension over what might loosely be termed "scholarly" and "general" opinions of Wilde has never been properly resolved. In fact it has become only more stark with the continuing brilliance of Wilde's reputation outside universities, testimony to which can be found in the proliferation of nonacademic critical writing on him. It can be quite plausibly argued that works by figures such as Peter Ackroyd, Neil McKenna, Neil Bartlett, Colm Tóibín, or by Wilde's grandson, Merlin Holland, have exercised more influence over the general reader than anything written in an academic monograph. Matters are not helped by the fact that the terms in which academics typically debate Wilde's literary reputation are hardly designed to attract the nonspecialist. They tend to centre on a dull pedantry over whether Wilde did or did not plagiarize the work of some long-forgotten late-nineteenth-century dramatist, or on the obfuscations of overdetermined theories of sexuality and textuality. Persuading the general reader, as well as the average student reader, that scholarship has something positive to contribute to their experience of a group of works which, on the surface, are not very obviously "difficult" or complex—compared to, say, those of contemporaries such as Walter Pater, Henry James, or Joseph Conrad—is an important task. It forms the central ambition of this book.

Our second and related ambition is to establish a clearer distinction between the enduring "personality" of Wilde through which, as we mentioned above, most readers encounter his works, and the literary merits of those works themselves. The theoretical insistence by New Criticism, and then by structuralism and deconstruction, on viewing texts simply as linguistic artifacts has almost no relevance to how the average reader experiences a work—certainly a work by Wilde which invariably comes to them already labelled and contextualized by a particular knowledge of his life. Who today can read *The Picture of Dorian Gray* without calling to mind the iconic photographs of Wilde and his own "dear boy," Lord Alfred Douglas, an identification which Wilde himself rather confusingly pointed to in *De Profundis* (even though he had almost certainly not begun his relationship with Douglas when he wrote that novel)? Often it is the notoriety of Wilde's life that attracts readers to the works in the first place. A first step, then, in bringing academic and popular opinion together has to be an acknowledgment of the existence and irresistibility of this biography which (oddly enough) turns out to hang ominously even over the critic concerned only with purely textual matters.

When he shaped his own career, as he tried assiduously to do throughout his life, Wilde actively promoted an identification of himself—or, more accurately, of an image he projected of himself—with his work. At first these images included the languid aesthete and then the dandy, both of whom could neglect or affront the niceties of British social mores. They were followed within months with an image of the sophisticated man of letters, of what in *De Profundis* once again Wilde called the "supreme arbiter of taste," and then that of the urbane socialite and man of the theatre, the toast, for two or three years at least, of London's fashionable West End. Although this self-promotion was initially a highly successful strategy, one which earned Wilde considerable publicity, its limitations were dramatically exposed during his trials in 1895 and his subsequent conviction for gross indecency. Wilde's literary works continued to be interpreted biographically, but via an image over which he had now completely lost control. Post-prison works, such as *The Ballad of Reading Gaol* and *De Profundis*, can be seen as his (or both his and Robert Ross's) attempts to recover some agency in that process of fashioning, to re-present his criminal personality as that of a tragic victim, whether of a vindictive British establishment or of an all-consuming passion for his apparently undeserving lover, Alfred Douglas. And it is the enduring quality of these latter images that has probably been the single most important factor in shaping Wilde's reputation through the late decades of the twentieth century and into the twenty-first. With the exception of Neil McKenna's recent work, which we have already mentioned and to which we shall return in later chapters, modern biographies have done relatively little to challenge these images: indeed popular films like Brian Gilbert's *Wilde* only reinforced them.

It would be foolhardy for the writers of any study to claim to be able to present the "real" man behind the myth of Wilde; but such a concession does not prevent one from drawing attention to the kind of biographical information that disturbs or problematizes that myth, and then showing how it can generate rather different readings of his literary output. To put this simply: the present book does not attempt to offer a new biography of Wilde; nor—as some critics might phrase it—does it aim to "re-try" him, or to deconstruct Wilde the cultural icon. Our initial focus is narrower and more modest: we are interested in exposing the extent to which myths about Wilde, particularly about his life, have shaped literary judgments, and then in establishing some grounds upon which biographically informed criticism might proceed. And those grounds, in turn, involve getting certain "facts" right and being rigorous about criteria of "relevance"—that is, about determining which sorts of facts about the life can be used to explain which sorts of literary qualities, and also how those facts can be used in the service of literary and aesthetic judgments. Contrary to expectations, we shall argue that those works that seem at face value most amenable to biographical readings, because they seem closest to the details of Wilde's life, often turn out to be most resistant to them, in the sense that the personal allusions which can be detected in them do not generate coherent or consistent interpretations of the works as a whole. Seeing Wilde's *oeuvre* as partly autobiographical, as a working out of some private preoccupation with his sexual identity, does not, we will suggest, do him any great service as a writer—nor, oddly, does it bring us much closer to understanding his complex personality.

Studying Oscar Wilde

In the next chapter we show how biographically motivated readings of Wilde's works have produced a body of assumptions about his literary talents which are so widespread that they have now virtually fossilized into "facts" about him. We then investigate the status of some of these "facts" by examining critically the accounts of Wilde's life that underpin them. Again our aim here will not be to provide an alternative biography of Wilde; instead we will be concerned with establishing the limits of biographical interpretation *per se,* by drawing attention to the insecurity of much of our knowledge of Wilde's life (particularly his sexual life) and to the general methodological difficulties involved in using the work as evidence for the "real" man. In subsequent chapters, we look more closely at how particular Wildean myths have evolved and the impact which they have had on our understanding of specific works. In chapter three we concentrate on that text which seems the most authentically autobiographical, which has consequently had the greatest impact on how Wilde's life and career have been conceived, and which also represents the most insistent blurring of the boundary between biography and criticism—namely, *De Profundis*. That document is surrounded by intriguing stories and legends and is known more by repute than in detail. Our exploration of its role in authorizing the most potent of modern biographical myths, that of the "tragic" Wilde, will thus centre on bringing to the reader's attention what might seem to be some rather complex and esoteric information about the way in which it was composed. We shall then try to show how those dry-as-dust scholarly facts can change our sense of the document's identity, and we shall explain the implications of that transformation for the ways we interpret and value it, and thus for its "use" in understanding Wilde's life. The chapter will close by setting out new grounds for a literary (as opposed to a biographical) appreciation of *De Profundis*, one which pays full attention to its artifactual nature, and which attempts to come to terms with qualities that have often been overlooked, such as its repetitions, inconsistencies in its argument, its uneven tone, and its loose, rambling structure.

Chapter four contests different elements of myths about Wilde: the idea of him as a "genius," an effortlessly engaging and erudite thinker, whose philosophizing places him (according to some modern critics) in a (basically German) tradition stretching from Immanuel Kant and Friedrich Schiller to Friedrich Nietzsche, and then to Walter Benjamin and Theodor Adorno. Unlike the popular "tragic Wilde," Wilde "the intellectual," as we might call him, is very much a creation of modern academics, one which derives mainly (though not exclusively) from that area of his life and that part of his *oeuvre* which are least well known to the general reader—that is, his undergraduate education in classics at Trinity College, Dublin and at Magdalen College, Oxford and his subsequent use of that education in his critical writing, particularly in the essays published in *Intentions*. Wilde's contemporaries, though acknowledging a certain showy cleverness in that volume, nevertheless tended to dismiss it as superficial or derivative. Such a judgment is clearly at odds with the originality and complexity that some modern scholars allege they find there. How do we explain this discrepancy? Is it inevitable that academic revaluations of Wilde's criticism, which typically draw attention to the depth and sophistication of his learning, will make it inaccessible to most general readers?

Chapter three tries to show the consequences of a lack of scholarship—that is, how errors or lacunae in readers' understanding of the composition of *De Profundis* can lead them to misidentify it. Chapter four, by contrast, draws attention to problems associated with what might be termed an excess of scholarly investigation. It examines the way in which an overzealous interpretation of Wilde's sources—an attempt to synthesize his diverse references into a coherent "philosophy"—can make him into a overly "difficult" writer. Our own analysis, by contrast, aims to restore to the general reader some feeling for the light-hearted wittiness of Wilde's critical prose by showing that his knowledge is not nearly as deep as has often been assumed, and that the ways in which it is displayed—in particular his use of citation, quotation, and allusion—are designed to prevent us from taking any of it too seriously. In short we shall try to demonstrate how scholarship, when appropriately deployed, can reveal Wilde's qualities as an entertainer, and can explain, too, why it was that his contemporaries were so much less impressed by his erudition than modern commentators tend to be.

Chapter five concentrates on what are Wilde's most popular and enduring works—the society comedies. These are also the works that seem to require the least elucidation by the academic community. Yet they have probably generated more scholarship than the rest of the *oeuvre* put together: in a sense, one might detect here a struggle for ownership, as academics vie with each other (and with the general reader) to find ever more esoteric layers of meaning in what are very accessible works. In this chapter, then, we begin by differentiating three distinct sorts of reference (or specialist knowledge) to which scholars have drawn attention in their attempts to explain the plays: the literary (that is, the specific literary traditions, such as the French "well-made play," upon which Wilde's dramas draw); the biographical (those "subtextual" allusions to Wilde's own sexual life); and the social or topical (that is, the plays' dependence on the intricate values and mores of late-Victorian etiquette). We then give some concrete examples of how such knowledge can be deployed to interpret the plays, and we pay particular attention to the ways in which these different layers of reference interact with each other. We will argue that what may seem to be the most relevant sort of knowledge to the general reader—the biographical—turns out to be the least useful, insofar as the occasional allusions to Wilde's personal life cannot be used for a coherent or consistent reading of any play as a whole. Moreover, and somewhat surprisingly, pursuing the plays' "gay" subtexts can actually make them seem more (rather than less) conventional to the extent that they can be seen as exhibiting elements of Victorian homophobia.

The same chapter—chapter five—also pays attention to a group of works often overlooked in studies of Wilde's career as a dramatist—his unfinished plays and scenarios, particularly *La Sainte Courtisane*, *The Cardinal of Avignon*, and *A Florentine Tragedy* (all of which are printed in the appendix). Like *Salome*, these three works have historical or biblical settings, and contain no topical references. They thus seem very far removed from the details of Wilde's own life. Yet we argue that it is these works, rather than the society comedies, which most reward biographically inflected readings, for it is in them that we see Wilde at his most "raw" and personal, using the drama to explore emotions that are closest to his own experiences. We suggest that the conflicts dramatized in *La Sainte Courtisane*, *The Cardinal of Avignon*, and *A Florentine Tragedy* make most sense in terms of Wilde playing out the anxieties which were produced by his own relationship with Douglas, a detail which in turn may explain why none was ever finished.

In chapter six we turn to Wilde's fiction and attempt to explain the reasons behind the popularity of *Dorian Gray*, particularly the conundrum of how the selfsame work could be viewed both as a straightforward morality tale and—as Edward Carson bluntly put it in the first (Queensberry's libel) trial—a "book putting forth sodomitical views." Today, with the hindsight of the trials, we are so habituated to reading Wilde's novel biographically that we can easily overlook its complexity and subtlety—that is, the nature of those stylistic clues that take us back to the biography in the first instance. We argue that *Dorian Gray* derives its suggestive power not from its expressive transparency, as writers such as Neil McKenna have tended to assume, but rather the opposite, from a highly contrived literary style which works by ellipsis and allusion, and which demands of its readers a fairly sophisticated literary education in order that they recognize and follow the chains of association which those allusions gesture towards. We shall then try to explain the mechanisms of this style by examining *Dorian Gray*, not as most critics and readers do, in relation to Wilde's other triumphs in the 1890s, such as the society comedies, but rather in relation to an earlier and often overlooked group of works, those short stories (mainly fairy tales) which he wrote in the late 1880s. We show how, in what may seem rather simple and straightforward tales such as "The Happy Prince" and "The Young King," Wilde developed the techniques which he would later use with such success in his novel.

Notes

1. Stefan Collini, *English Pasts: Essays in History and Culture* (Oxford: Oxford University Press, 1999), 313.

2. These figures are the guide prices taken from the catalogue of Sotheby's auction of Wilde material that took place in London on 29 October 2004; see 88, 89, 92–93, 108.

3. Grant Allen, "The Decay of Criticism," *Fortnightly Review*, 31 n.s. (March 1882), 340.

4. Unsigned obituary notice, *Pall Mall Gazette*, (1 December 1900), 2; reprinted in *Oscar Wilde: The Critical Heritage*, Karl Beckson, ed.(1970; London: Routledge, 1997), 229–30.

5. F. O. Matthiessen, "The Responsibilities of the Critic"; quoted in Morris Dickstein, "The Critic and Society, 1900–1950," in A. Walton Litz, Louis Menand and Lawrence Rainey, eds., *The Cambridge History of Literary Criticism. Volume 7. Modernism and the New Criticism* (Cambridge: Cambridge University Press, 2000), 323.

6. Mark Jancovich, "The Southern New Critics," *The Cambridge History of Literary Criticism. Volume 7*, 207.

7.   T. S. Eliot, "Tradition and the Individual Talent," *Selected Essays* (London: Faber & Faber Ltd., 1951), 17.

8.   Christopher Craft, *Another Kind of Love: Male Homosexual Desire in English Discourse, 1850–1920* (London: University of California Press, 1994), 111.

Works Cited & Consulted

Ackroyd, Peter. *The Last Testament of Oscar Wilde*. London: Hamish Hamilton, 1983.

Bartlett, Neil. *Who Was That Man?: A Present for Mr Oscar Wilde*. London: Serpent's Tale, 1988.

Holland, Merlin. *The Wilde Album*. London: Fourth Estate, 1997.

McKenna, Neil. *The Secret Life of Oscar Wilde*. London: Century, 2003.

Tóibín, Colm. *Love in a Dark Time*. London: Pimlico, 2002.

| II | Lives of Wilde:
Facts and Fictions

THE EFFORTS of Wilde's earliest biographers, writing in the first half of the twentieth century, have consistently been dismissed by their late-twentieth- and twenty-first-century counterparts. The reason for this state of affairs is simple: many of the players who had roles in Wilde's life were still alive for several decades after his death, and consequently any story of Wilde's life had to exhibit a sensitivity to their feelings, and more formally (and particularly in the case of anything written about Lord Alfred Douglas) to be alert to the swingeing penalties that British libel laws can exact.[1] Early biographies have thus been treated cautiously, as representing only partial accounts of their subject's life. Moreover, some of those biographers were only too well aware of the disadvantages of openly associating themselves with a figure who had endured constant public vilification in the early years of the twentieth century, and as a consequence were as much concerned with rewriting their own role in Wilde's life as with their ostensible subject. This is also true of those biographies written by "friends" of Wilde, such as Robert Harborough Sherard and Frank Harris, who competed with each other for the honour of being remembered as Wilde's rescuer or champion.

The charge of unreliability can also be easily proved in the several accounts of Wilde written by Alfred Douglas; those narratives were a series of attempts at self-justification and thus self-fashioning, particularly after his marriage in 1904 to Olive Custance when it was important for him to mark out some distance from his former, openly homosexual, self. In an obvious sense this partisanship, whether it exists in the form of an *apologia* or of condemnation, is a loss, for it undermines the reliability of the testimony of those who were the main witnesses to Wilde's life. Moreover, such reservations are also applicable, though for slightly different reasons, to the life of Wilde written by his second son, Vyvyan Holland (in 1954, with a sequel published in 1966). As a family member (although he could not have known nor remembered his father particularly

13

well) Holland's work could boast the privilege of inside information. He certainly had access to many documents (both letters and manuscripts) unknown to earlier writers, and for a time it was this quality of his accounts of his father that made them difficult to rebut or supersede, even though they were incomplete and one-sided.

The first significant milestone in Wilde's biography, then, in the sense of establishing the foundations for a more secure critical appraisal of the life, and one moreover which could be contested by others, can be dated to Rupert Hart-Davis's 1962 edition of Wilde's letters. For the first time, scholars with no personal connection with Wilde had the opportunity to examine for themselves the evidence of the day-to-day minutiae of his passions and friendships; more importantly, they also had the means to assess the claims made by earlier biographers, since the *Letters* included copious correspondence between Wilde and figures such as Sherard, Harris, and Douglas. Given this wealth of information, it may seem surprising that so few new biographies were immediately forthcoming: with the exception of a small crop of studies in the mid-1970s— including H. Montgomery Hyde's *Oscar Wilde* (1975), Louis Kronenberger's *Oscar Wilde* (1976), and Sheridan Morley's *Oscar Wilde: An Illustrated Biography* (1976), a volume which does not even cite the *Letters*—a full quarter of a century passed before the appearance of Richard Ellmann's monumental and posthumous *Oscar Wilde* (1987).

This hiatus can, however, be explained (at least in part) by those critical fashions in literary studies that we mentioned in chapter one, and which had the cumulative effect of excluding Wilde from serious academic attention. More particularly, the dominance in the 1950s, 1960s, and early 1970s of New Criticism and structuralism made the writing of biography a less respectable academic pursuit; certainly, it is significant that none of the biographies of Wilde published in Britain in the 1970s was written by an academic. Furthermore, the principal historicist alternatives to text-based criticism, influenced as they were by Marxist historiography, tended to understand Victorian literary history in terms of the ways in which literary works allegedly reproduced and normalized bourgeois ideologies. Such a view favoured a concentration on the realist novel as a form whose representational properties could be most readily and easily explained in terms of its political functions. As a consequence, Wilde's interests in poetry, drama, and criticism (as well as in nonrealist fiction) tended to make him irrelevant to such a narrative.

By contrast, the influence of gay and gender studies in the late 1970s and 1980s, and in particular the emphasis in Anglo-American feminism (or gynocriticism) on the interrelationship between expressivity and sexuality, gave a new prominence to biography as a key critical tool, as well as to the biographies of those particular artists and writers whose sex or gender identity had allegedly marginalized them from mainstream culture. It was against the background of this changed intellectual climate that a new biography of Wilde, by one of the foremost academic biographers of the century, may have seemed to be a worthwhile enterprise.

The length, detail, and narrative fluency of Ellmann's biography immediately marked it out from all previous lives. Warmly received by most reviewers and by the general reading public, it remains almost two decades after its first publication the standard biography, the account of Wilde to which the majority of readers—scholars, students, and our common reader—will go first. This is not to ignore the fact that there have been many criticisms of Ellmann's work, both on the grounds of its accuracy and in terms of the fundamental way in which he conceived of Wilde's life—that is, of what he omitted from his account. There have also been several biographies since Ellmann's, including those by Gary Schmidgall, Joseph Pearce, Melissa Knox, Barbara Belford, and Neil McKenna. However, although each of these works was motivated by an attempt to challenge particular aspects of Ellmann's account—usually and significantly his treatment of Wilde's sexuality—none has succeeded in replacing it, in the sense of offering a more complete or comprehensive account of the whole life. Certainly it is Ellmann's Wilde that has had, and continues to have, the most significant influence on how readers understand Wilde's literary works. Ellmann's *Oscar Wilde*, then, remains the starting point for considering that biographical imperative we mentioned in the previous chapter.

The Evidence for the Life

Most assessments of biographies typically begin with attention to "facts"—to, that is, the evidence upon which a story of the life has been constructed. So— in the case of Wilde—what is the status of those facts and the evidence that they provide for us? Although it is obviously impossible to corroborate such a claim, we can be certain that after Wilde's conviction in May 1895 the atmosphere of London became acrid with the smoke of destroyed incriminating evidence. Moreover, following Wilde's bankruptcy even more material disappeared, whether accidentally, legally, or illegally. In Wilde's correspondence and in that of his literary executor, Robert Ross, as well as in Stuart Mason's *Bibliography of Oscar Wilde*, we find occasional mentions of Wilde having made gifts of manuscripts to friends, manuscripts that were subsequently sold on at public auction, presumably to private collectors. The periodic reappearance of such materials (a good example of which was the sale in March 2004 of a manuscript of "The Soul of Man under Socialism," hitherto assumed to have been lost) suggests that many documents may still survive in private collections, and that unknown individuals are continuing, albeit possibly unwittingly, to exercise an unseen control over that image of Wilde we discussed above. In this way, the evidence for Wilde's life is different from that of many other literary figures. So, for example, we know that there are few surviving records that give details of Shakespeare's life; but for Wilde, what we think we know about the nature and extent of the evidence is continually having to be revised.

An equally intractable problem has to do with the treatment of the evidence that is in the public domain. Here we need to acknowledge from the outset that it is almost certainly true that even the most scrupulous biographer cannot come objectively to Wilde's life. So many of the events in it have elicited a moral response for so long a period of time that to sift through the evidence has always involved a degree of prejudging. Even the most sympathetic of scholars have tended to ignore those details which do not fit their particular preconceptions of his career. Moreover examples of such prejudice can be found in works that one would not, at first glance, expect to exhibit such bias, such as H. Montgomery Hyde's *The Trials of Oscar Wilde* (1948). Though Hyde advertised his work as a reliable record of the trial proceedings, Merlin Holland's more recent transcript in his *Irish Peacock and Scarlet Marquess* (2003) reveals that, in his account of the first trial (the libel case brought by Wilde against Queensberry), Hyde judiciously edited various exchanges, perhaps in order to present Wilde's performance in the witness box in the best possible light, polishing some of Wilde's statements to make them seem wittier than they in fact were. Hyde also excluded those statements by other witnesses that pointed to a more sordid side to Wilde's "loves" that dared not "speak" their name.

In a similar way, Holland's recent revised and considerably expanded edition of the *Letters* indicates that in his earlier collection Rupert Hart-Davis had also silently excluded certain categories of correspondence, particularly those relating to the minute details of Wilde's writing career. Hart-Davis's 1962 Wilde is probably a more glamorous figure than Holland's and Hart-Davis's 2000 counterpart. However the biographer or critic, for whom such material is a crucial factual resource, was never in a position to see such editing (or, if we care to use a harsher term, such censorship). It is this invisibility that matters most, for it means that the materials with which the critic or biographer has to work have already been shaped into a preexisting narrative of some sort or other: not only do we not know the full extent of the evidence, we are never entirely clear about the ways in which the material which is in the public domain has been structured or informally edited.

Perhaps more regrettably, this shaping or troping of material is to be found even in the ways in which unpublished archive resources have been organized. A particularly striking example can be seen in the filing practices of the largest collection of Wildeiana, that held in the William Andrews Clark Memorial Library, now part of the University of California in Los Angeles. Until a recent project to microfilm the collection (completed in 1999), that material had been ordered for the researcher into two main classes, those labelled "catalogued" and "uncatalogued." The fact that for many years this second body of documents was stored together in boxes meant that few scholars bothered to examine it in any detail. Those who did (like Peter Raby) were amazed to find crucial pieces of evidence, such as the original manuscript of Wilde's letter to George Alexander containing the first known scenario of *The Importance of Being Earnest*, or the financial records of Wilde's earnings in the West End theatre stored alongside other, far less important information. There are several possible reasons for such oversights, none of which should reflect adversely on the staff of that library. The first might be simply accidental; the second an understandable pressure on resources and time; and the third a failure to recognize the particular significance of a document. (There is, after all, no reason for a librarian to be constantly abreast of research of any or all parts of a library's holdings.) The unfortunate upshot of all this, though, was that an inevitable prioritizing of evidence took place, and this process once again invisibly shaped conceptualizations of Wilde's life and career.

Taken together, these caveats amount to an acknowledgment that "facts" about Wilde's life—the evidence from which biographies are constructed—are almost never neutral: so there are values involved in deciding whether certain factual details come into the public domain in the first instance, and in what forms; there are more values involved in assessing the status of particular facts;

Wilde Archives   Given the chaos that accompanied the bankruptcy proceedings brought against Wilde in 1895, in which the contents of his house were offered for sale, it is perhaps surprising that so many materials relating to his life and particularly to his writing career— letters, notebooks, manuscripts, typescripts, proofs, and so forth—have actually survived. Much credit in this respect must go to Robert Ross who was responsible for rescuing and later (in his role as Wilde's literary executor preparing the first *Collected Edition* of Wilde's works) for recovering many important documents. Although some of this material remains in private hands, a considerable amount of it can be readily accessed in the collections of public libraries in Great Britain and the United States. The most important of these Wilde archives include (in the U.S.) those located in the William Andrews Clark Memorial Library at the University of California, Los Angeles; the Harry Ransom Humanities Research Center at the University of Texas, Austin; the Berg, Arents Tobacco, and Frohman Collections in the New York Public Library; the Rosenbach Foundation in Philadelphia; the Pierpont Morgan Library; Princeton University Library; and the Beinecke Library at Yale. And in the U.K.: the British Library (including the recent bequest of Lady Eccles and the Lord Chamberlain's collection of the licensing copies of plays); the Herbert Beerbohm Tree Archive in the Bristol Theatre Collection, University of Bristol; and the Ross Collection at the Bodleian Library, University of Oxford.

and there are still further values involved in interpreting their significance and relevance to Wilde's life.

A useful example of the complexities that can ensue when such values are in competition with each other can be seen in the bitter arguments that have surrounded Wilde's alleged cause of death. Ellmann, in common with some earlier biographers, asserted that "Wilde's final illness was almost certainly syphilitic in origin" (Ellmann, 545). At the time when Ellmann was writing there was no single conclusive piece of evidence that pointed to this diagnosis; rather, it was an inference which he drew from a variety of pieces of what we might term circumstantial evidence. Recognizing the seriousness of his assertion—then (as now) the link between syphilis and sexual behaviour gives the disease a particular stigma—Ellmann somewhat unusually provided a long justificatory footnote:

> My belief that Wilde had syphilis stems from statements made by Reginald Turner and Robert Ross, Wilde's closest friends present at his death, from the certificate of the doctor in charge at that time ... and from the fact that the 1912 edition of [Arthur] Ransome's book on Wilde and Harris's 1916 life (both of which Ross oversaw) give syphilis as the cause of his death. Opinion on the subject is however divided, and some authorities do not share my view of Wilde's medical history. Admittedly the evidence is not decisive—it could scarcely be so, given the aura of disgrace, shame, and secrecy surrounding the disease in Wilde's time and after—and might not stand up in a court of law. Nevertheless I am convinced that Wilde had syphilis, and the conviction is central to my conception of Wilde's character and my interpretation of many things in his later life. (Ellmann, 88)

Syphilis: The Nineteenth-Century Artist's Disease   In the late nineteenth century, in the days before the discovery of penicillin, there was, of course, no proper cure for this devastating illness. It led in its tertiary stage to mental deterioration, particularly aphasia or what was then termed a "softening of the mind," and eventually death. Moreover, its "appropriateness" as a judgment on the sexually licentious artist resided, at least in part, in the ways in which it ravaged both body and mind. Infamous and infamously defiant late-nineteenth-century syphilitics included the French writers Charles Baudelaire (who once commented that "the day a young writer corrects his first proofs, he's as proud as a schoolboy who's just caught the pox") and, a little later, Alphonse Daudet. Both wrote about the consequences of living with the many and varied afflictions syphilis visits on the sufferer, as well as (the sometimes worse) discomforts of the proposed remedies, which including frequent purging, bizarre diets, and bathing in freezing cold water. Baudelaire's close friend and publisher, Auguste Poulet-Malassis, who visited him a few months before his death, wrote poignantly of how the famous poet had "lost his memory of language and figurative signs."

Few statements can be as revealing of a biographer's method. As we see, the actual evidence for the diagnosis of syphilis comes from uncorroborated "statements" made by two of Wilde's friends at the time of his death, men without medical qualifications who were almost certainly deeply distressed by the events to which they were witnesses. (That Ransome and Harris repeat Turner's and Ross's account lends it only notoriety, not authority.) Ironically, the doctor's death certificate (which Ellmann later quotes) does not mention syphilis at all: the diagnosis is rather of "méninge encéphite" (encephalitic meningitis). It is a leap of interpretation to assume that the swelling of the lining of Wilde's brain was a symptom of syphilis. We must presume that Ross, Turner, Ransome, Harris, and Ellmann (though apparently not the figure best qualified to know, the doctor himself) came to this conclusion because the diagnosis of syphilis fitted with a particular narrative of Wilde's life—it represented an irresistibly tragic ending to a career destroyed by an overwhelming sexual appetite. As Ellmann admits, he is "convinced" it was syphilis, because it is that illness which is "central" to his conception of Wilde's "character."

The same might be said of Melissa Knox's later *Oscar Wilde: A Long and Lovely Suicide*. Her psychoanalytic reading of Wilde's life, which centred on his alleged sexual guilt, required a sexually contracted disease for him to feel guilty about—and naturally enough it is syphilis which best fits the bill. Unsurprisingly, perhaps, Wilde's grandson, Merlin Holland, made strenuous attempts to correct this "diagnosis" with the counterargument that "the medical and literary press" had run articles "supporting" his view that "the 'death by syphilis' theory" was "radically unsound."[2] However, this in its turn was countered by the allegation (from Knox's advocates) that Holland had restricted access to Wilde's estate,

---

continued   He then went on to quote a contemporary medical book on aphasia which noted that "when you see an aphasic who appears to be in possession of his mental faculties, though he has lost the ability to express himself, how many times have you said of certain animals 'if only they could speak'" (Pichois & Ziegler, 361). Daudet, in particular, produced a remarkably unsentimental and blackly humorous account of the physical pain his syphilitic neuropathy caused him. Physicians in Paris devoted to caring for syphilitic patients included Jean-Martin Charcot, Freud's collaborator, working at his famous clinic, La Salpêtrière, and Georges Gilles de la Tourette, a pupil of Charcot. Part of the attraction of a diagnosis of syphilis in Wilde's case is that it enlists him in this French Romantic tradition of transgressive writers, as well as explaining what some have perceived as a falling away in his creativity in the last years of his life following his release from prison in 1897.

and thus (it was implied) to precisely the sort of evidence that would eventually corroborate her views. It needs to be stressed here that no party in this dispute can be described as completely "disinterested"; likewise, the evidence, such
as it survives, can be interpreted in a number of ways. Encephalitic meningitis
can indeed be a symptom of tertiary syphilis; but it can also have several other causes. Thus the weight one gives to this "fact" about Wilde's death is entirely dependent upon the other sorts of facts one aligns it with, and here Holland
is certainly correct in observing that there are details about Wilde's health in
his final months which are not readily compatible with a diagnosis of syphilis.
Moreover the selection of, or emphasis upon, those "other facts" in turn depends
on what Ellmann, with admirable candour, terms one's preexistent "conception
of Wilde's character."

Sorting out the rival claims of Wilde biographies is not, then, just a matter of assessing the status of particular pieces of evidence. Equally important is
the task of laying bare the values and assumptions which have shaped the narratives that interpret such evidence. Put more straightforwardly: understanding
the biography is as much about finding out the purposes for which the narrative of the life is being used as it is about uncovering who Wilde really was (if
indeed such an ambition could ever be fully realized). Moreover, we need to be
clear about these matters when we attempt to clarify the relationship between
biography and literary-critical judgments made about the work. And we need
to acknowledge that it has rarely been the story of Wilde the writer that has
interested his biographers; rather the principal source of interest has been the
trajectory of Wilde's sexual life. As a consequence, his literary works, as we have
noted, have most often been viewed (both by the academic community and
many thousands of "home" readers) as expressions or extensions of attitudes
formed by Wilde's own sense of his sexual identity. As Ellmann cogently puts it
apropos of *The Picture of Dorian Gray*: "Wilde put into the book a negative version of what he had been brooding upon for fourteen years and, under a veil,
what he had been doing sexually for four.... Through his hero Wilde was able
to open a window into his own recent experience" (Ellmann, 297). Such a commonplace correlation between incidents in Wilde's life and events which take
place in his fiction, though, tends to leave unanswered some important questions concerning the precise nature of the relationship between Wilde's sexuality and creativity. These can usefully be brought into focus by means of a simple
thought experiment.

Wilde's Sexuality

How would we read Wilde's literary works if it were suddenly discovered that
they had been written by a straight writer, a woman, or even a closet gay writer, one never tried, let alone imprisoned for his sexual life (a figure, for example,
such as Wilde's exact contemporary, the poet A. E. Housman)? Put another way,

can we imagine *The Importance of Being Earnest* having been written by Arthur Wing Pinero, Henry Arthur Jones, or even Elizabeth Robins? Or *The Picture of Dorian Gray* by Joseph Conrad? Such questions do not somehow seem comparable to inquiring whether some of Shakespeare's works might have been written by Bacon (as some literary historians have done at intervals in the last two centuries). The attribution to Bacon, although almost certainly incorrect, is at least reasonable; but assigning *The Importance of Being Earnest* or *The Picture of Dorian Gray* to one of Wilde's contemporaries seems inherently implausible (although, interestingly, it is possible to imagine different authors for some of Wilde's fairy tales, such as "The Happy Prince" or "The Selfish Giant"— works which, as we argue later, have been read by children without the obscuring lens of Wilde's biography). Such a reaction is an indication of how deeply engrained our retrospective reading of Wilde's creativity is, one always coloured by knowledge of the man revealed during the trials. But it also raises questions about the identity of that figure of Wilde to whom the novel or the plays seem so indissolubly tied. Here it is perhaps worth reiterating that of several personas which Wilde himself actively cultivated—the aesthete, dandy, socialite, or man of the theatre—none was explicitly or openly homosexual, and it is to be doubted (as Alan Sinfield has argued) whether many of Wilde's contemporary readers actually knew prior to the trials that the married man with two children was himself leading a "double life."[3] These are questions to which we will return. First, though, we need to disentangle the meanings of the terms "the gay Wilde" or "Wilde the homosexual" to try to ascertain the nature of that sexual identification through which the works are so persistently read.

It may come as a surprise to some to learn that there is no single nor reliable story of Wilde's sexual life. Ellmann's biography can rightly lay claim to be the first academic study to present that sexuality in a positive light—that is, to see it as being inextricably linked to Wilde's creativity. In Ellmann's view, Wilde's sexual orientation was not an unfortunate and rather troublesome aberration, as it had been for a tradition of apologists from Sherard to Montgomery Hyde. Rather for Ellmann it was the defining core of Wilde's personality. Given this claim, it is surprising to find that Ellmann's conception of what that sexual life actually amounted to is rather empty, perhaps to the point of naivety. We are told of Wilde's male "friendships," of his engaging personality, and of his emotional attachments to a series of attractive young men, as well as about his generosity in love (even to his wife). As Ellmann confided to one of the present authors, in his view the secret of Wilde's life was simple: it was one of love.[4] And its tragedy was that the main object of that love—Alfred Douglas—was an unworthy recipient of it. Such a powerfully romantic reading of Wilde's sexuality, in which many of the rather obvious distinctions between love and sexual appetite tend to be elided, is conspicuous for what it fails to disclose, or for terms which it does not use. When we read Ellmann's biography, we find that it is strangely difficult to get much sense of Wilde as an actual sexual being, of the numbers and frequency of his sexual partners and liaisons, or of his own sexual pleasures, or indeed of the differences that might have existed between his homosexual and heterosexual relationships. There is an ironically Victorian coyness in Ellmann's descriptions of Wilde's actual sexual life, for if we are to judge by Ellmann's account, not much sex seems to have happened.

Early critics of Ellmann, though, did not generally pick up on this limitation, possibly because the sympathy with which he portrayed a homosexual lifestyle was so novel, and possibly because the tragic trajectory of his biography fitted so well with what we have termed the Wilde "myth." Those reviewers who did raise objections to the biography tended to focus upon small factual errors (such as confusions of names or dates) or upon Ellmann's overdependence on unreliable source materials (such as those "witness" accounts of his deathbed scene which we mentioned earlier). To be sure, among the reviewers there was the occasional voice who complained about the lack of attention given to Wilde's writing life, or rather the lack of a fit between Ellmann's account of Wilde's sexuality and his actual methods of composition.[5] On the whole, though, the main impact of Ellmann's work was to spur scholars into politicizing the myth that his biography had so successfully consolidated—that is, into viewing Wilde's homosexual identity as formed less by the particularities or details of his actual sexual practices (about which, as we have said, Ellmann was remarkably reticent) than by those contemporary homophobic ideologies which marginalized and criminalized him. Thus, for example, some historians followed up hints in Ellmann's life about possible connections between Wilde's trial and the homosexuality of Lord Rosebery (later to become Prime Minister), seeing the activities of the prosecution (for example, their decision not to call Douglas as a witness) as an attempt to cover up a potential homosexual scandal at the very highest echelons of British political life. Other scholars, notably Ed Cohen, took up this idea of Wilde as a political "scapegoat," arguing that in 1895 it was

---

The Power of Wilde's Name & "Dirty" Books   Wilde's name has had such potency that it has—not surprisingly—led many to identify him with anonymous or forged works, several of them sexually explicit. The most famous of these was the apparent discovery of a whole cache of Wilde manuscripts by Fabian Lloyd, Constance's brother and so Wilde's brother-in-law. They are now held in the Clark Library and were quickly revealed to be forgeries written by Lloyd himself in an attempt to cash in on Wilde's name. A similar kind of fraud was that practised by the publisher Charles Carrington, who tried to pass off a translation of the *Satyricon* of Petronius Arbiter as a work by Wilde. (The *Satyricon* had a kind of totemic if scurrilous reputation in late-nineteenth-century culture and came to be associated with numerous writers; Charles Baudelaire, for example, was reputed to have agreed to work on a translation of it.)

homosexuality itself, rather than Wilde, which was on trial. In this view, once again, the particularity of Wilde's own sexual behaviour was of less concern than the opportunities his case allegedly offered for a specific "construction" of the homosexual by a homophobic media. Pursuing this line of argument, Alan Sinfield has also argued that Wilde's trial marked the moment when "the image of the queer emerged."[6]

It is worth emphasizing at this point that these extensions to, or elaborations of, Ellmann's biography had very little to say about Wilde's literary career, or what for brevity we can call the literary (as opposed to the political) value of his writings. Rather they concentrated on documenting Wilde's centrality to a history of gay rights. Moreover, what has mattered most in that history has been Wilde's iconic status: as a highly visible "sign" he allowed other kinds of attitudes—particularly homophobic ones, or class prejudices, or even discrimination based on ethnicity—to come into view. As a consequence Wilde's writings have tended to be of interest principally insofar as they can be subsumed into this larger political narrative: put crudely, insofar as they can be interpreted as interrogating or subverting the values and attitudes of the culture which criminalized him. And in this process, as we have said, precise details about Wilde's actual sexual behaviour, and thus information allowing Ellmann's romanticized reading of the life to be controverted, have generally been neglected. In fact, until Neil McKenna's *The Secret Life of Oscar Wilde* was published in 2003, there were few biographies that directly took issue with the details of Ellmann's depiction of Wilde's sex life.

The "Franker" Biographies

Gary Schmidgall's *The Stranger Wilde* (1994) was explicitly motivated by a dissatisfaction with what he termed the "discreet" dispensation of an earlier generation of biographers (a group in which he included Ellmann). By contrast, Schmidgall promised to give the reader a more "inconvenient" portrait

---

continued   The most enduring attribution of authorship concerns Wilde's supposed contribution to the nineteenth-century pornographic novel *Teleny*, which continues to be reprinted with his name on the cover. In other words it is Wilde's name that continues to sell the work rather than any intrinsic merit it might possess. The legend of *Teleny*'s composition was that the manuscript was circulated among a group of friends which included Wilde. Each added chapters or episodes and passed the work on. Scholarly opinion over its authenticity remains divided. Not only is there no consensus about which parts Wilde may (or may not) have written, there is no concrete evidence that he ever wrote material of this kind.

of a (now) famous icon, one which gave fuller attention to the "ramifications" of Wilde's homosexual identity—to, that is, his lack of sympathy with "closeted" gay contemporaries, such as Walter Pater or Henry James. Such claims, though, were not based on any new evidence about Wilde's actual sexual practices, but rather on what was at heart a programmatically autobiographical reading of the literary works and a problematic equating of late-nineteenth- and late-twentieth-century homosexual experiences. These culminated in Schmidgall imagining Wilde as a *habitué* of late-night "talk-shows." Schmidgall, then, told us no more about Wilde's actual sexual behaviour than Ellmann had done, and in this respect his account of Wilde's sexual psychology—Wilde's allegedly greater willingness to be "out"—lacked both novelty and depth. The same point can be made of Melissa Knox's *A Long and Lovely Suicide*, to which we have already alluded. Like Schmidgall's book, Knox's controversial account of Wilde's sexual identity was not based on new evidence; rather it depended (once again) on a rereading of his literary works, only this time from the viewpoint of the psychoanalyst in her chair interrogating Wilde on the couch. So although Knox could certainly claim to offer the most radically new view of Wilde's sexuality since Ellmann, for many scholars (and certainly for non-Freudians) the authority of her account was compromised, and perhaps vitiated, by a number of flaws in her methodology—that is, by her simplistic assumptions about literary creativity (which paid no attention to the artifactual and institutional nature of literary works) as well as her assumptions about a straightforwardly expressive relationship between emotion and language.

Why Was Alfred Douglas Never Prosecuted for Gross Indecency?   Numerous readers have wondered why Wilde's relationship with Douglas did not form part of Wilde's indictment for gross indecency, and why, in the light of their very public relationship, Douglas was never prosecuted following Wilde's conviction in 1895. According to H. Montgomery Hyde, the issue was brought up by the foreman of the jury in Wilde's third trial, when he noted, "if we adduce any guilt ... it applies as much to Lord Alfred Douglas as to the defendant." The judge, Mr. Justice Wills, agreed, but pointed out that the observation was irrelevant to Wilde's case. Further light is shed on this matter by letters published by Merlin Holland in *Irish Peacock & Scarlet Marquess* between the Hon. Hamilton Cuffe (then Director of Public Prosecutions) and Charles Gill (who acted as junior counsel for the Marquess of Queensberry in the libel case brought by Wilde). Gill had written to Cuffe about whether a "prosecution ought to be instituted against Lord Alfred Douglas on account of his connection with the case of Oscar Wilde and Alfred Taylor" (Taylor ran a male brothel, but refused to give evidence against Wilde, and was tried and convicted for gross indecency along with him.) In Gill's view a prosecution against Douglas would not succeed because the evidence against him could not be corroborated.

Advertised as "the greatest contribution to Wilde scholarship" since Ellmann's "magisterial biography," Neil McKenna's startlingly graphic *The Secret Life of Oscar Wilde* (2003) was (like Knox's and Schmidgall's studies) explicitly conceived as a corrective to Ellmann's idealized view of Wilde's sexual self. That said, once again McKenna does not challenge the basic premise of Ellmann's book in that he too sees Wilde's personality and creativity defined by his sexuality. He understands Wilde's uninhibited pursuit of his desire in quasi-heroic terms, as that of a "brave champion" who exhibited a "courageous" commitment to "'the Cause,'" one of gay rights. For McKenna, Wilde was a member of a "modern day Theban Band [of] warriors and lovers willing and prepared to embrace death rather than surrender" (McKenna, 396). McKenna also shares the propensity of Ellmann (and once more of Knox and of Schmidgall) to interpret the literary works in straightforwardly biographical terms, to the extent that the chief value of what McKenna terms Wilde's "highly autobiographical" writings lies in what they reveal about his "secret life" (McKenna, xiv). The principal distinctions of McKenna's account, then, are to be found in his very different conception of what Wilde's sexual life actually amounted to, and the quality of the new evidence which he provides to substantiate it.

McKenna's biography is self-consciously concerned with what he terms Wilde's sexual "behaviour"—that is, with the pleasure Wilde took in sexual activity once he had "surrendered" to the "overwhelming" nature of his attraction to young men, and the ways in which he then sought to satisfy his compulsive appetites. McKenna sees sex as a practice: he wants to trace what exactly Wil-

---

continued   He also felt that a jury would be sympathetic to Douglas because of his youth: given "the difference in their ages and the strong influence that Wilde has obviously exercised over Douglas … I think that Douglas, if guilty, may fairly be regarded as one of Wilde's victims." Cuffe then passed this information on to a minister of state at the Home Office indicating that he agreed with Gill, adding that "irresponsible persons may say and very likely will say that he [Douglas] goes unprosecuted because of his position in life" (Holland, 294–96). No proceedings were ever brought. Later historians have indeed thought that Douglas's "position in life" was the determining factor. They point to the fact that if Douglas had been brought to court, cross-examination might have implicated senior individuals in government. Douglas Murray notes that Douglas's elder brother, Lord Drumlanrig, private secretary to Lord Rosebery (a known homosexual, who at the time was then Minister for Foreign Affairs) had died in 1894 in mysterious circumstances in a shooting accident just prior to his wedding. Joseph Baylen and Robert L. McBath found evidence that later, when he was Prime Minister, Rosebery ordered British representatives in Italy to monitor Douglas's and Wilde's activities in that country.

de did, with whom, and where. So he unapologetically lays before the reader details about Wilde's alleged fondness for oral sex, the "disgusting" stains on the bed-sheets of his room at the Savoy Hotel, his "hunting" and sharing with Douglas (and occasionally with Ross) of young male prostitutes or "pick-ups," and his taking advantage of his wife's (and children's) absence to make assignations with young men at their Tite Street home. In charting such behaviour, McKenna exposes a sexual life that for some readers will seem to be little more than a studied, exploitative, and sometimes sordid promiscuity. McKenna's own emphasis, though, is on the tensions between what he terms this "generalised" lust, an "addiction to sex … frequent sex, with as many people as possible," and the "ideal and idealised love," defined by personal qualities such as fidelity, loyalty, and devotion, which are precisely the terms by which Wilde typically troped his relationship with Douglas (McKenna, 188).

A good example of the differences between Ellmann's and McKenna's treatments of Wilde's sexual behaviour can be seen in their respective accounts of Wilde's and Douglas's visit to Algiers in early 1895 during the rehearsals of *The Importance of Being Earnest*. To the best of our knowledge, only one short letter by Wilde written during this trip has survived. Addressed to Robert Ross, it describes in mock pastoral terms the "beauty" of the surroundings, the "lovely" Kabyle boys, and "an excursion into the mountains of Kabylia" where "shepherds fluted on reeds" and where Wilde and Douglas were "followed by lovely brown things from forest to forest" (*Complete Letters*, 629). The principal source of evidence for Wilde's and Douglas's activities are the writings of André Gide, particularly his autobiographical volume *Si le grain ne meurt* (1924), in which Gide describes meeting Wilde and Douglas in the walled city of Blidah, and their taking him on a tour of the town's nightlife, one which ended in a barroom brawl. A few days later Gide met up with Douglas and Wilde again, this time back in Algiers; Gide recounts how Wilde procured for him a young flute-playing Tunisian, "Bosie's boy," Mohammed, with whom he later spent the night in a room opposite to that occupied by Wilde and another "boy" (Douglas meantime had returned to Blidah in pursuit of yet another Arab boy, one "Ali"). Ellmann retells these events using both Gide's and Wilde's words, but in such a way that Gide's sexual behaviour is the centre of the narrative and that of Wilde reduced to something of an amused bystander. So Wilde is described merely as having "made the arrangements" for Gide's rendezvous with Mohammed (who is just "an Arab boy with a flute"), while the "arrangements" themselves are left unspecified, and observations about Wilde's own nocturnal adventures are simply omitted. Moreover, Ellmann's dominant image of Wilde's Algerian perambulations is an oddly nonsexual one; he is pictured as going "through the streets" followed by a "band of petty thieves" whom he "observed … with joy" and to whom he "scattered money" (Ellmann, 405). The blatancy of what we would now call sex tourism is conveniently overlooked by Ellmann.

Not so McKenna: his account of the Algierian excursion is much more detailed and it stresses from the outset its sexual purpose. He points out for the uninformed reader that Algiers was well known in French gay circles as an ideal location for gay sex tourism: "Algiers was no different to London, other than that the supply of boys seemed unending and that, for Bosie in particular, boys—some as young as thirteen or fourteen—were readily available" (McKenna, 324). This emphasis upon the youth of the male prostitutes is another detail carefully omitted by Ellmann. So too is the sharing of sexual partners, which McKenna sees as an intrinsic part of the sexual dynamic—establishing an "erotic bond of sorts"—linking Wilde, Bosie, and in this case, Gide. McKenna gives Wilde considerably more agency than Ellmann does, casting him in the role of an experienced and determined sexual predator. Wilde, then, is a "habitué" of the café where the initially "puzzled" André is introduced to Mohammed, and he enjoys a "night of passion" with his own "*darbouka* player" (McKenna, 327). McKenna also reads Wilde's report of his activities to Ross in explicitly sexual terms, glossing Wilde's reference to "lovely brown things" as referring to "beautiful boys wherever they turned, seemingly all of them smiling sexual invitation." Indeed the reference to fluting shepherds loses all its overtones of bucolic innocence and becomes instead "probably an oblique reference to oral sex" (McKenna, 324).

An initial comparison between these two accounts might lead one to conclude that Ellmann, whether through tact or possibly distaste, is guilty of romanticizing practices that might otherwise be labelled as child prostitution or pedophilia, and that his biography is therefore profoundly misleading if not irresponsible. By contrast, McKenna is much more aware of the nature of the activities he is describing. As he baldly puts it: "Neither Oscar nor Bosie had any sense that their pursuit of boys was wrong, or that paying them for sex might be exploitative. They were used to paying renters for sex in London" (McKenna, 324). Such a judgment, though, tends to overlook the uncomfortable fact that neither Ellmann nor McKenna has concrete evidence to substantiate his particular version of events in north Africa. As we noted above, both rely heavily on Gide's memoirs, but given Gide's complex reactions to his own sexuality, these cannot unquestioningly be taken to be accurate. Several modern Gide scholars—including those explicitly sympathetic to their subject—have acknowledged that his writings are considered by some to be "so far-fetched" that they ought to be viewed as the product of an "over-fertile imagination."[7] McKenna, too, will admit to the possibility of unreliable memoir evidence, although he tends to dismiss the problem. For example, while noting that another of his sources (the unpublished autobiography of Trelawny Backhouse) is "not always accurate or, indeed, true," he justifies using it on the grounds that it has "the ring of authenticity" to it (McKenna, 153). A further difficulty is that this "ring" derives largely from its similarities with other equally untrustworthy sources, such as the memoirs of Douglas or John Addington Symonds.[8]

In the light of these problems it could be argued that Ellmann's consciously elliptical account of the Algiers visit is merely an acknowledgment of the uncertain status of the evidence he is relying upon: as with any good judge, he omits what he considers unsubstantiated hearsay. Likewise, McKenna, for all his apparent candour, is sometimes guilty of his own tendency to romanticize. For example, he describes how Wilde's encounter with another Arab boy narrowly avoided disaster when the latter's plans to "trap [Wilde] for robbery and possible murder" were thwarted by Wilde's sexual experience and expertise: "after Oscar had sex with him, he was, apparently, 'ready to lay down his life for him'" (McKenna, 328). Most readers will perhaps be a little suspicious of this rather hackneyed idea that the power relations involved in prostitution can somehow be dissolved both through the pleasure of sex and by the consummate sexual mastery of an older man. Moreover, those who carefully examine McKenna's endnotes will observe with dismay that the source for the anecdote turns out to be a letter from Laurence Housman to George Ives which dates from 1933: this "apparent" fact, then, derives its authority from a memory recalled four decades after the event, and from a man who could not possibly have been a witness to what he describes.

Unfortunately there is no reliable way to adjudicate between Ellmann's and McKenna's stories: we do not know with certainty what transpired among Wilde, Douglas, Gide, and their various Arab "boys" during that trip to Algiers. It is certainly possible to speculate about their sexual behaviour, based on the knowledge that Algiers was indeed a well-recognized destination for European sex tourists. But the plausibility of such speculation will depend as much upon the authority of the narrative which interprets the evidence (that is, to use Ellmann's phrase once again, upon the biographer's "conception of Wilde's character") as it does on the status of the evidence itself. In this respect, it is worth noting in passing that McKenna's acceptance of Gide's account, and thus his confident assertions about Wilde's and Douglas's sexual promiscuity, derive from his attempt to construct what he terms a "psychologically" coherent and convincing account of a homosexual lifestyle; that lifestyle in turn (from the evidence given in the trials) appeared to involve extremely frequent casual sex—what McKenna terms a "two-year binge of intense and unremitting sexual activity with dozens of boys and young men; an endless cycle of pursuit and capture, of desire and satiation" (McKenna, 217), exemplified by Wilde and Douglas "hunting singly, or as a pair" to bring boys back to the Savoy Hotel in London in order have sex "either *à trois*, or sequentially" (McKenna, 222–23). "Addiction" is the term McKenna most frequently invokes to explain such appetites, and in so doing he gives Wilde's behaviour a recognizably modern pathology and thus, we might infer, a fashionable and perhaps not wholly appropriate relevance to twenty-first-century sexual anxieties.

Whether or not McKenna's description and diagnosis of Wilde's sexual behaviour is more correct, or more plausible, than that given by Ellmann is not in itself a literary question, though it certainly has had considerable relevance for how Wilde's literary works are to be interpreted. As we noted earlier, both Ellmann and McKenna read a work of fiction such as *The Picture of Dorian Gray* as a disguised autobiography, and so both agree that the novel is about homosexuality. In Ellmann's view it is "one of the first attempts," though "appropriately covert," to "bring homosexuality into the English novel" (Ellmann, 300); for McKenna, it is "a celebration of the nature of sexual desire and sexual pleasure between men," "'designed,' 'intended' and 'understood' by its readers to be a book about sodomy and those men who practised sodomy" (McKenna, 127). The questions which are begged here are numerous. To what extent is biography—in this case a certain preconceived view of Wilde's character—driving the interpretation of the novel, rather than, as Ellmann and McKenna would have us believe, the novel providing evidence for the life? Second, there is the issue of the extent to which the novel is therefore deriving its value from its connection with the biography. And third, there is the question of whether and how that value changes as the biography—in this case, the sexual life—is revised. We will return to these questions in later chapters. For now, though, it will be sufficient to give some further illustrations of the complexities involved in them.

Sexuality, Creativity, & the Trials

Both Ellmann's and McKenna's accounts of Wilde's sexuality draw extensively upon contemporary correspondence, mainly that of Wilde and Douglas, but also from some of the other men with whom they were involved, such as Robert Ross, John Gray, André Raffalovich, and Adrian Hope. However, the language of such letters, particularly those which McKenna and Ellmann see as "love tokens," can present the biographer with some difficult problems. Wilde, in common with many of his male correspondents, tended to describe his encounters with young men, and his feelings for and about them, in elaborately affected, quasi-classical, and often rather flippant terms, all of which make it difficult to ascertain whether or not, or to what extent, he is writing seriously. Given the climate of the time, it is of course to be expected that expressions of male-male desire would necessarily be coded, even in private correspondence. Much scholarship has been devoted to deciphering the classical allusions by means of which such relationships were typically articulated, at least among classically educated men such as Wilde.[9] For the same reasons, though, such disguise, if disguise it is, makes it virtually impossible to distinguish between real sentiment and what may be mere pose or exaggeration, fantasy, or a shared joke. An example will perhaps make the dimensions of this problem clearer.

McKenna's understanding of Wilde's sexual development involves a transition from what he terms early "love affairs" with "young poets"—specifically Rennell Rodd, Richard Le Gallienne, and André Raffalovich—to a later, more promiscuous and predatory involvement with male prostitutes. McKenna's evidence for Wilde's relationship with one of those poets, Le Gallienne, whom he claims Wilde "loved" after his marriage, derives from some surviving correspondence which was apparently initiated by Le Gallienne in September 1887 when he sent Wilde his first book of poetry. Le Gallienne subsequently took up an invitation to meet Wilde, and later stayed at Tite Street in June 1888 and March 1889; in the period between these dates the two men exchanged further books, verses, and letters. The exchanges included a volume by Le Gallienne inscribed with a poem commemorating their very first encounter. It begins: "With Oscar Wilde, a summer-day | Passed like a yearning kiss away, | The kiss wherewith so long ago | The little maid who loved me so | Called me her Lancelot" (*Complete Letters*, 367).

The language of Wilde's and Le Gallienne's letters is certainly effusive, increasingly so as their acquaintance develops. So Wilde talks of Le Gallienne as the "young poet who came here so wonderfully and so strangely," and of their meeting to "make music," and later of his hopes that Le Gallienne's "laurels are not too thick across your brows for me to kiss your eye-lids" (*Complete Letters*, 367, 397, 457). Le Gallienne himself is equally fulsome, writing to Wilde that the "thought that you sometimes recall me is sweet as a kiss & it is blessed to know that but a little while & I shall be with you once more…. I have news to tell you in which I think you will rejoice with your true-lover" (*Oscar Wilde Revalued*, 77–78). And to John Lane he joked: "suffice it | I have never yet more fascinating fellow [i.e., Wilde] met, | and O! how sweet he was to me | is only known to R. le G" (Beckson, 193). But is such "talk" evidence of a sexual relationship?[10] Or is it merely a pose, a self-conscious and ironic indulgence of both men? If the language were serious, would Le Gallienne have used it again to Lane, who later wished to distance himself from Wilde's homosexuality? McKenna believes that it does constitute evidence of a sexual relationship, unequivocally asserting, apropos of Le Gallienne's poem, that

> The yearning kiss in question was literal as well as literary. Something more corporeal had happened that summer afternoon between Oscar and the twenty-two year old Le Gallienne…. There can be no doubt that Oscar seduced Richard Le Gallienne that summer afternoon; and no doubt that Le Gallienne was ready and willing to be seduced….The same month that he met and had sex with Oscar, Le Gallienne was also found staying with the journalist and poet Gleeson White and his wife in Christchurch, Hampshire, a town which was later to house a small but important colony of Uranian poets and writers (McKenna, 89).

In point of fact, and *pace* McKenna, there is plenty of room for doubt, and other scholars have been much more cautious in their speculations about the nature of Wilde's and Le Gallienne's relationship. For example, Karl Beckson focuses exclusively on their shared literary interests, with Le Gallienne cast not as Wilde's lover but merely his "log-roller" (Beckson, 194). Ellmann is also rather more circumspect, barely even hinting at a sexual intimacy. Citing some of the same evidence as McKenna, he includes an additional—and in his view, rather telling—comment made by Le Gallienne to a friend in 1888: that Wilde's language was "very rich" (Ellmann, 267; his source is Louise Jopling). That language was also of course self-consciously literary, as were Le Gallienne's own responses: both men wrote to each other using the exaggerated "purple prose" that would later be found in works such as *The Picture of Dorian Gray* and *The Sphinx*. So in the same letter where Wilde talks of kissing Le Gallienne's eyelids, he also describes his friend's poetry as "rich and Dionysiac and red-veined" with "that true ultimate simplicity that comes, like the dawn, out of a complex night of many wandering worlds" (*Complete Letters*, 457).

It is precisely these sorts of stylistic similarities that seem to have led McKenna to conclude that the language shared by *The Picture of Dorian Gray* and his letters is compelling evidence that Wilde's fiction is deeply autobiographical. Yet it needs to be acknowledged that the same observation could lead one to the very opposite conclusion: namely that Wilde's and Le Gallienne's letters, far from disclosing "real" feelings, and thus being authentic windows into their subjects' private lives, are merely a lighthearted literary game played by two self-consciously poetical writers. In this respect, rather than the novel being autobiographical, we might just as convincingly conclude that the letters are a form of fiction, and that they are certainly elaborate linguistic constructions. Moreover, other questions need to be asked about such material. What value accrues to it by virtue of being a "coded" reference to homosexuality? Would we be more or less interested in Le Gallienne's poetry, or Le Gallienne as a poet, if we knew for certain that his relationship with Wilde was a sexual one and not a mere "literary" friendship?

McKenna's and Ellmann's reading of a work such as *The Picture of Dorian Gray* as a novel fundamentally "about" homosexuality is obviously of importance to historians such as Ed Cohen who wish, as we have noted, to see Wilde's life and work as key "events" in a history of gay rights. But what relevance does (or could) such a reading have for those who wish to read the novel primarily for its literary value—for, say, its stylistic qualities, its intertextuality, or its narrative strategies? Here we ought to distinguish between, on the one hand, the role played by Wilde's writing in accounts of his sexual behaviour and sexual psychology and, on the other, the bearing of his (disputed) sexuality on judgments about the merits of his writing *as* writing. Too often the distinctions between these question are elided, so that Wilde's literary works are read as an expression of (and thus in turn become evidence for) his sexuality, and that sexuality in turn becomes the main key to unlocking the meaning of his literary works. In such viciously circular reasoning an important question is often overlooked: that is, how far could a work such as *The Picture of Dorian Gray* lay claim to critical attention for other reasons than exhibiting sexual desires and sexual practices which were at the time illegal (an issue to which we return in chapter six)?

On the novel's first publication in Britain there were a number of reviewers who insinuated a connection between rumours about Wilde's sexuality and the themes of the story. And those opinions typically came from figures—particularly W. E. Henley—who had known Wilde personally for some time. In this sense, they were not reviewing the novel, but—in the manner of many contemporary critics—reading the man via a review of the novel. However, there is surprisingly little concrete evidence to suggest that Henley's views were representative and that Wilde's writings had been widely viewed—that is, by readers who did not know him personally—in terms of their homoeroticism. Of course had they been so interpreted, and had Wilde therefore been given a reputation as a dangerous and morally subversive writer, instead of simply posing as one, he could hardly have achieved his popular successes on the relentlessly commercial West End Stage, a cultural arena which always fought shy of public controversy. Such an observation does not constitute evidence that Wilde's works were not "about" homosexuality, nor about *his* homosexuality (we suggested in chapter one that it is virtually impossible to adduce such a negative proof). It does nonetheless alert us to the existence of a range of interpretations available from the novel which are not overtly sexual or even biographical, and this in turn suggests that there were (and are) grounds for evaluating Wilde's works (and more particularly *The Picture of Dorian Gray*) other than those of self-disclosure. But this observation leads us to ask why these other grounds have been so routinely set aside in favour of autobiographical readings.

One of the reasons why such prominence has been given to the conjunction of Wilde's sexual and literary careers can be traced back to his trials, and in particular to the use made by Edward Carson, Queensberry's defence counsel, of some of Wilde's letters to Douglas (one of which included a sonnet), of *The Picture of Dorian Gray*, and of some of the maxims Wilde had recently published in the *Chameleon*. It is worth reminding ourselves that unlike the case successfully brought in 1888 against Emile Zola's British publisher, Henry Vizetelly, the Queensberry libel trial was not about an obscene publication, nor was it a case of literary libel. The trial was provoked by a card that Queensberry had left for Wilde in the Albemarle Club which identified him as "posing" as a "somdomite [*sic*]." Moreover, the introduction by Queensberry's counsel of "evidence" to be found in literary works may have come as something of a surprise to Wilde; certainly he could not have guessed that it would form a part of Queensberry's defence until he learned of the latter's Plea of Justification only a couple of days before the actual trial was due to start.

Most of that plea is concerned with listing instances and acts of "indecency and immorality" committed with named individuals. Only at the very end (almost as an afterthought) do we find the two elements of the plea that relate to Wilde's writings. Specifically they claimed that Wilde "did write and publish and cause and procure to be printed and published with his name on the title page thereof a certain immoral and obscene book [that is, *The Picture of Dorian Gray*] ... which said work was designed and intended ... and was understood by the readers thereof to describe the relations intimacies and passions of certain persons of sodomitical and unnatural habits tastes and practices." The plea further claimed that Wilde "joined in procuring the publication of the said last mentioned obscene work [the *Chameleon*] ... published his name on the contents sheet ... as its first and main contributor and published in said magazine certain immoral maxims as an introduction to the same under the title 'Phrases and Philosophies for the Use of the Young'" (Holland, 290). Both these works, according to Queensberry's plea, "were calculated to subvert morality and to encourage unnatural vice." They may have been added to the plea to justify the claim in Queensberry's card that Wilde was "posing" as a sodomite, should the evidence of his "unnatural habits" prove inconclusive.

The first point we should be alert to here is the restricted number of literary works which Queensberry's counsel named. *The Picture of Dorian Gray* and "Phrases and Philosophies" amount to only a small fraction of Wilde's *oeuvre*: the poems, all the plays, the short fiction, and the journalism were passed over. Moreover, the case was not that *The Picture of Dorian Gray* and "Phrases and

---

The Victorians & the Importance of Literary Biography   It was not unusual for Victorian reviewers to connect literary works and the lives of their authors, and literary biography was a popular genre. Famous examples include Elizabeth Gaskell's *Life of Charlotte Brontë* (1857), John Forster's *Life of Charles Dickens* (1872–1874), and John Cross's *George Eliot's Life* (1885). Writers' autobiographies—such as John Ruskin's *Praeterita* (1885–1889)—were equally popular. This interest in biography culminated in Sir Leslie Stephens's monumental *Dictionary of National Biography* (1882–present; after 1890 its editorship was taken over by Sir Sydney Lee) in which one of the longest entries is devoted to Shakespeare, a figure for whom there is relatively little secure biographical information. This inevitably led to a situation in which the writer's life was constructed from the work, and the work reinforced opinions about the life. In the Queensberry libel trial Carson's dissolving of the distinction between life and art would not then have seemed unreasonable. Indeed hostile reviews of works of literature often took the form of thinly veiled attacks on the personal lives of their authors. Algernon Swinburne, Dante Gabriel Rossetti, and Walter Pater had all suffered in this way.

Philosophies" were in any sense representative of Wilde's general intentions as a writer; rather, they were cited as specific and special cases. The singling out of *The Picture of Dorian Gray* may have been prompted by some of those isolated reviews (which we mentioned earlier) that had greeted its first publication in *Lippincott's Monthly Magazine*. Although not explicitly accusing Wilde of proselytizing homosexuality, comments had been made about the novel's "disgusting sins and abominable crimes" and its suitability only for "outlawed noblemen and perverted telegraph boys."[11] This was an allusion to the Cleveland Street scandal of 1889 in which a house in Westminster had been raided by the police, and in which telegraph boys from the General Post Office situated nearby had been found to have been offering sexual services to aristocratic customers. Such comments made the referent of the reviewers' objections clear and Wilde, unsurprisingly, had written numerous replies in defence of his story. That said, it needs to be stressed again that not all reviews had taken this line; American readers in particular seemed much more inclined to view the novel as a straightforward (and valuable) morality tale. It seems utterly implausible that American reviewers were collectively more naive than their British counterparts; it is just that they were not in possession of that inside information of some of Wilde's English reviewers, and as a consequence could more easily separate, in D. H. Lawrence's phrase, the teller from the tale. The evidence of "Phrases and Philosophies" was somewhat less secure, in that in this instance it was much more difficult to establish a direct connection between Wilde's aphorisms and specific sexual offences; here it was more the case that Carson was hoping to establish guilt by association—that Wilde's agreement to have his work published in the *Chameleon* aligned him with the allegedly immoral attitudes of that publication's other contributions, particularly the story entitled "The Prince and the Acolyte" by the magazine's editor, John Francis Bloxam.

In his opening remarks for the prosecution, Wilde's (that is, the prosecuting) counsel Sir Charles Clark spent a good deal of time on what he termed the "very curious allegations" regarding Wilde's literary works, probably because he thought that they were the most easy to rebut. And the case that he presented was straightforward: he aimed to demonstrate that the works in question did not necessarily lend themselves to the "inferences" listed by the defence, arguing that *The Picture of Dorian Gray* had been "five years ... upon the bookstalls and at bookshops and in libraries" and the epigrams in "Phrases and Philosophies" were no different in kind to those "which many of us have enjoyed when being interchanged in dialogue by the characters in such a play as *A Woman of No Importance*" (Holland, 40–41). Clark also took pains to establish the longevity and distinction of Wilde's reputation as a man of letters. Since the publication in the early 1880s of his first volume of poetry, Wilde, according to Clark, had become "a very public person indeed, laughed at by some, appreciated by many but at all events representing a special and particular aspect of artistic literature, which commended itself greatly to many of those of the foremost minds and most cultivated people of our time" (Holland, 28–29). In his cross-examination of Wilde, Queensberry's counsel, Edward Carson, tried to undermine Clark's case by contesting what he termed the "natural meaning" of the disputed works, by which he meant the meaning most readily available to the majority of readers (whom he called "ordinary" individuals): that they were about, or were inciting, illegal acts such as sodomy. And he also tried to force Wilde to concede that his writing was deeply autobiographical, that he was depicting incidents "in his own life." Carson's tactic was to try to convince the jury that only a man of what he called a "sodomitical" nature could have written such material.

Like some modern critics and readers, then, Carson was proposing a straight-forwardly expressive relationship between an author and his work, one which Wilde, in his turn, tried to counter by distinguishing between the function of a literary persona (a mask adopted by the literary artist) and the life and feelings of the real author. So Wilde consistently contested Carson's suggestions by insist-ing on a distinction between "novels and life," and emphatically reminded the court that he had written "a work of fiction." Likewise, Wilde absolved himself on artistic grounds of any responsibility for the "misinterpretations" that might be placed on his work by individual readers and which told far more against them and their values than against himself, the author. With particular regard to *The Picture of Dorian Gray*, he stressed that the reader did not discover mean-ings "in" the text, but rather—in a manner that would, in abstract terms at least, find sympathy with some other modern critics—projected onto it what he or she wished to find there. His argument was that "each man sees his own sin in Dorian Gray. What Dorian Gray's sins are, no one knows. He who finds them has brought them.""Only brutes and the illiterate," Wilde suggested, could pos-sibly have read his novel in the manner suggested by Carson (Holland, 78, 81). In this way Wilde tried to deflect the allegation of "sodomite" away from him-self—as an artist—and onto his readers, a group for whose beliefs he could not possibly be held responsible.

It is hard to judge who came out best from these courtroom exchanges. We should remember that by far the largest part of Carson's cross-examination cen-tred on the more serious and damning aspects of Queensberry's Plea of Justifi-cation, those numerous counts of gross indecency which Wilde had committed with young men. It was the evidence relating to these activities, overwhelming and irrefutable as it turned out to be, rather than Wilde's literary work, which brought about the collapse in the prosecution's case. This point needs to be stressed: it is commonly suggested that Wilde's literary art—in fact, art in gener-al—was on trial as much as the man. But this is just not true. Wilde was not tried and convicted because of anything he had written (the famous cross-examina-tion over *The Picture of Dorian Gray* belongs only to the libel trial, where Wilde was prosecuting and had not yet been, in strictly legal terms, accused of anything). Mr. Justice Clark's summing up (at the close of Wilde's first trial for gross indecency) gave the jury only four questions to consider, none of which mentioned his literary works. Carson's cross-examination of Wilde about his writing in the case against Queensbury was more than anything else part of a rhetorical strategy made by an extremely clever advocate who had known Wilde at Trinity College in Dublin, and knew better than most the weaknesses in the way he argued. The fact that it was seen as such by Wilde's counsel (and apparently by some members of the first jury in the case brought against Wilde by the Crown) should act as a reminder of the problems we encounter with "autobiographical" modes of interpretation: however tempting they might be, they can never be substantiated. Moreover, they also suffer from being always post hoc—as Wilde's counsel, Clark cogently put it, *The Picture of Dorian Gray*, that allegedly "sodomitical" book, had been available "upon the bookstalls and at bookshops and in libraries" for five years prior to the trial. As we noted earlier, no one during that time had seen fit to bring a case against it under the obscenity laws in the way in which the Crown had prosecuted Vizetelly. If *The Picture of Dorian Gray* was as manifestly about sodomy as Carson (and, later, McKenna) alleged, then there certainly would have been grounds for some kind of prosecution of both Wilde and his publisher, Ward, Lock.

On the other hand, though, Carson did win from Wilde the concession that certain passages in *The Picture of Dorian Gray* could be misconstrued so as to "convey the impression that the sin of Dorian Gray was sodomy" (Holland, 78–79). Of course the mere possibility of such an interpretation in no way proved (or proves) that the novel was written with the clear intention that it should be so read; nor does it go any way towards proving that such a reading accurately reflected the disposition or desires of the author. As Clark had curtly pointed out in his opening for the prosecution, "there is always a difficulty, of course, when upon a plea of this kind a statement is made referring to a particular book, because it puts one into the difficulty of considering what that book is" (Holland, 41). Yet Carson's proposition was a powerfully suggestive one, and his method of cross-examination—his rapid movement between statements about how readers interpreted the novel to questions about the details of Wilde's own life—was designed to consolidate it as a "fact" in the minds of the jury. If Carson could repeatedly suggest that Wilde himself was a homosexual, or that he moved within homosexual circles—if he could fix this image in the jury's minds, as he later successfully did—then what he claimed to be the so-called "natural meaning" of *The Picture of Dorian Gray* would begin to seem much more persuasive, more self-evident than it was. And in that process the distinction, which Wilde had insisted on, between who a writer is and what he writes about, would become irrevocably blurred.

Can We Imagine Robert Louis Stevenson
Writing *The Picture of Dorian Gray*? If Not, Why Not?

We can see the latent power of such suggestions by briefly comparing critical reactions to *The Picture of Dorian Gray* with those to Robert Louis Stevenson's near-contemporaneous *The Strange Case of Dr. Jekyll and Mr. Hyde*. It has now become a critical commonplace to reiterate Wilde's own contention about his novel, that nothing in the story is made explicit, and that Dorian's "sins" are never named. Likewise, and by extension, the precise nature of the relationships among the three main male characters, Lord Henry Wotton, Basil Hallward, and Dorian himself, is always deliberately withheld from the reader. At a time when male and female lives were much more clearly demarcated, and men habitually socialized in each other's company, often in the absence of women, a Victorian readership would not necessarily find anything remarkable when they encountered such a strictly gendered fictional world. At the same time, though, the relationships among the three men often appears claustrophobic and competitive; moreover it seems to centre on secrets, blackmail, and a celebration of the male body. The language in which the men describe their attachment to and interest in each other can be seen as ambivalent in that it appears to borrow terms more usually associated with the representation of male-female relationships. Similarly many of the settings in which Wilde places his male characters remove them from more usual Victorian male middle-class or aristocratic environments, those of professional work, or politics, or the public domain in general. By contrast, Basil, Dorian, and Lord Henry are most frequently found in the home, or in what can be loosely described as domestic settings, even if that domesticity is entirely male and more to do with exquisite tastes and rare objects than hearth, homeliness, and the raising of children. There is also a relative absence of narrative interest in female characters: many critics have pointed out how the role of Sybil Vane was "written up" for the 1891 book version of the novel. In addition the style of the novel has often been remarked upon. The overdetermined descriptive language, with its excessive use of adjectives and intensifying adverbs to do with the senses, has been taken to be suggestive of an aesthetic or a Decadent sensibility; historically (since the early 1870s, at least) those two labels had been used to connote or code sexual aberrance or excess.

For a century of readers, including Carson, Ellmann, and McKenna, it is precisely these sorts of elements that combine to form what they see as a homoerotic dynamic to the novel, one in which the tensions among the three main characters can only be fully understood in terms of male-male desire. Is it the case, though, that these features are necessarily homoerotic? As we shall detail later, some critics have seen this depiction of male aristocratic society as a critique of class and of a male bourgeois work ethic, rather than as a sexual ethic. Stevenson's *The Strange Case of Dr. Jekyll and Mr. Hyde* also concentrates almost exclusively on a male world, one which is again characterized by hidden desires and impulses, by secrets and blackmail, by differences between outside appearances and inner moral realities, and by a lack of interest in female characters. And there have been a number of modern critics who have insisted that Stevenson's novel, too, works by means of a submerged homoerotic dynamic which connects and explains the unusual tensions in the relationships among the main male characters and their failure, when threatened, to call upon the usual social mechanisms of policing and control, or to invoke the possibility of redress in law. At the same time, though, a homoerotic reading of Stevenson's novel will strike most readers as being much more provocative, and certainly more surprising, than a similar reading of *The Picture of Dorian Gray*. We have no evidence that Victorian reviewers interpreted *The Strange Case of Dr. Jekyll and Mr. Hyde* in such a way; nor is it an interpretation which comes readily to most modern readers when they encounter the novel for the first time. Those academic studies that claim to find a homoerotic subtext have had virtually no influence on the general reader and such a subtext has rarely, if ever, figured in the work's numerous dramatic and film adaptations. And one obvious reason for the relative resistance of *Jeykll and Hyde* to a homoerotic interpretation lies in the way Stevenson made an appeal to the Victorian reader via his romanticized, heterosexual authorial persona—one which, we might add, was as much a construction, as much a product of media hype, as Wilde's more effetely Decadent self-image. The dominant public perception of Stevenson, first as a dashing and glamorous adventurer, and then as an ill and tragically weakened married man who removed himself to a South Sea island, hardly lent itself to support personal sexual iconoclasm, let alone gay subtexts in his work.

Our aim in replaying Carson's and Wilde's exchanges, and then in comparing *The Picture of Dorian Gray* with *The Strange Case of Dr. Jekyll and Mr. Hyde*, has been to remind ourselves of the kinds of assumptions that have to be in place if the expressive value of literary works—their "authenticity"—is to be defined in terms of their connections to the author's sexual life, or to assumptions about his or her sexual identity. It is important to remember that the accusation that Wilde "did write and publish and cause and procure to be printed and published with his name on the title page thereof a certain immoral and obscene book" did not require Carson to prove that Wilde was guilty of immoral and obscene activities in his own life. Likewise, then, we should also recognize that our evaluation of what exactly works such as *The Picture of Dorian Gray* have to say about homosexuality does not have to depend on establishing the work's closeness to Wilde's own sexual practices. In forming a critical judgment about the novel we should try to separate two issues which Carson, and many literary critics since, have deliberately blurred. The first is: what (if anything) does *The Picture of Dorian Gray* (or any other work in Wilde's *oeuvre*) have to say about (homo)sexuality? And the second is: do those depictions of sexuality have any interest or value in and of themselves apart from their alleged relationship to Wilde's own life, knowledge of which, as we have noted above, is still relatively insecure?

There is a more telling point to be made against seeing Wilde's literary works as crudely expressive of his sexuality, and this is also to be glimpsed in the libel trial. As we noted, only a fraction of Wilde's writing was mentioned in the court proceedings: so even if the case for seeing autobiographical elements in *The Picture of Dorian Gray* can be sustained, it still leaves the major part of the *oeuvre* unaccounted for. A theory of expressivity cannot be established on the basis of a few passages taken in isolation from one novel. It is worth reminding ourselves how resistant some of Wilde's other writing has been to readings of this sort. And it is also worth pointing out that when other works (notably *A Woman of No Importance* and *The Importance of Being Earnest*) have been read for their gay subtexts, those readings (as we argue in chapter five) are difficult to square with their overall dramatic structures, with their initial receptions, and with their enduring popularity among basically conservative British theatrical audiences.

There is also the issue of what we do with the evidence—mainly from contemporary reviews—about how Wilde's works were actually read at the time of their publication (rather than with the hindsight of the evidence that came to light during the trials). As we have said, it is certainly the case that some readers saw *The Picture of Dorian Gray* in terms of a scandalous portrayal of male–male desire but, as we have also said, many others did not. Moreover the worst of the British reviews came from individuals who seem to have known in advance what they were "looking for" in the book. In the terms in which Wilde put it, they found exactly what they "brought with them." Much the same can be said of "The Portrait of Mr. W.H.," another work often read nowadays for its homoerotic subtexts. However, as Horst Schroeder pointed out many years ago, hostile responses to Wilde's essay/story were the exception rather than the rule. He claims that the vast majority of reviewers saw "no harm in the story and discussed it not from the point of view of morality, or rather immorality, but in the first place from the point of view of Shakespearean criticism."[12] Significantly, the most barbed review of "Mr. W.H." came from the same source as the most vituperative comments about *The Picture of Dorian Gray*—from the *Scots Observer*, edited by that former colleague and later bitter rival of Wilde, the arch-conservative W. E. Henley, Stevenson's model for the pirate Long John Silver in *Treasure Island*.

Wilde's Place in a History of Sexuality

Fittingly, such a perception of the discrepancy between modern readings of Wilde's works and the evidence of how the majority of contemporary readers responded to them has led some historians to reexamine the whole issue of the kind of sexuality which the works express. Here some of the most searching criticism of anachronistic readings of Wilde's writings have been made by Alan Sinfield and a little later by Joseph Bristow. Both critics have suggested that such readings have been driven by modern concerns about homosexuality—that it is these concerns which in turn inform the identification and the interpretation of the works' alleged homosexual codes. Broadly speaking, Sinfield and Bristow argue that the modern reader tends to equate the "effeminacy" associated with the behaviour of Wilde's dandies with homosexuality even though, from the point of view of the cultural historian, there is little actual evidence for making such a connection in the years leading up to Wilde's trials. As a consequence what the modern reader takes to be markers of gender politics might have appeared to original readers in the first instance as class markers, in the sense that representations of the excesses of the dandy were invariably understood to be comments on aristocratic privilege rather than on sexual identity. Such a reading has the advantage of preserving elements of the transgressive nature of Wilde's heroes, but it gives to them a very different politics. It has the added merit of accounting for some contemporary objections to his work.

Arguments like those of Sinfield and Bristow, which attempt to distinguish between what was interpreted as effeminate behaviour on the one hand, and homosexual (or in Carson's terms, "sodomitical") behaviour on the other, in their turn have encouraged a wider-ranging debate about the historiography of gay culture in the late nineteenth century and the nature of Wilde's precise role in it. The idea that Wilde's trial marked the emergence of the homosexual as a distinct "type," an observation which can be traced back to, and which has in turn received its authority from, the work of Michel Foucault, and which (as we noted) was developed by Sinfield, is now itself coming under scrutiny. So, too, is the assumption that the 1890s marked a particularly high moment of homophobia—a moment in what has been seen as a general homosexual panic. For example, through a meticulous examination of numerous legal cases, H. G. Cocks has argued that "sodomy" was named "openly, publicly, and repeatedly" from 1780 onwards, and that there is no evidence to see the 1890s as a uniquely homophobic decade. As a consequence, Cocks argues that there is no compelling evidence for Wilde's trial being seen as a hugely significant defining moment which materially changed attitudes towards the sexual behaviour of homosexuals.[13] Cocks even contests one of the fundamental received truths of queer theory, that the Labouchere amendment to the Criminal Law Amendment Act of 1885, under which Wilde was convicted, was pivotal in the policing of sexuality. That act, in his view, did not substantially change the law; it merely codified what had been happening on a piecemeal basis in common law for a long period. In keeping with this revisionary tendency, Matt Cook has recently claimed that amendments to the 1898 Vagrancy Law (which passed into law well after Wilde's trials, and which criminalized public soliciting or importuning) did much more to change the policing of homosexuality than Labouchere's famous amendment. Cook also draws attention to the roles played by less prominent homosexual activists, such as George Ives, in bringing about real changes in the public perception of male-male desire. All of this runs counter to the views of a generation of earlier critics, such as Elaine Showalter, who argued that the 1890s was a singular decade, one marked off by its acute anxieties about gender and sex roles.

These debates are not of course about literary issues, nor are they much concerned with the role of literary works in the history of gay culture. However they do have important implications for the critic of Wilde's literary works. We have argued that the interest in reading Wilde's work autobiographically, stemming as it did from the trials, was part of a larger project of rehabilitating his reputation by giving him a central role in the history of gay rights. However, if that history is now being questioned, then the *raison d'être* for such a reading is also weakened, if not undermined. If the argument for a generalized homosexual panic—that is, for a heightened anxiety about homosexual activity in the years leading up to Wilde's trials—is flawed, then one of the central justifications of expressive autobiographical readings of his works is lost. We might put all this another way round and say that if arguments about a homosexual panic are exaggerated, then Wilde's reasons for wishing to use his works to proselytize for what McKenna calls the "Cause" are by the same token undermined.

Raising questions about Wilde's motives for writing leads to what is perhaps the most substantial objection to a straightforward identification between his literary works and his sexuality. Other details of Wilde's biography—that is, his letters to his publishers, to his literary friends, his self-advertised desire for fame, his constant need for money—all these point to a range of quite separate motives for writing, some of which manifestly conflict with a desire to explore, in however coded a manner, his sexual identity. To treat Wilde's works as expressing aspects of his life involves a profoundly impoverished view of both his personality and of literary creativity in general, one which separates the composition of individual works from much of what philosophers have for some years identified as the institutional qualities of art. Such a treatment also elides real distinctions to be made about different sorts of works, written in different genres, on different occasions, and for different audiences, different purposes, and for different publishers. It does not even acknowledge, let alone attempt to explain, what sociologists of texts are now calling the bibliographic codes of literary works.[14] That is, it says little about a work's reception and almost nothing about its sales, because it fails to notice the social, and so the produced, nature of any text—that decisions about pricing, format, print run, and so on, invariably have a commercial (and therefore a social) rather than simply expressive origin. Equally importantly, autobiographical, and particularly psychosexual, views of creativity have nothing to say about collaboration, particularly in those genres, such as the drama, which depend upon a host of co-creative agents, principally actors, managers, and directors. (It is worth reminding ourselves also that Wilde worked most successfully in a wholly commercial theatrical environment, and none of the theatre managers with whom he collaborated would have any interest in staging a work which ran even the smallest risk of offending an audience, let alone of incurring the wrath of the state censor, the Lord Chamberlain's Chief Examiner of Plays.) This is a qualification particularly important in Wilde's case, because there is strong and consistent evidence that at every stage in his career as a writer both of fiction and of drama he solicited advice from more experienced colleagues and frequently acted on that advice.

And so ...

Where have all these qualifications led us? Initially they suggest that the question of whether Wilde's literary works are "about" his homosexuality cannot be satisfactorily answered by a recourse to details of his own sexual life. We can be confident about this claim for several reasons. First, many details of Wilde's sexual life are still unknown, and some of the most important questions about it will probably never be answered. Even McKenna's book relies on testimony from the trials, much of which is not necessarily reliable, and certainly not capable of being generalized to explain the whole of Wilde's sexual experiences. Second, and as we have already suggested, there is a considerable dispute among cultural historians about whether there could have been a readership (beyond Wilde's own intimate circle) for the coded references to homosexuality which his works allegedly contain. After all, reduced to their bare bones, arguments about subtexts in a literary work are invariably tautologous: we cannot prove the existence of hidden meanings. If we could do so, they wouldn't be hidden, or have to be hidden, in the first place. All we can do is try to identify a body of readers for whom those readings would have been relevant, and try to find a persuasive reason for an author to address them. In the case of Wilde, neither of these avenues has been satisfactorily explored. And this reservation in turn leads to a third caveat. There is a great deal more to Wilde's life (or to anybody else's, for that matter) than sexual behaviour, and many more possible ways of explaining literary creativity. So even if we were disposed to accept the premise that Wilde's personality was formed and then driven by his sexuality, we are not as a consequence justified in ignoring or neglecting those many other details which affected how his works were written, and which cannot be understood in terms of sexual orientation. To give a graphic example of this point: Wilde's disputes with his publisher Leonard Smithers over the pricing and print runs of *The Ballad of Reading Gaol* (generally Wilde's complaints were entirely related to the amount of money he would earn from the poem) probably had as much to do with his overall artistic conception of that work as his years in prison for gross indecency did.

Here perhaps we should confess to a vested interest in this debate about the limits to the amount of work which an autobiographically expressive aesthetic will do for us. Our example of Wilde's disputes with Leonard Smithers is taken from an earlier attempt to discuss Wilde's creativity in terms which deliberately resisted giving priority to his sexuality and which focused instead on the materialist preconditions for professional authorship in the late nineteenth century. In that study we argued that the mundane and the unglamorous aspects of authorship can be seen as inevitably possessing a powerful formative agency. The point of marshalling such information was not to offer it as an alternative to, say, Ellmann's or McKenna's version of creativity; nor indeed as an alternative to autobiographical interpretation *per se*. It was merely to point out that this kind of information has an equal claim to our attention when we try to understand what motivated Wilde, not least because it often leads to a concept of authorial intention which conflicts with one understood primarily in terms of his sexual identity. To put this simply, and perhaps in somewhat reductive terms: it is difficult to reconcile our knowledge that, for Wilde, writing was often and necessarily a commercial activity with the idea that he wished to use his literary works to subvert bourgeois sexual morality. At the same time, though, we also need to acknowledge that the majority of modern readers are likely to be attracted to Wilde precisely because of his sexual notoriety, and it is thus his sexuality—rather than those more mundane aspects of his life—which will continue to be seen as the driving force of his personality, and so the most important element in his creativity. Carson's legacy, if not wholly welcome, has certainly been enduring.

Such an acknowledgment obviously places the academic critic in a distinctly odd position *vis-à-vis* that "general reader" to whom, as we noted in chapter one, he or she has—or should have—certain responsibilities. How can scholarship about Wilde—whether it is to disavow notions of authorial intention altogether, or whether it is to present a less glamorous and more commercially motivated intending author—be made relevant to these general readers' experience when it seems to fly in the face of what they most want to know? Or rather, when it seems simply to disable or contradict the kind of reading to which many are so strongly attracted? As we have suggested, one can contest on scholarly grounds many of the details (as well as the overall argument) of McKenna's biography: that his autobiographical reading of the literary works is simplistic and tautologous, and that his sensationalized account of Wilde's sexual promiscuity is based on what is often clearly unreliable evidence and an anachronistic conception of sexual identity. Yet McKenna's biography—like the evidence from Wilde's trials—gives the modern reader a powerfully dramatic portrait, one which it is difficult to modify, let alone supplant. The main challenge of the remainder of this book, then, is to try to show the positive elements of what will often seem like a negative activity—that of undermining or disabling some of the most cherished popular myths about Wilde and his works, including the idea that his writing is—as McKenna puts it—"highly autobiographical." We begin, in the next chapter, by looking at the notion of his life as a "tragedy," and we shall concentrate on *De Profundis*, that work which seems on the face of things to be the most authentically autobiographical because it was not published in his lifetime and was therefore apparently free from the taint of those commercial interests which we have mentioned.

Notes

1. It is worth reminding American readers that British law does not define freedom of speech in the same way as American law, and that laws of slander, defamation, and libel are different in the two countries.

2. Merlin Holland, "Comments on Susan Balée's Review of *Oscar Wilde: A Long and Lovely Suicide* by Melissa Knox," *Victorian Studies*, 39 (1996), 539–41.

3. See Alan Sinfield, *The Wilde Century* (London: Cassell, 1994); and "'Effeminacy' and 'Femininity': Sexual Politics in Wilde's Comedies," *Modern Drama*, 37 (1994), 34–52.

4. A comment made during a private conversation between Ian Small and Richard Ellmann in the early 1980s.

5. The most important of these was Joseph Donohue's observation that Wilde's creativity continued well after his release from prison: Wilde wrote and saw through press *The Ballad of Reading Gaol* (1898) and carefully and systematically revised *The Importance of Being Earnest* and *An Ideal Husband* for publication in 1899. See Joseph Donohue, "Recent Studies of Oscar Wilde," *Nineteenth-Century Theatre*, 16.2 (1988), 123–36.

6. Sinfield, *The Wilde Century*, 121.

7. Jonathan Fryer, *André & Oscar: Gide, Wilde and the Gay Art of Living* (London: Constable, 1997), 116.

8. So are we really to believe, as McKenna seems to do, Douglas's assertion, made in his *Autobiography*, that "'at least ninety per cent' of his contemporaries [at Winchester] had sex with other boys" and that the "remaining ten per cent were doomed to celibacy by circumstance rather than by choice" (McKenna, 153)?

9. See, for example, Richard Jenkyns, *The Victorians and Ancient Greece* (Cambridge: Harvard University Press, 1980); for an account more closely focused on Wilde's use of classical culture, see Linda Dowling, *Hellenism and Homosexuality in Victorian Oxford* (Ithaca: Cornell University Press, 1994).

10. There is the added complication that Le Gallienne's handwriting, especially in those letters which McKenna quotes, is often very difficult to read.

11. Comments which appeared in an unsigned notice in the *Scots Observer*, 5 July 1895, 181; reprinted in *Oscar Wilde: The Critical Heritage*, Karl Beckson, ed., 75. Further details of the reception of the *Lippincott* version of *Dorian Gray* can be found in *The Complete Works of Oscar Wilde. Volume III. The Picture of Dorian Gray*, Joseph Bristow, ed. (Oxford: Oxford University Press, 2005), xliv–li.

12. Horst Schroeder, *Oscar Wilde, 'The Portrait of Mr. W.H.'—Its Composition, Publication and Reception* (privately printed: Braunschweig, 1986), 15.

13. See H. G. Cocks, *Nameless Offences: Homosexual Desire in the Nineteenth Century* (London: Tauris, 2003). The thesis against which Cocks is arguing can be usefully seen in works such as Peter Gay, *The Bourgeois Experience*, 2 vols. (Oxford: Oxford University Press, 1984–1986).

14. The role of bibliographic codes in interpreting literary works has been theorized most cogently and accessibly by Jerome J. McGann in *The Textual Condition* (Princeton: Princeton University Press, 1991); for an application of his ideas to Wilde's texts, see Nicholas Frankel, *Wilde's Decorated Books* (Ann Arbor: University of Michigan Press, 2000).

Works Cited & Consulted

Baylen, Joseph and Robert L. McBath. "A Note on Oscar Wilde, Alfred Douglas and Lord Rosebery, 1897," *English Language Notes*, 23 (1985), 42–48.

Beckson, Karl. *The Wilde Encyclopedia*. New York: AMS Press, 1998.

Belford, Barbara. *Oscar Wilde: A Certain Genius*. New York: Random House, 2000.

Bristow, Joseph. *Effeminate England: Homoerotic Writing After 1885*. New York: Columbia University Press, 1995.

Cocks, H. G. *Nameless Offences: Homosexual Desire in the Nineteenth Century*. London: Tauris, 2003.

Cohen, Ed. *Talk on the Wilde Side: Towards a Genealogy of Discourse on Male Sexualities*. New York: Routledge, 1993.

The Complete Letters of Oscar Wilde. Merlin Holland and Rupert Hart-Davis, eds. London: Fourth Estate, 2000.

Cook, Matt. *London and the Culture of Homosexuality, 1885–1914*. Cambridge: Cambridge University Press, 2003.

Daudet, Alphonse. *In the Land of Pain*. ed. and trans. Julian Barnes. London: Jonathan Cape, 2002.

Douglas, Alfred. *Oscar Wilde and Myself*. London: John Lang, 1914.

_____. *Without Apology*. London: Martin Secker, 1938.

_____. *Oscar Wilde: A Summing-Up*. London: Duckworth, 1940.

Ellmann, Richard. *Oscar Wilde*. London: Hamish Hamilton, 1987.

Fryer, Jonathan. *André & Oscar: Gide, Wilde and the Gay Art of Living*. London: Constable, 1997.

Gay, Peter. *The Bourgeois Experience*. 2 vols. Oxford: Oxford University Press, 1984–1986.

Guy, Josephine M. and Ian Small. *Oscar Wilde's Profession: Writing and the Culture Industry*. Oxford: Oxford University Press, 2000.

Harris, Frank. *Oscar Wilde: His Life and Confessions*. New York: printed and published by the author, 1916; rev. ed. London: Constable, 1938.

The Letters of Oscar Wilde. Rupert Hart-Davis, ed. London: Hart-Davis, 1962.

Holland, Merlin. *Irish Peacock and Scarlet Marquess*. London: Fourth Estate, 2003.

Holland, Vyvyan. *Son of Oscar Wilde*. London: Hart-Davis, 1954.

_____. *Time Remembered. After Père Lachaise*. London: Gollancz, 1966.

Hyde, H. Montgomery. *The Trials of Oscar Wilde*. London: Hodge, 1948.

_____. *Oscar Wilde*. New York: Farrar, Straus, and Giroux, 1975.

Knox, Melissa. *Oscar Wilde: A Long and Lovely Suicide*. New Haven: Yale University Press, 1994.

Kronenberger, Louis. *Oscar Wilde*. Boston: Little, Brown, 1976.

Mason Stuart [Christopher Millard]. *Bibliography of Oscar Wilde*. London: T. Werner Laurie Ltd., 1914.

McKenna, Neil. *The Secret Life of Oscar Wilde*. London: Century, 2003.

Morley, Sheridan. *Oscar Wilde: An Illustrated Biography*. London: Weidenfeld and Nicolson, 1976.

Murray, Douglas. *Bosie: A Biography of Lord Alfred Douglas*. 2000; London: Hodder & Stoughton, 2001.

Pearce, Joseph. *The Unmasking of Oscar Wilde*. London: Harper Collins, 2000.

Pichois, Claude and Jean Ziegler. *Baudelaire*, trans. Graham Robb. 1989; London: Vintage, 1991.

Raby, Peter. "The Making of *The Importance of Being Earnest*," *Times Literary Supplement*, 4629 (December 20, 1991), 13.

Schmidgall, Gary. *The Stranger Wilde*. London: Abacus, 1994.

Sedgwick, Eve Kosofsky. *Epistemology of the Closet*. Berkeley: University of California Press, 1990.

Sherard, Robert Harborough. *The Life of Oscar Wilde*. London: T. Werner Laurie, 1906.

Showalter, Elaine. *Sexual Anarchy: Gender and Culture at the Fin de Siècle*. New York: Viking, 1990.

Small, Ian. *Oscar Wilde Revalued*. Greensboro: ELT Press, 1993.

| III | *De Profundis*:
Tragedy and the Art
of Self-Fashioning

TOWARDS THE END of the previous chapter we mentioned that the most potent of modern myths of Wilde was that which understood him as a tragic victim. It is easy to see how the general outline of this myth came about. We have to imagine a man at the height of his creative powers and the toast of London's West End theatre suddenly finding himself incarcerated for a two-year sentence in a number of dingy Victorian prisons, principally at Holloway (in London) and at Reading. He had been imprisoned for practices that he did not consider to be criminal; he was deprived (as he saw matters, unfairly) of contact with Lord Alfred Douglas, the person he most wanted to hear from; he learned of the death of his mother well after the event; he was tortured by the knowledge that he could not see his two sons; he was denied access (until well into1896) to the reading and writing materials that had hitherto been central to his life; and finally he was forced to spend most of his time alone or in silence, forbidden to converse with other prisoners except in furtive whispers which if discovered could be punished by solitary confinement.

Given all this Wilde could all too easily appear to himself as the central player in an absurd comedy, and to outsiders as a deeply tragic figure for whom imprisonment was the appropriate nemesis for overweening hubris. At some point in late 1896, by now provided with pen and paper through the good offices of the prison authorities, Wilde commenced, as he put it, to "show his life to the world," to write "of the past and of the future, of sweet things changed to bitterness and of bitter things that may be turned into joy" (*Complete Works*, II: 141, 37). The resulting manuscript, which is addressed to "Dear Bosie" (that is, Wilde's lover, Douglas), has passed into literary history. It has come to be known—rather deceptively, as it turns out—as *De Profundis*, or "from the depths" (the title that translates into that phrase, one taken from the Psalms, was Robert Ross's and not Wilde's).

Uniquely among Wilde's works *De Profundis* appears to have been composed in isolation from all of the usual institutions of literary production, and thus seems to possess an expressive immediacy absent from the other more self-consciously fashioned works in the *oeuvre*. More particularly, it seems to exist beyond the reach of those commercial interests that recent historians have seen as central to late-nineteenth-century authorship. The popular history of *De Profundis* hints at a dynamic connecting expression, authentic experience, and emotional intensity. The image of Wilde conjured up by the work's title, that of the lonely agonized prisoner pouring out his soul in a work of cathartic emotional and spiritual release, invites us to read the resulting document as a frank and sincere exploration of the self. It should thus come as little surprise to discover that of all Wilde's works it is *De Profundis* that has been most consistently appropriated for biographical readings—Isobel Murray suggests it can be seen as "partial autobiography" (Murray, xiii)—and as a consequence, it is *De Profundis* that has probably held the greatest sway over the manner in which Wilde's life, and in particular his character and his creativity, have been conceptualized. In the light of all this, it is strange to find that while *De Profundis* may be the most infamous of Wilde's works, it is also the least analysed.

Murray's label prompts a number of questions. First, how accurate or how useful an account of Wilde's life is *De Profundis* if we do consider it to be "partial autobiography"; in other words, what kind of "life" of himself does Wilde give to us? Second: would there be many readers of *De Profundis* if it were not so intimately tied to such a famous (or notorious) historical person? We could pose these questions in a rather different way. Do we value *De Profundis* principally for the insights it gives us into Wilde the man, either directly (in terms of

---

Myths About Literary Creativity   The stories that have accumulated to explain the creation of *De Profundis* have elements in common with myths about the creation of a number of other literary works, such as Coleridge's claim that "Kubla Khan" was composed in an opium-induced hallucination, or Lloyd Osbourne's explanation of the composition of *Dr. Jekyll and Mr. Hyde* by his stepfather, Robert Louis Stevenson. Osbourne reported that it was the direct transcript of a dream, drafted out in a frenzied burst of activity over a mere three days only for the manuscript to be burned (a result of the objections of Stevenson's wife, Fanny) and entirely rewritten in a subsequent three-day period: "an astounding feat," Osbourne wrote, "sixty-four thousand words in six days" (Stevenson, *Works*, V: vii, xi). Accounts such as these marginalize the element of calculation and contrivance in literary creativity. In them the author is so closely identified with the work that he appears almost to be possessed by it, and as a consequence is unable to censor his thoughts. That lack of control in turn allows him to disown full responsibility for his writing—as Douglas was to report Wilde later doing apropos of *De Profundis*.

informing us of events in his private life) or indirectly (in exhibiting aspects of his personality)? And if so, then how secure are those insights? Or, is the work valuable in and of itself, as a piece of what modern critics have termed life-writing, and therefore as a meditation on the nature of suffering and redemption? If we follow this second path, then we also need to ask why the piece is so rarely considered as a whole, and why some of its most obvious literary short-comings—such as its repetitions, its rambling structure, its frequent contradic-tions—have been so rarely commented upon? Here it is worth stressing that it is an emphasis on the privacy and intimacy of the document that typically per-mits these kinds of limitations to be explained away. As Richard Ellmann ably put it: "as an apologia *De Profundis* suffers from the adulteration of simplicity by eloquence, by an arrogance lurking in its humility and by its disjointed structure. But as a love letter it has all the consistency it needs" (Ellmann, 484).

De Profundis: Its Texts & Its Identity

What difference does it make if we replace the label of "partial autobiogra-phy" with that of "love letter"? Is Ellmann's label any more appropriate than Murray's or, for that matter, than that of Robert Ross? Oddly enough, if we take the time to look at the evidence closely, it turns out that it is not at all clear whether the manuscript even represents a single document, let alone pos-sesses a single identity: that is to say, although the folio bearing the number "1" begins with "Dear Bosie" and the folio bearing the number "40" concludes with "Your affectionate friend, Oscar Wilde," the folios in between are so varied in character—in the amount and kind of corrections, the style of the handwrit-ing, the sort of material discussed—that it is possible that initially they derived from quite separate documents.[1] Moreover, even if we do assume that the man-uscript constitutes a single letter, it was one which was never actually received in that form by its addressee, Alfred Douglas. According to Robert Ross (the most significant player in the entire textual history of the work), Douglas was only sent a "typed copy" of the manuscript, and whether or not he actually received that typed copy, and what relation it bore to the manuscript itself, are vexed issues.[2]

The vast majority of readers will not normally concern themselves with these questions about the textual integrity and social status of Wilde's prison manu-script. Moreover, they are details that are routinely overlooked in the romanti-cized mythology of its composition to which we alluded earlier. So recently, for example, Julia Prewitt Brown has written of *De Profundis* as being composed "in an exalted state of mind," an observation that could only be made by someone who had never looked at the manuscript itself (Brown, 105). Yet, as we shall try to show, these questions of integrity and status are particularly significant when we think about the manuscript's autobiographical functions—that is, about both its expressive honesty and its role in forming myths about the "tragic" Wilde.

In assigning such a vital role to names, it is obviously important that we are as clear as possible about our own labels. So in the discussion that follows we will distinguish between what we term Wilde's "prison manuscript," that heavily revised handwritten document of 55,000 words written on both sides of forty often barely legible folios, which he put together in his prison cell (it is currently held in the British Library), and the subsequent printings of it, or parts of it, by various hands. These include the portions of the manuscript that Ross published under the title of *De Profundis* in 1905 and 1908, and the text which Hart-Davis produced in his 1962 edition of Wilde's correspondence (reprinted in Merlin Holland's and Hart-Davis's enlarged edition of the correspondence in 2000, and reprinted too at the hands of several other editors). We shall refer

---

Swallows and Amazons & the "Missing" Typescript of De Profundis   It will come as a surprise to some readers to learn that a key (if unwitting) player in the textual transmission of Wilde's prison manuscript was a writer who is best known today as the author of a sequence of children's stories, beginning with the famous *Swallows and Amazons* (published in 1930). Some years before this work, however, Arthur Ransome (1884–1967) had also published a book on Wilde entitled *Oscar Wilde: A Critical Study* (1912). In that work he suggested that the versions of *De Profundis* that Ross had published in 1905 and 1908 had derived from a letter addressed not to Ross (as a reader might have justifiably concluded from those editions) but rather to Alfred Douglas. The very fact that Ransome had dedicated *Oscar Wilde: A Critical Study* to Ross made it clear to Douglas that Ross must have been the source of this information. Douglas, aware of how damaging this revelation could be to his reputation, immediately wrote to Ross demanding an explanation. Ross defended Ransome by arguing that Douglas, having received a typed copy of Wilde's prison manuscript, must have always known the origins of the published editions of *De Profundis*. Douglas furiously denied this and issued writs for libel against author, publisher, printer, and bookseller. Publisher and printer apologized and withdrew but Ransome and the Times Book Club went to court. The action was heard in the High Court of Justice, King's Bench Division, on 17 and 18 April 1913. Ransome and the Times Book Club defended themselves by producing Wilde's manuscript (which had been lodged by Ross in the British Library some years earlier), which proved that Ransome's account was true.

In a letter to Ross of 1912 (now housed in the Ross Deposition in the Clark Library, and reproduced by Douglas Murray), Douglas explained matters as follows: "As you must be perfectly well aware, I have never, until I saw it stated in Ransome's book, had the slightest inkling that the MS of *De Profundis* was a letter addressed to me by Wilde or that there was any connection between the letter you sent me in 1897 (which I destroyed after reading the first half dozen lines) and the book" (Douglas Murray, 171). Some years later, in his *Autobiography*, Douglas gave a fuller, though different, version of events:

to these last items as Wilde's "prison letter" in order to distinguish them from Ross's editions. If we look in more detail at Wilde's prison manuscript, and try to ascertain what sort of a document it is, *textually speaking*, what do we find?

As we have noted, much of the biographical importance that attaches to Wilde's prison manuscript comes from the fact that it was never published in his lifetime. It is a commonplace assumption that manuscripts are documents which in some way represent more "authentic" expressions of a writer's thoughts. This assumption in turn rests on a further and apparently equally commonplace observation, that a manuscript somehow embodies the "aura" (to adapt Walter Benjamin's phrase) of a historically real figure. Consequently it is seen as a tangible physical connection with the past and so seems to be the closest possible wit-

---

continued

> I did not know of the existence of the *De Profundis* MS till years after Wilde's death. … All I can say with certainty is that on one occasion after I met Oscar again, after his release from prison, I reproached him about something or other in the course of a discussion we had, and he said words to the following effect: "Surely you are not bringing up against me what I wrote in prison when I was starving and half mad. You must know that I didn't really mean a word of what I said." It immediately and naturally occurred to me that he was referring to this letter of Ross's which was supposed to have contained extracts of things he had said or written against me in prison, and I replied to the effect that I had really not done more than glance at the letter, and that as soon as I saw what it was about I tore it in pieces and threw the pieces away. (Douglas, 135)

Although Douglas did admit to receiving from Ross some form of typescript with comments by Wilde about him in 1897, he consistently denied having taken proper notice of it, and therefore denied, too, being able to connect it with the text of Wilde's prison manuscript (in fact Douglas also persisted in claiming that the typescript he received must have been completed before Wilde left prison). It is impossible to know whose version of these events—that of Ross or Douglas—is true. Ross may have sent Douglas an edited transcript of the prison manuscript (though it is hard to see why he would have gone to the bother of doing so). Douglas may have read much more of the typescript which he received than he was prepared to admit, and may also have believed that in burning it he had destroyed the only copy, and therefore any evidence that Ransome could use to defend himself. What may be more significant, however, is the fact that during the action against Ransome the manuscript was read out in court and therefore further transcripts of it were made by reporters. These were subsequently published in part in many newspapers. Inaccurate and incomplete as these were, this was the first time that the material that Ross had omitted in his editions came into the public domain, and therefore in some ways they represent the first publication of those parts of Wilde's prison manuscript.

ness to a writer's creative intentions. Such familiar views of manuscripts have in turn received powerful intellectual reinforcement from some long-established traditions of academic text editing. Theorists such as W. W. Greg argue that any movement away from the manuscript towards a printed text inevitably involves a process of textual corruption because the mechanisms of printing always require the agency of other hands. It was this conviction that gave the rationale to the production of modern variorum editions; it was (and is) assumed that such a process of excavation gets us back to some indefinable "essence" of a work, and thus closer to a writer's mind in the throes of creation.

The Prison Manuscript

Given this fetishization of manuscript evidence, it may come as something of a surprise to realize that the text printed in all editions of the *Letters* is in fact a mediation of Wilde's prison manuscript. Textual scholars know well that the transposition of handwriting into type inevitably involves any number of editorial interventions and compromises. In the case of the prison manuscript these are numerous and include the following: a standardization of accidentals, principally punctuation, spelling, and paragraphing; the omission of Wilde's many deletions of passages; and the rendering invisible of his frequent reordering of material and his insertion of new thoughts. In the *Letters* there are also no indications of those places where Wilde's handwriting is so cramped or blotted as to be difficult to read, and thus no sense that there are plausible alternative readings for certain words and phrases. There are also occasions where Wilde's

---

Manuscript Evidence & Editorial Practice   There are four ways in which modern textual editors can treat the evidence which manuscripts provide (technically, documents such as manuscripts have been known as "witnesses" to a text or, more recently, as "versions"). They may, as W. W. Greg and Fredson Bowers have argued, view a manuscript as the primary and most authoritative witness to a writer's creative intentions. It follows from this that any copy made from the manuscript entails the possibility (and with early manuscripts, the likelihood) of textual corruption. When they are faced with multiple manuscript copies of a work—frequently the case with Wilde's *oeuvre*—these editors still have to decide which one has priority and why. Second, an editor may see publication as a necessary part of the creative process, one in which the writer is given the opportunity to revise and refine first thoughts. In this view, the editor may grant authority to the first published edition of a work, or to the last edition which the writer oversaw before he died, or—hypothetically—to any one in between. Here manuscripts are of interest insofar as they represent an early stage in the creative process. In contrast to the Greg-Bowers line of argument, publication *per se* is not seen as a censoring, coercive, or corrupting activity, although in the case of Wilde it is certainly true that some periodical publishers (and theatre managers) were more controlling than others.

hand is clear, but where his text has been silently "corrected" by the modern editor. In other words, a manuscript which is extremely unfinished, and in places barely legible, is re-presented in type as a coherent and assured narrative.[3] As a consequence, the experience of reading the text in print and the account of its composition which we hypothesize from that reading are profoundly altered. Where the manuscript is chaotic, full of false starts and cancellations, the printed text gives the appearance of order, polish, and fluency.

Even more surprising perhaps is that the physical appearance of the manuscript—in particular the ways in which the pages are numbered and the fact that only some of the folios are revised—does not correspond to the view that it was the product of a single set of intentions. Some folios are obviously fair (or "top") copy, with Wilde writing in a tiny hand both on and between the lines of the paper. Elsewhere the writing is larger, more spaced, the corrections more numerous, and the frequency of Wilde's deletions and false starts much more striking. With this second sort of folio we do indeed seem to be closer to a mind in the throes of composition. Interestingly, though, there is no sense of sequence in the relation of "rough drafts" to fair copy. So it is not the case that we have, say, the first third of the document in fair copy, and the rest in draft because the writer ran out of time or paper: rather fair copy and draft are mixed throughout the manuscript. Moreover there is clear evidence that the last and first sentences on certain folios have been corrected to fit one page to the next, with the numbering of the folios themselves adjusted accordingly (so we find

---

continued   The third option for an editor is to give authority to what has been termed a "social" text—that is, a text that has had wide social currency and influence, but which does not necessarily have the full authority of the writer. A good example is to be found in a famous line in Act I of *The Importance of Being Earnest*, where Lady Bracknell comments on Jack's dead parents. The best-known form of this line, the one most often heard in performance, was in fact the result of a revision made by Robert Ross when he published the play in his 1908 *Collected Edition*: "To lose one parent, Mr Worthing, may be regarded as a misfortune; to lose both looks like carelessness." The authority for this revision is not known. Wilde's final (i.e., 1899) version of this line is more concise: "Both?—that seems like carelessness." Finally, some editors may construct what they consider the best possible version of a work by combining elements of some or all surviving witnesses. Such texts are referred to as "eclectic" texts, and are best known from the editorial practice employed in some editions of Shakespeare's plays. The complex textual condition of *De Profundis* has made eclectic editing the best way of reconciling the competing claims to authority among the surviving witnesses (which include Wilde's prison manuscript and various extant, and often undated, typescripts which derive from it).

folios 3 and 3A following folio 2 and preceding folio 4). The nearest modern analogy would be to the digital process of cutting and pasting in a word processor. In other words, most of the physical evidence, together with the few references we have in Wilde's other correspondence, point to the manuscript being a kind of *cento*, a composite document made up of several different pieces of work, some of them false starts, which may have been written at different times during those long and interminably dull prison days, and with quite different purposes in mind.

Only part of the prison manuscript seems to have started life as a letter to Douglas. The first known reference to such a letter occurs in Wilde's correspondence with his friend More Adey, in a letter of 18 February 1897. There Wilde talks of working "on the most important letter of my life," one which will "deal ultimately ... with the way in which I desire to meet the world again." But he also complains about needing to finish it in a few days' time so that he can send it to Ross to "copy ... out carefully," so that Adey can check that copying; then and only then can the letter itself be forwarded on to "A.D." (*Complete Letters*, 678). This sense of urgency seems to have been induced by Wilde's desire to receive some sort of reply from Douglas before he left prison (Wilde's expected release date was three months hence). Significantly, the end of the manuscript does indeed contain instructions to Douglas as to the form his response should take. "Write to me," Wilde implores, "write to me with full frankness about yourself: about your life: your friends: your occupations: your books" (*Complete Works*, II: 154).[4] So it seems that Wilde did not really want a short or unconsidered response; perhaps he hoped for something nearer the length of his own letter. More particularly, Wilde appeared to want some sort of response to his

---

Wilde's Habits of Composition   Fortunately there are a number of Wilde's works—particularly the society comedies—for which virtually complete sequences of manuscript and typescript drafts have survived and these help us put together a picture of how he typically composed. In the case of the plays, Wilde began by sketching out a rough scenario, and this was followed by the composition of discrete and freestanding blocks of dialogue. This is to say that in the earliest stages of writing, lines are not generally assigned to particular characters, and in subsequent drafts, when characters' names had been filled in, Wilde frequently distributed and redistributed speeches among them, with apparently little regard to how this affected characterization of minor roles. It seems that the jokes were developed first (several notebooks have survived that contain lists of epigrams), and Wilde then tried to shape dramatic exchanges around them. Of more significance, perhaps, is the fact that his revisions do not develop in a simple linear fashion: lines, speeches, and sometimes act endings deleted from early drafts reappear in later ones. From this we can deduce that Wilde probably worked with several different drafts in front of him at the same time, and that the movement between first and final thoughts was therefore relatively fluid.

objections (which we describe more fully later) about an article Douglas had written on him for the *Mercure de France*, and a dedication that Douglas planned to include in an edition of his own *Poems*.

Whatever document Wilde was working on when he wrote to Adey he did not manage to finish it, and we may surmise that his intentions towards it changed. A full six weeks later, in a letter dated 1 April 1897, and this time addressed to Ross, Wilde writes again about his "letter to Alfred Douglas," informing Ross that it is now finished, and Ross is to expect it shortly. (In fact Ross did not receive the letter because the prison authorities refused permission for it to be sent.) In that letter of 1 April Wilde also repeated his instructions about copying, although this time they were more complex: Wilde asked for *two* typed copies of the whole manuscript to be made, one for himself "on good paper such as is used for plays ... [and with] a wide rubricated margin," and one for Ross, his newly appointed literary executor; and he also requested two further typed copies of specific passages "welded together" with anything else that Ross might judge "good and nice in intention"; these were to be sent to some close friends so that they might know something of "what is happening to my soul" (*Complete Letters*, 781–82). Such instructions seem to refer to a rather different document from the letter Wilde had conceived when he had written to Adey on 18 February.

How Should We Read the Manuscript?

The manuscript Wilde had to hand on 1 April was apparently much longer, and also in places rather less personal in that there were now passages that were suited to eyes other than those of Douglas, Adey, and Ross. More important-

---

continued   Of course the very fact that so many early drafts of Wilde's works have survived at all is strong evidence of the value that he placed on them. He seems to have been reluctant to discard any of the material he wrote, and was always alert to the possibility that lines composed for, and then deleted from, one work could at a future date be transposed into another. Interestingly this pattern of dramatic composition is confirmed by the surviving manuscripts of Wilde's prose writing, particularly the essays collected in *Intentions*. There too, we find evidence that the manuscripts submitted as printer's copy to the periodicals in which the essays were first published were also composite documents made up of corrected fair-copy pages, corrected fair-copy interleaved pages (numbered, as in the prison manuscript, 2a, 13a, 23a, 34a, and so forth) as well as corrected pages retained from earlier drafts. There is also evidence that Wilde was willing to reuse manuscript material from other works: so an early fragmentary manuscript of "The Decay of Lying" contains in it a renumbered manuscript page from one of Wilde's reviews for the *Pall Mall Gazette*. Likewise, some passages deleted from drafts of *An Ideal Husband* were later used in *The Importance of Being Earnest*.

ly, though, it would surely have been much too lengthy for Ross to have had copied twice (and in two different ways), sent to Douglas, and Douglas to have replied, before Wilde was released from prison, as those instructions at the end of the manuscript indicate. Put another way, it seems very unlikely that Wilde's injunction to Douglas on the last folio—"Write to me with full frankness"— was actually the last part of the manuscript to be composed. It is much more probable that they belonged to an earlier piece (the letter Wilde had hoped to have finished within a few days when he wrote to Adey in February) which he had subsequently expanded by rewriting some passages and interpolating material from other documents.

This sequence would explain why some folios are much more heavily corrected than others. It would also explain why some of the passages, such as those on *Hamlet* or on the life of Christ, read as if they had their origins in a different kind of intellectual activity from recriminations against Douglas. In all likelihood they were a reaction to Wilde's prison reading (which included the Gospels in Greek and Ernest Renan's *Vie de Jésus*, as well as Shakespeare) and were only later, to use Wilde's own term, "welded" to try and form a whole (presumably during that six-week period from February to April). We seem then to have a composite document, made of different pieces composed at different moments; interestingly and importantly, such a description explains the confusing repetitions and shifts in time in the prison manuscript.

These repetitions and shifts are more troublesome than most critics have hitherto acknowledged. For example, Wilde's friendly soliciting at the end of the manuscript for further information about Douglas's proposed article on him seems flatly to contradict an earlier comment in which he talks of the "ridiculous *Mercure* … with its absurd affectation" and of his own "orders" for "the thing [i.e., Douglas's article] to be stopped at once" (*Complete Works*, II: 76). This angry report brooks of no negotiation. Why then (apparently later) represent himself as undecided, to the extent of asking Douglas to "quote" from the article, as it is "set up in type" (*Complete Works*, II: 154)? We will return to these sorts of contradictions later, but our main point for the moment is that by the time the 1 April letter was written, the manuscript which Wilde had before him no longer seemed to be just a letter to Douglas; it now had a more public dimension, to the extent that Wilde seems to have envisaged revising it at a future date, perhaps with publication in mind. Why else might Wilde have specified a copy of his manuscript for his literary executor, if he did not intend it, at some point and in some form, to be made public? (Significantly in his instructions in the February letter Wilde mentions only one copy "for me," whereas the later instructions specify one for Ross and one for himself.) This sense that the "letter" was by now no longer simply a letter, and looked like something more public and intended for fuller publication, might well have been why the authorities in Reading Prison decided to withhold the manuscript until Wilde's release.

What conclusions can we draw from these details about the composition and physical appearance of the manuscript? They do not in any simple way under-write assumptions about its expressive authenticity. If anything they point us in the opposite direction, for they remind us that it is a contrived document, parts of which, as we have already said, were in all likelihood conceived with pub-lication in mind. For example, in one of the most frequently quoted passag-es, occurring near the beginning of the manuscript, Wilde compares himself to Byron, a figure also publicly feted and vilified:

> I was a man who stood in symbolic relations to the art and culture of my age.... Few men hold such a position in their own lifetime, and have it so acknowledged.... Byron was a symbolic figure, but his relations were to the passion of his age and its weariness of passion. Mine were to something <more wonderful> /<?true> more noble,\ more permanent, of more vital issue, of <wider> /larger\ scope. (*Complete Works*, II: 94–95)

Wilde's summation of his life here does not seem to be addressed only to Doug-las; it feels more as if Wilde is self-consciously fashioning a version of his life for posterity, and perhaps attempting to control the shape of subsequent narratives about him. Of course Wilde's narrative hardly lives up to his advertising of it, in that the personality that emerges from it is frequently some way short of being "noble." So passages like the one above coexist with those of petty recrimina-tion (in the obsessive recounting of arguments), hubristic self-assertion (in Wil-de's comparison of his own suffering with the agony of Christ), and lachrymose self-pity. The personality that Wilde presents in the whole manuscript is a bun-dle of contradictions. However the tendency to see the manuscript as the prod-uct of a single and consistent creative act has led critics to try to reconcile these disparate modes and moods, and the trope that best allows such an accommoda-tion is that of tragedy—or more particularly, a tragedy born of an overwhelming love affair. So the story of Wilde's personal life, revealed through and exempli-fied by the emotional twists and turns of the prison manuscript, becomes that of a prodigiously talented man, in his own words, "brought low" through his desires; those desires in turn metamorphose into an intoxication and obsession with a life of "sensual ease" that culminates in his nemesis, in which he describes himself staggering "as an ox into the shambles" (*Complete Works*, II: 95, 43). The power of this self-dramatization can be seen in its closeness to the life mapped out in Ellmann's biography; it has also informed the work of those many crit-ics and historians who wish to see the trials and his imprisonment as the defin-ing moment of Wilde's life.

However, a recognition of the manuscript's artifactual nature should alert us to the possibility that the complex and conflicting personality we find in it might be the result of rather more prosaic circumstances, of Wilde's inexpert (or unfinished) "welding" together of documents initially composed separately and with different audiences in mind: that is, that the "personality" he chose to exhibit in a private remonstration with Douglas was very different from the more elevated sufferer he wished to construct for posterity. Moreover, both of these personas may have had an element of artifice to them and should not necessarily be taken as indications of the "real" Wilde. We should acknowledge that Wilde's copying instructions to Ross and Adey indicate that he wrote (at least at times) with a sense of an audience in mind; that this audience was always more numerous and complex than the manuscript's ostensible recipient, Alfred Douglas; and that some aspects of the personality that Wilde exhibits in the manuscript have a performative element to them.

Where do these observations take us? They should make us much more cautious about interpreting the prison manuscript, in its entirety, either as a "love letter" or as "partial autobiography." And this in turn suggests that self-disclosure may be neither the most secure nor the most appropriate ground for evaluating it. Certainly we should be aware that in those parts of the manuscript in which Wilde does examine his personal life with Douglas, his version of events may not be particularly reliable. His construction of himself as an aggrieved victim may have more to do with rhetoric than reality, and thus Wilde's tragic persona may also be largely a fiction. In this scenario what we learn about Wilde from the prison manuscript is not so much who the "real" man was as the facility and inventiveness of his "self-fashioning." Likewise if, as we have suggested, some of the details of its composition entitle us to treat the prison manuscript as a semipublic document, then we need to confront head-on the problems of its structure and tone. That is, it will no longer be sufficient to explain away the repetitions and stylistic inconsistencies as aspects of (or evidence for) Wilde's volatile emotional state.

In the remainder of this chapter we will pursue these two possibilities in more detail, beginning by reconsidering Robert Ross's abridged editions of the manuscript; these represent the first attempt to place before the public a literary work. As we will explain, Ross's use of Wilde's manuscript has been controversial; but it still has much to tell us about the document's textual integrity and its identity.

Robert Ross's *De Profundis*

It is worth reminding ourselves that Ross was able to produce his editions of *De Profundis* because rather than sending the prison manuscript to Douglas, he kept it himself, apparently sending Douglas one of the typed copies instead. It is not clear whether Ross took this course of action on his own initiative, or whether it had been suggested to him by Wilde. When the two men were together in Dieppe after Wilde's release they would have had plenty of time to discuss the manuscript, and it is difficult to believe that it would not have been the focus of a great deal of their conversation. The consequence of Ross's decision was effectively to transfer "ownership" of the manuscript from Douglas to Ross; with this move its identity as a "love letter" was immediately compromised. In his preface to his 1905 edition of *De Profundis*, Ross refers to Wilde's manuscript simply as "the last work in prose he ever wrote" (*Complete Works*, II: 311). (We might note that private letters are rarely given the status of "works." Ross seems to be making a distinction between the manuscript as "letter" and as literary work.) Then, in order to establish authority for his volume, he quotes some sections of Wilde's 1 April 1897 letter to him, describing them as Wilde's "instructions" for the "publication" of *De Profundis*. Ross carefully edited the excerpts from Wilde's letter in order to remove all reference to Douglas, as well as any sense that *De Profundis* had ever been intended as a private document. For example, Wilde's comment—"Whether or not the letter does good to his narrow nature and hectic brain, to me it has done great good"—was reproduced by Ross as the more generalized: "Whether or not the letter does good to narrow natures and hectic brains, to me it has done great good" (*Complete Works*, II: 311). The implication is that Wilde, from the outset, had thought of his manuscript (or parts of it) as having some form of public life; he had, according to Ross, "mentioned its existence to many other friends." This erasure of Douglas by Ross has usually been interpreted as a form of censorship, one motivated by Ross's personal animosity, his fear of libel, as well as his attempt to restore some of Wilde's damaged reputation. Ross's excisions from the manuscript itself—he omits all the passages in which Wilde speaks directly of his relationship with Douglas—have also been seen in the same light, and as a result both his 1905 and 1908 editions have tended to be overlooked by both critics and literary historians.

What has not been realized is that the text of Ross's 1905 edition in fact corresponds closely to those parts of the manuscript which Wilde himself specified as making up a version which he considered safe for the eyes of his friends. Moreover, on the manuscript itself these passages are marked off in blue pencil. In his preface to the 1905 edition Ross did not quote Wilde's instructions in his 1 April letter about the passages that were "good and nice in intention," presumably because he did not, at that time, wish to give readers the impression that the manuscript had been heavily edited. However, Ross was considerably more open in the preface to his 1908 edition, declaring his intention to issue only "portions" of the manuscript, though describing this decision as being "in accordance with the writer's wishes." He then explained what those portions amounted to:

> *I need only say here that* De Profundis *is a manuscript ... cast in the form of a letter to a friend not myself; that it was written at intervals during the last six months of the author's imprisonment on blue stamped prison foolscap paper. Reference to it and directions in regard to it occur in letters addressed to myself.... With the exception of Major Nelson* [i.e., the governor at Reading

Prison] ... *myself, and a confidential typewriter, no one has read the whole of it. Contrary to a general impression, it contains nothing scandalous. There is no definite scheme or plan in the work; as he proceeded the writer's intention obviously and constantly changed; it is desultory; a portion of it is taken up with business and private matters of no interest whatever.* (*Complete Works*, II: 314–15; Ross's italics)

There are several ways of reading this passage. For critics disposed to be hostile to Ross, it may look like evidence of duplicity: having hinted in 1905 at the manuscript's public existence, Ross is now forced to acknowledge that virtually "no one has read the whole of it," though he quickly glosses over this discrepancy by commenting that the passages he excised are mere "business and private matters of no interest whatever." To focus on Ross as a censor, however, is to overlook other important details in his statement, such as his description of the manuscript as having been composed over "six months" with "constantly" changing intentions. We know that Wilde often composed rapidly; the implication here is that he wrote in fits and starts over a relatively long period of time, a suggestion that is confirmed by the physical state of the manuscript. We are emphasizing this point about the manuscript's composition because it is important to acknowledge that Ross's editing is really doing no more than formalizing existing transitions in the manuscript's argument and style to which Wilde had drawn attention in his 1 April letter. The question that is begged, then, is not so much to do with where Ross "disjoints" the text, but whether or not the material that he leaves out compromises the manuscript's literary (as opposed to its biographical) value. To put this another way: we might ask whether, as Wilde's literary executor, Ross did a good job.

Ross's 1905 edition in fact printed approximately one-fifth of the text of the manuscript. As one might expect, the "business and private matters" that he omitted include all references to the day-to-day details of Wilde's life with Douglas which are dwelt on so obsessively and repetitively in the full manuscript—that is, the meals and the arguments they had together, Douglas's (homosexual) "trouble" at Oxford, his forced trips to Egypt, the reconciliation between Douglas and Wilde in Paris, Wilde's interviews with Douglas's mother, Lady Queensberry, the tensions over the article in the *Mercure de France*, and so on. Ross also suppressed personal names: so Douglas becomes —— and Ross himself R——. What remained to Ross, after these excisions, were two long, abstract digressions (as we have noted, on *Hamlet* and on the life of Christ) as well as numerous shorter asides almost certainly suggested by the books to which Wilde had access in prison (so comments on Dante, Goethe, and the Old Testament are frequent). The effect of this editing is to take away much of the particularity, and some of the pettiness, of Wilde's emotional responses. The personality of Wilde is still in evidence on every page of Ross's edition, but now it is defined largely in relation to literary and biblical tropes. In other words, the Wilde of Ross's text suffers in a recognizable literary tradition. So his first explicit allusion is a strategy to clothe himself in the garb of the most famous suffering poet of the nineteenth century. Like Tennyson, Wilde is a "lord of language" and like Tennyson in *In Memoriam*, Wilde too testifies to the poverty of mere "words" to convey the depth of his suffering.

One or two examples will make this distinction between the tormented artistic type (which Ross's editing exhibited) and the recriminating individual (which he excluded) a little clearer. Ross chooses to open his text with a self-conscious literary and biblical re-creation of a suffering persona. The generalizing "we" is inclusive, and the power of the rhetoric does not require for its effect a knowledge of the particularity of Wilde's case. Ross edits Wilde into a figure of suffering humanity; the emotions described are exactly those which answer to Wilde's own account of his life as "something more noble, more permanent, of more vital issue, of larger scope":

> … Suffering is one very long moment. We cannot divide it by seasons. We can only record its moods, and chronicle their return. With us time itself does not progress. It revolves. It seems to circle around one centre of pain. The paralysing immobility of a life every circumstance of which is regulated after an unchangeable pattern … this immobile quality, that makes each dreadful day in the very minutest detail like its brother, seems to communicate itself to those external forces the very essence of whose existence is ceaseless change. Of seed-time or harvest, of the reapers bending over the corn, or the grape gatherers threading through the vines, of the grass in the orchard made white with broken blossoms or strewn with fallen fruit: of these we know nothing and can know nothing.
>
> For us there is only one season, the season of sorrow. The very sun and moon seem taken from us…. It is always twilight in one's cell, as it is always twilight in one's heart. (*Complete Works*, II: 159)

The contrast with the beginning of the full manuscript could not be starker. Its tone results from a personal mixture of admonition, anger, and self-pity. Wilde's sense of outrage and grievance (evidenced in the insistent repetition of first-person singular verbs) is the dominant note, and is particular to the circumstances which occasioned it, his life with Douglas:

> Dear Bosie,—
>
> After long and fruitless waiting I have determined to write to you myself, as much for your sake as for mine…. Our ill-fated and most lamentable friendship has ended in ruin and public infamy for me, yet the memory of our ancient affection is often with me, and the thought that loathing, <*illeg. word*> /bitterness\ and contempt should forever take that place in my heart once held by love is very sad to me: and you yourself will, I think, feel in your heart that to write to me as I lie in the loneliness of prison-life is better than to publish my letters without my permission or to dedicate poems to me unasked, though the world will know nothing of whatever words of grief or passion,

of remorse or indifference you may choose to send as your answer or your appeal. (*Complete Works*, II: 37)

Where Ross's *De Profundis* is strikingly lyrical, the manuscript rebukes; where Ross's Wilde attempts to encompass the totality of human suffering within a larger temporal scheme, the manuscript articulates a series of incidents which demonstrate only the petty power politics between the older, famous writer and the careless disciple and lover trading on that fame.

Taken as a whole, Ross's *De Profundis* possesses a thematic and tonal coherence; as a meditation on suffering articulated via a literary canon that includes Dante, Wordsworth, Goethe, Augustine, and Shakespeare, it is reminiscent of the dense allusiveness of Wilde's earlier (and published) critical essays. The following passage, for example, would not look at all out of place in *Intentions*:

> Art has made us myriad-minded. Those who have the artistic temperament go into exile with Dante and learn how salt is the bread of others, and how steep their stairs; they catch for a moment the serenity and calm of Goethe, and yet know but too well that Baudelaire cried to God—
>
> > O Seigneur, donnez-moi la force et le courage
> > De contempler mon corps et mon coeur sans dégoût.
>
> Out of Shakespeare's sonnets they draw, to their own hurt it may be, the secret of his love and make it their own; they look with new eyes on modern life, because they have listened to one of Chopin's nocturnes, or handled Greek things, or read the story of the passion of some dead man for some dead woman whose hair was like threads of fine gold, and whose mouth was as a pomegranate. (*Complete Works*, II: 177)

Is it helpful to call this simply a letter? Such a passage demands to be read in explicitly literary terms, for its intertextuality and for its abstract (as opposed to personal) account of integrity. This is not to deny that Ross's text gains much poignancy and power from the knowledge that the intellectual abstractions for which Wilde gropes have arisen from a need to revalue or to give meaning to his own particular experiences. But the logic of his argument does not depend on that particularity; moreover, the rhetoric is constantly pulling the reader towards what is seen as a truth about human lives in general. For example, Wilde's allusion in the following passage (in Ross's 1905 edition) to his loss of access to his children is utilized not so much to evoke pity for his own plight, but as an opportunity to make a more abstract comment about the nature of self-knowledge:

> Suddenly they [my children] were taken away from me by the law. It was a blow so appalling that I did not know what to do, so I flung myself on my knees, and bowed my head, and wept, and said, "The body of a child is the body of the Lord: I am not worthy of either." That moment seemed to save me. I saw then that the only thing was for me to accept everything. Since then—curious though it may sound—I have been

happier. It was of course my soul in its ultimate essence that I had reached. (*Complete Works*, II: 176)

Here Wilde registers his emotions in a highly stylized, almost theatrical manner: and this is because it is not so much the "reality" of his own grieving with which he is concerned, but a theological intellectualization of the meaning of loss. Moreover, the rhetoric directs us to dwell on the value of that abstract meaning rather than the intensity of Wilde's own particular emotions. We are invited to understand, as Wilde does, that the only appropriate response to the vulnerability that loss induces is an acceptance of our fate which returns us to a childlike state of innocent simplicity. This sort of writing, then, works very differently from the recriminations against Douglas with which the manuscript begins; there Wilde's emotional responses are only ever particular. The power of that writing arises from a visceral, but fundamentally private, reliving of specific past events. Take for example the following passage (omitted from Ross's edition) in which Wilde admonishes Douglas over his extravagance:

> But your surrender of your little allowance did not mean that you /were ready to\ g<a>ive up <*3 illeg. words*> /even one of your most\ superfluous luxuries, or /most\ unnecessary extravagances.... My expenses for eight days in Paris for myself, you, and your Italian servant were nearly £150: Paillard alone absorbing £85. (*Complete Works*, II: 63)

It is the nature of the details, the meticulousness of Wilde's accounting, that is striking here. At the same time, though, there is no meaning to the amounts of money specified apart from some private quarrel between Wilde and Douglas. The bitterness of Wilde's tone may allow us to make some inferences about his state of mind; but we do not move beyond the specifics of a particular personality. Here it is worth recalling two of Wilde's artistic injunctions in the Preface to *Dorian Gray*: "To reveal art and conceal the artist is art's name" and "From the point of view of feeling, the artist's craft is the type." Nothing could be more foreign to Wilde's literary aesthetic than the idea of self-revelation so commonly attributed to the prison manuscript when it is considered solely as a letter: a tortured replaying of the intimacies of his life with Douglas may have been important—at some moments of his imprisonment—for Wilde's own mental well-being (and possibly, in his eyes, necessary for any future reconciliation with his lover), but this was not such stuff that art was made on. Ross's editing of the prison manuscript—undertaken at Wilde's direction—could thus be seen as an attempt to do honour to these precepts: in omitting what he deemed "private," Ross was simply excising that material which lacked artistic value as Wilde himself had defined art.

De Profundis & **Autobiography**

Of course, for modern readers it is the self-revelatory aspects of the life Wilde chose to "show to the world" which are of most interest. As we have said, this preference has been largely due to the way the prison manuscript has been represented to them—as a private letter which was locked up in the British Museum for half a century. The public literary work, which Ross tried to excavate, is very much submerged in that letter, existing among details of Wilde's relationship with Douglas. At first sight the reader of the manuscript is often overwhelmed by the sheer abundance of those details, and this reinforces the impression that Wilde is revealing a great deal. But first impressions can be deceptive. Although Wilde's story of his life covers around four to five years from 1892–1897, it is not arranged chronologically. Rather Wilde dwells obsessively on a surprisingly small number of what he saw as the key events in his life with Douglas. They include Douglas's attempt to publish some of his own poetry and his correspondence with Wilde in the *Mercure de France*; the role Wilde played in "rescuing" Douglas from the clutches of blackmailers; Douglas's trip to Egypt; and Douglas's alleged neglect of Wilde when the latter was ill in Brighton in 1894. Wilde's recounting of these events is repetitive; and because they are often not dated, and are described in different ways, many readers will not realize that the same memories are being rehearsed again and again. If we wish to value the manuscript for its self-disclosure, we certainly need to look much more carefully at these events and the consistency with which they are retailed.

A good example of the complexities we encounter is to be found in Wilde's accounts of Douglas's "trouble" in Oxford; it was probably blackmail following a homosexual scandal, which if made public would have threatened his family with disgrace, and possibly Douglas himself with imprisonment. Wilde alludes to it in a passage near the beginning of the manuscript: "The gutter and the things that live in it had begun to fascinate you. That was the origin of the trouble in which you sought my aid, and I … out of pity and kindness gave it to you" (*Complete Works*, II: 38). Some pages later, Wilde returns to the same incident, but is more expansive:

> Our friendship really begins with your begging me in a most pathetic and charming letter to <come to you *2 illeg. words*> /assist you\ in a position appalling to any one, doubly so to <an undergraduate> /a young man at Oxford\: I do so, and ultimately through your using my name as your friend with Sir George Lewis, I began to lose his esteem and friendship, a friendship of fifteen years standing. When I <lost> /was deprived of\ his advice and help and regard I <lost> /was deprived of\ the one great safeguard of my life. (*Complete Works*, II: 58–59)

The obvious point to note here is that only a careful reader would gather that Wilde is referring to the same event—that is, having apparently dealt with his first meeting with Douglas, he is now returning to it. However, this chronological complexity is the least interesting part of the repetition, although one needs to be alert to the fact that the passages refer to the same event to see what is at issue. In the first passage Wilde characterizes his willingness to help Douglas as a morally admirable decision, one inspired by "pity and kindness." By contrast, in the second rehearsing of the incident Wilde presents himself as being importuned by Douglas and later regretting his generosity. More precisely he uses this incident to blame Douglas for his (Wilde's) estrangement from his legal adviser, George Lewis, and this in turn, in Wilde's view, becomes central to his later downfall. How near is this to the truth? It certainly is the case that Lewis could not act for Wilde during the trials, but that inability was not, directly at least, Douglas's doing. Lewis had already been engaged by Queensberry, and when Lewis realized that Wilde wished to secure his services, he assured Wilde that "although I cannot act against him [Queensberry] I should not act against you"; and following the committal proceedings for Queensberry, Lewis passed the case to Charles Russell and never appeared in court afterwards either acting for or against Wilde (Holland, 300). So Wilde, far from losing Lewis's "esteem and friendship," was rather the recipient of his enduring loyalty.

One explanation for these different interpretations of the same event might relate to Wilde's changing moods, not so much about Douglas as about himself. Thus in the first passage the incident allows him to fashion a version of his life in terms that hint at a generosity of spirit; but in the second case he sees himself merely as a victim. What is important is that we actually gain very little insight into the nature of the "trouble" at Oxford, nor how, nor why, it was Wilde who came to Douglas's assistance. Little, then, has been revealed.

Another example of this confusing repetition of the same event concerns an incident which took place in the middle of April 1895—before Wilde's conviction, that is. Douglas had seen fit to publish in the *Star* a letter which in his view defended Wilde's conduct. Wilde recalls the event as follows: "I remember <you sent me> /your producing\ with /absolute\ pride a letter you had <addressed to> /published in\ one of the halfpenny newspapers about me.... You appealed to the '*English sense of fair play*,' or something very dreary of that kind, on behalf of '*a man who was down*'" (*Complete Works*, II: 71). This passage occurs at a point about a third of the way through the prison manuscript. Towards the end of the manuscript, Wilde returns to that letter, indeed to the exact phrases he had used to describe Douglas's actions there, but with no signal that he has already discussed the event: "You must remember that a patronising and Philistine letter about 'fair play' for a 'man who is down,' is all right for an English newspaper. It carries on the old traditions of English journalism in regard to their attitude towards artists" (*Complete Works*, II: 173). We can explain such a repetition in terms of a simple lapse of memory, understandable in a long document. But there is a much more disconcerting unsignalled repetition of material in Wilde's manuscript which also concerns Douglas's attempts to publish material on Wilde.

On this occasion Douglas wanted to include some of Wilde's letters to him to accompany an essay he had written for the *Mercure de France*. The memory of it is for Wilde like an open wound. So barely one hundred words into his manuscript, he alludes to that attempted publication as he reveals his hopes that his words will cause Douglas to "feel in your heart that to write to me as I lie in the loneliness of prison-life is better than to publish my letters without my permission or to dedicate poems to me unasked" (*Complete Works*, II: 37). Some sixteen thousand words further on Wilde revisits the same event, describing the role of another friend, Robert Harborough Sherard, in thwarting Douglas's plans:

> Robert Sherard ... comes to see me, and amongst other things tells me that in that ridiculous 'Mercure de France,' with its absurd affectation of being the /true\ centre of literary corruption, you are about to publish an article on me with specimens of my letters. He asks <was> me /if it really was\ by my wish. I was greatly taken aback, and much annoyed, and gave orders that the thing was to be stopped at once. (*Complete Works*, II: 76)

Scarcely a few hundred words later, the hurt surfaces again, and Wilde describes a visit he is required to make to the prison governor at Wandsworth to hear a request made by Douglas. The governor

---

"Trafficking with Merchants for His Soul": Douglas's Attempts to Publish Wilde's Correspondence   Wilde's objections to Douglas's desire to publish some of their private correspondence were not made just on personal grounds, that he feared his privacy might be further invaded. His opposition was also a matter of principle; it derived from a long-held view that the public's appetite for details about artists' biographies was degrading for all parties, and that an appreciation of an artist's personality should derive from an appreciation of his art, and therefore had nothing at all to do with knowledge of his private life. On learning that Keats's love letters to Fanny Brawne were to be sold at auction at Sotheby's in March 1885 Wilde composed a sonnet (published the following year) lamenting the exposure of the personal details of their relationship. It begins: "These are the letters which Endymion wrote | To one he loved in secret, and apart. | And now the brawlers of the auction mart | Bargain and bid for each poor blotted note, | Ah! For each separate pulse of passion quote | The merchant's price: I think they love not art, | Who break the crystal of a poet's heart | That small and sickly eyes may glare and gloat!" (*Complete Works*, I: 165–66). Wilde expressed similar sentiments throughout his career, in the Preface to *Dorian Gray*, and in *Intentions* where he wrote: "The private lives of men and women should not be told to the public. The public have nothing to do with them at all." (Ross, ed., *Intentions*, 313)

reads me out a letter you had <sent to him to say> /addressed to him in which you stated\ that you proposed to publish an article "on the case of Mr Oscar Wilde," in the Mercure de France ... and were anxious to obtain my permission to publish extracts and selections from ... what letters? The letters I had written to you from Holloway Prison: the letters that should have been to you things sacred and secret beyond anything in the whole world! These actually were the letters you proposed to publish for the jaded *décadent* to wonder at, for the greedy *feuilletoniste* to chronicle. (*Complete Works*, II: 78)

A mere couple of hundred or so words further on still we find Wilde returning to the theme, apparently unaware of the fact that the topic has already been broached three times before:

What did interest /them\ [i.e., the French] was how an artist of my distinction ... could ... have brought such an action. Had you proposed for your article to publish the letters, endless I fear in number, in which I had spoken to you of the ruin you were bringing on my life, of the madness of moods of rage that you were allowing to master you to your own hurt as well as to mine, and of my desire, nay my determination to end a friendship so fatal to me in every way, I could have understood it, though I would not have allowed such letters to be published. (*Complete Works*, II: 81)

A little later, Wilde goes back to the interview with the prison governor, once again apparently unmindful of the fact that he has mentioned the details of the episode very recently:

You could write to the Governor of Wandsworth Prison to ask my permission to publish my letters in the "Mercure de France."... Why not have written to the Governor of the Prison at Reading to ask my permission to dedicate your poems to me, whatever /fantastic\ description you may have chosen to give them? Was it because in the one case the magazine in question had been prohibited by me from publishing <any> /letters\, the /legal\ copyright of which, as you are of course perfectly well aware, was and is vested entirely in me? (*Complete Works*, II: 84)

Even if we accept the proposition that the manuscript is a kind of *cento*, this fourfold repetition of the same incident in the space of so short a stretch of text is not easy to understand, except in terms of an obsessive mind working out its demons. Four-fifths of the way through the letter—in other words, some twenty thousand words later—Wilde once more calls to mind Sherard's role as a censor, this time to make explicit the contrast between those friends who had stayed loyal to him, and kept his interests at heart, and those (like Douglas) who had (apparently) acted thoughtlessly and selfishly:

When Robert Sherard heard from me that I did not wish you to publish any article on me in the *Mercure de France*, with or without letters, you should have been grateful to him for having ascertained my wishes on the point, and /for\ having saved you from without intending it, inflicting more pain on me than you had /done already\. (*Complete Works*, II: 132)

Finally and almost incomprehensibly, Wilde concludes the prison manuscript by making solicitous enquiries about the state of the article that he had bitterly deprecated so many times before:

> [L]et me know all about your article on me for the "*Mercure de France.*" I know something of it. You <*illeg. word*> /had better\ quote from it. It is set up in type. Also, let me know the exact terms of your Dedication of your poems. If it is in prose, quote the prose; if in verse, quote the verse. /I have no doubt that there will be beauty in it\ ... /Tell me about your volume and its reception\. (*Complete Works*, II: 154)

It is very difficult to see how this comment could have been written by Wilde after he had learned of Sherard's intervention: here Wilde implies that he knows relatively little of the content of the *Mercure* essay; he is also uncharacteristically optimistic about Douglas's other proposal, anticipating that the dedication in the volume of poems (also to be published by the *Mercure*) will have "beauty in it." The attitude to Douglas's actions is so inconsistent that it is difficult to make sense of Wilde's constant rehearsing of it except in terms of a simple loss of narrative or structural control.

On other occasions the reliability of the manuscript seems to be compromised by an opposite quality, an overzealous control that amounts to a form of deception. So Wilde refers to a trip to Egypt made by Douglas in 1893, and in so doing he relates conversations he had with Douglas's mother, Lady Queensberry, over his apparent concern with Douglas's health:

> I had myself, with your knowledge and concurrence, begged your mother to send you to Egypt away from England, as you were wrecking your life in London. I knew that if you did not go it would be a terrible disappointment to her, and for her sake I did meet you, and /under the influence of great emotion, which even you cannot have forgotten\, I forgave the past. (*Complete Works*, II: 48)

A letter by Wilde dated 8 November 1893 helps to explain what is going on here. Wilde had written to Lady Queensberry expressing concerns about Douglas's well-being and advising that she "send him abroad to better surroundings"—"to the Cromers in Egypt if that could be managed, where he would have new surroundings, proper friends, and a different atmosphere" (*Complete Letters*, 575).

An ill-informed reader would not be aware of the fact that a trip to Egypt to work with the British ambassador, Lord Cromer, was a convenience that suited many parties. It allowed Douglas to escape from a possible scandal at home which had threatened to embroil him, Ross, and Wilde. Although precise details are now lost, the broad outline of that affair can be summarized as follows. Robert Ross had met a sixteen-year-old youth, subsequently identified as either Philip Danney or Alfred Lambart. Ross invited the youth, at that time a pupil of a school in Bruges, to stay with him in London, where Ross seduced him. Ross later introduced Danney/Lambart to Douglas. Depending upon which source we go to, Douglas fell in love with the youth or seduced him (or both), and took him back to Goring to spend a weekend there—to sleep first with himself and then with Wilde. The youth returned to Bruges, where his headmaster Briscoe Wortham found out the details of the incident. Wortham was convinced that Wilde (as well as Ross and Douglas) was involved sexually with his pupil. The youth's father informed the police, but refused to press charges against either Ross or Douglas because, as Ross's solicitor—again Sir George Lewis—pointed out, a successful prosecution by the father would also have involved the prosecution of his own son.

In outline these are the details omitted from Wilde's account. One reason for Wilde's lack of candour may be explained by the fact that other eyes, especially those of the prison authorities, would have been a party to compromising information. But of course there was no need for candour, for Douglas would have known exactly what Wilde was alluding to. However this issue of what we can call "partial disclosure" forces us to confront our temptation to treat the manuscript autobiographically. What appear to be the most authentically private moments—in that they answer best to the title of a personal letter—paradoxically tell us least; or, rather, what they do tell us is misleading, for not only do they withhold what is for the modern reader vital information, they also allow Wilde to present himself in a not wholly truthful light.

A second example of this absence of candour concerns the reconciliation of Douglas and Wilde in Paris. Immediately after the Egyptian exile, Wilde describes himself as being reluctantly persuaded to meet Douglas for one last time in the French capital; he also describes Douglas eagerly travelling solidly for a week to that rendezvous. The problem is that both parties disagree absolutely about what actually happened in Paris. Here is Wilde's account of that meeting, and his reasons for consenting to it:

> You had yourself often told me how many of your race there had been who had stained their hands in their own blood.... Pity, my old affection for you, regard for your mother ... the horror of the idea that so young a life, and one that amidst all /its ugly\ faults had /still\ promise of beauty in it, /should come to so revolting an end\, mere humanity itself—all these ... must serve as my excuse for consenting to <3 illeg. words> accord you one /last\ interview <at any rate>. When I arrived in Paris, your tears, breaking out again and again all through the evening, and falling over your cheeks like rain as we sat, at dinner first at Voisin's, at supper at Paillard's afterwards: <your joy at> /the unfeigned joy you evinced at\ seeing me <again> ... your contrition, so simple and sincere, at the moment: made me consent to renew our friendship. (*Complete Works*, II: 50)

As a piece of rhetoric, Wilde's "recollection" of Douglas's tear-stained face and his own succumbing to it is powerfully moving. However, and quite characteristically, Douglas's recall of the same events was different, and he later dismissed Wilde's version as those "purely imaginary scenes at Voisin's and Paillard's" (Douglas, 41). Here Douglas uses "imaginary" in a derogatory sense because he is contesting the truth of Wilde's statements. Ironically, however, the term "imaginary" does seem apposite, but only if we see the writing as a self-fashioning, as an act of the imagination.

Intertextuality & Self-Fashioning

Most readers of Wilde's prison manuscript will probably not notice his repetitions nor be able to detect the misrepresentations that we have described. Taken in its entirety, the document is exceptionally difficult to summarize or to paraphrase, or even to recall in detail. This is partly a result, as we have noted earlier, of its lack of an organizational structure and its consequently meagre paragraphing, far more noticeable in the manuscript than in any printed version. The experience of reading it tends therefore to be impressionistic; we come away from it with a sense of Wilde's moods, rather than of his argument. Does it matter, then, if the events that generate those moods turn out to be rather limited in number, and that Wilde's recall of them can be demonstrated to be unreliable or biased?

The answers to these questions depend a great deal on what we initially decide to "do" with the document. Those who are still inclined to treat the prison manuscript as partial autobiography might argue that its inconsistencies and lack of polish merely demonstrate its authenticity as a witness to Wilde's emotions. But even if we follow this path, we still encounter problems which have to do with the way emotions are registered. Sometimes they are highly stylized, almost theatrical in tone (as in a passage that we quoted, in which Wilde describes himself on his knees, head bowed, and weeping); but on other occasions, they seem extraordinarily raw, the venomous contempt for Douglas scarcely controlled. On these occasions one can almost feel Wilde working himself up as he writes, and the emotion on display may have more to do with his mood at the moment of composition than at the time of the events that are being recalled—the emotions are, as it were, being "cooked up." It is interesting that in his prison manuscript Wilde often repeats lines he had given to Mrs. Arbuthnot in the last act of *A Woman of No Importance*, especially at those moments when she self-righteously dramatizes herself as a casualty of Lord Illingworth's sexual predation and duplicity. About halfway through his manuscript Wilde imagines what his life will be after his release from prison: "The external things of life seem to me now of no importance at all. You can see to what intensity of individualism I have arrived, or am arriving rather, /for the <way> /journey\ is long, and 'where I walk there are thorns'\" (*Complete Works*, II: 97). Wilde's quotation and figuring of himself as an outcast are very reminiscent of a speech he had given to Mrs. Arbuthnot in Act IV: "For me the world is shrivelled to a palm's breadth, and where I walk there are thorns" (Ross, ed., *A Woman of No Importance*, 170). A little later, as if to confirm that the play was indeed uppermost in his mind, Wilde uses the first part of Mrs. Arbuthnot's line:

"for me 'the world is shrivelled to a handsbreadth,' and everywhere I turn <I see> my name is written on the rocks in lead" (*Complete Works*, II: 101). It is as if Wilde, in his own mind, has temporarily morphed into a character from one of his own plays, but as the melodramatic victim and not in the role we would most expect, the dandy.

What if we set aside the idea of self-disclosure, and instead consider the manuscript for its literary merit—that is, as a work the main ambition of which is to describe in generalized terms the nature of suffering and redemption? Here we also encounter difficulties. We need to acknowledge that the manuscript is uneven to the point of inconsistency, and that Ross's editing of it should be revalued. In literary terms, Ross's *De Profundis* is a much "tighter" work; moreover, it is not necessarily any less authentic than the text printed by Hart-Davis. Both, after all, are mediations of Wilde's prison manuscript; it is just that each was undertaken with a different purpose in mind, and with a different sense of the manuscript's identity and of Wilde's intentions towards it.

Considering Wilde's manuscript as a literary work should also make us pay more attention to the origins of the tropes through which he presents his suffering. The tendency to see Wilde's manuscript as originating in his own experience has done no great justice to Wilde's reputation as a writer, for it has tended to obscure the richly layered literary allusiveness by which he "constructs" himself. At its best the prison manuscript contains wonderfully moving prose, which exhibits Wilde's skill in synthesizing different sources and traditions into a coherent and wholly new voice, so much so that the modern reader can no longer easily perceive the elements of that synthesis. To explore this aspect of Wilde's work, we need to be fully aware of those traditions which inform his depiction of suffering. In brief they include: a use of biblical language and biblical tropes; a reading of suffering in the work of previous writers, particularly Dante and Spinoza; and a use of classical allusions. Such a study might allow us to evaluate the prison manuscript in a way removed from the specificities of biography, particularly Wilde's relationship with Douglas.

Early on in the prison manuscript, sandwiched between his repeated indictments of Douglas's treatment of him in Brighton, Wilde offers the following generalized comment on the life of the prisoner:

> [W]e who live in prison, and in whose lives there is no event but sorrow, have to measure time by throbs of pain, and the <memory> /record\ of bitter moments. We have nothing else to think of. Suffering ... is the means by which we exist, because it is the only means by which we become conscious of existing; and the remembrance of suffering in the past is necessary to us as the warrant, the evidence of our continued identity. Between myself and the memory of joy lies a gulf no less deep than that between myself and joy in its actuality ... each day I have to <pass> /realise\ ... [that] my life, whatever it had seemed to myself and /to\ others, had all the while been a real symphony of sorrow. (*Complete Works*, II: 51)

This contrast between an identity formed from "sorrow," as opposed to one defined by "joy," is central to Wilde's intellectualization of suffering. Moreover the insight seems to derive directly from his own experience—seems, that is, to be a perfect example of the link between expressive authenticity and emotional intensity. Yet the proposition does not originate with Wilde at all; rather it comes in the first instance from Spinoza. Moreover, it was an idea with which Wilde was well acquainted long before his imprisonment. For example, in Part II of "The Critic as Artist" we find the following comment made apropos of Ernest's discussion of the value of the emotions evoked by works of art: "We weep, but we are not wounded. We grieve, but our grief is not bitter. In the actual life of man, sorrow, as Spinoza says somewhere, is a passage to a lesser perfection" (Ross, ed., *Intentions*, 174).

The allusion is to a passage in Spinoza's *Ethics* (from Part III, Definitions of the Emotions): "Tristitia est hominis transitio ad minorem perfectionem." Two entries on Spinoza in Wilde's *Commonplace Book*, a document from the 1870s, suggest that he may have studied, or at least read, the *Ethics* as an undergraduate. What may be more significant in tracing the origins of this allusion is Matthew Arnold's essay "A Word More About Spinoza," which first appeared in *Macmillan's Magazine* in 1863, and was reprinted as "Spinoza" in the first edition of *Essays in Criticism*. Arnold quoted this very line from the *Ethics* and translated it literally as "Sorrow is man's passage to a lesser perfection" (Arnold, ed. Super, III: 177). Walter Pater, too, had alluded to the lines in his *Imaginary Portraits* (1887) when he described the upbringing of the young Sebastian van Storck: "'Joy,' he

---

Wilde & the Question of Intertextuality   Few issues have divided critics as much as Wilde's use of sources. The central difficulty derives from the complex way in which he registers those sources. In his prose fiction he occasionally uses direct quotation and sometimes paraphrase. Only rarely does he give an author's name or a work's title. In the plays and in *Intentions* quoted material is hardly ever signalled textually (by, say, the use of quotation marks), and frequently Wilde reuses passages from his own (earlier) work. So *Lady Windermere's Fan* and *A Woman of No Importance* borrow aphorisms and jokes from *Dorian Gray*. The very terms critics use to describe these varied practices are fraught with difficulty because they impose judgments on Wilde in advance. So whether a critic uses verbs such as "copied," "repeated," "quoted," or "plagiarized" presupposes a particular intention towards a compositional practice. Along with this attribution of intention goes a judgment about the integrity of that practice (so the notion of plagiarism usually carries with it an association of deception or bad faith). In this respect one of the most intriguing of Wilde's manuscripts is his lecture on the poet Thomas Chatterton, given in December 1886 in Birkbeck College, London. In the following January the *Century Guild Hobby Horse* advertised its forthcoming publication, but the lecture never appeared. Wilde's seventy-page "manuscript" is part of the Clark collection, where it remained unexamined for many years.

said, anticipating Spinoza ... 'is but the name of a passion in which the mind passes to a greater perfection or power of thinking; as grief is the name of the passion in which it passes to a less'" (Pater, 105). Most significantly of all, in his review of *Imaginary Portraits* for the *Pall Mall Gazette* in June 1887, Wilde had singled out precisely this narrative moment, and had commented on how Pater's hero Sebastian "[e]arly in youth is stirred by a fine saying of Spinoza" (Ross, ed., *Reviews*, 172–73).

Whatever the origins of Wilde's knowledge of Spinoza, he clearly liked the passage from the *Ethics*, and it seems to have lodged firmly in his mind, for it was recalled some years later in a moment of considerable stress and tension. In the Queensberry criminal libel trial Wilde was asked the following question in relation to one of his "Phrases and Philosophies for the Use of the Young," a work which, in Queensberry's Plea of Justification, had been cited as evidence that Wilde, in his writing, was "posing" as a "sodomite":

> CARSON: Listen to this:"Pleasure is the only thing one should live for, nothing ages like happiness." Do you think pleasure is the only thing that one should live for?

> WILDE: I think self-realisation—realisation of one's self—is the primal aim of life. I think that to realise one's self through pleasure is finer than to realise one's self through pain. (Holland, 75)

It seems that Spinoza's proposition had become so assimilated to Wilde's own mental repertoire that it had virtually become his own (certainly the allusion is no longer signalled as an allusion). As a result, we can easily fail to recognize the

---

continued   It turned out to be "composed" of large passages physically cut out from the pages of what were in the 1880s the two most recent biographies of Chatterton, Daniel Wilson's *Chatterton: A Biography* (1869) and David Masson's *Chatterton: A Story of the Year 1770* (1874). The cut passages were pasted onto folio sheets with a few linking passages composed by Wilde. The lecture ends with an unacknowledged quotation of a sonnet on Chatterton by Dante Gabriel Rossetti. Of course we do not now know how Wilde delivered his lecture and whether those debts were acknowledged, but the fact that it was apparently withdrawn from publication suggests that on this occasion Wilde was being disingenuous. Significantly one of the critical essays in *Intentions*, "Pen, Pencil, and Poison," contains similar sorts and amounts of textual borrowings. On this occasion they are taken from the introduction to W. Carew Hazlitt's 1880 edition of *Essays and Criticisms by Thomas Griffiths Wainewright*; most of them are unacknowledged. No manuscript of "Pen, Pencil, and Poison" survives, and as a consequence it is tempting to conclude that Wilde composed it in the same cut-and-paste manner as he used in his Chatterton lecture.

extent to which Wilde's experience is being "constructed" through a literary commonplace, one certainly well known to some of Wilde's contemporaries.

The same observation might be made about Wilde's use of biblical allusions. There are in fact two quite distinct ways in which Wilde's reading of the Bible informed his prison manuscript. The easiest to decipher concerns overt allusions to biblical stories or characters: for example, the following represents one such clearly signalled quotation: "The song of Isaiah, '*He is despised and rejected of men: a man of sorrows and acquainted with grief: and we hid as it were our faces from him,*' had seemed to him to be prefiguring of himself, and <was fulfilled> /in him\ the prophecy /was fulfilled\" (*Complete Works*, II: 115). But there are many other, less obvious references; for example, the following passage seems to draw on a wide range of embedded biblical verses from Ezra 5:7 (the "prison-house"), Psalms 45:8 ("myrrh and cassia"), Genesis 18:27 and Job 30:19 (both of which mention "dust and ashes"), Isaiah 12:3 (the "wells of salvation"), and Isaiah 31:1 (where the desert blossoms "like a rose"):

> It is not a thing for which one can render /formal\ thanks in /formal words\. I store it in the treasure-house of my heart. I keep it there as a /secret\ debt that I am glad to think I can never possibly repay. It is embalmed and kept sweet by the myrrh and cassia of many tears. When Wisdom has been <bitter> /profitless\ to me, Philosophy barren, and the <words> /proverbs\ and phrases of those who /have\ sought to give me consolation <have been> as dust and ashes in my mouth, the memory of that little, lovely, silent act of Love has <has been so beautiful to me that it seems to me to have> unsealed for me all the wells of pity: <has> made the desert blossom like a rose, and <3 illeg. words> /brought\ me out of the bitterness of lonely exile into <illeg.word> /<something like>\ harmony with the wounded, <and> broken <heart of the great> /and great heart of the world\. (*Complete Works*, II: 85)

On an initial encounter, the preponderance of first-person pronouns (in contrast to the inclusive "we" in the passage from Isaiah) gives a sense of the immediacy of Wilde's emotions. However, a closer inspection shows us that the whole cadence of the passage is informed by an intimate knowledge of the King James Bible, one that would have been shared by all late-nineteenth-century British Protestant (and therefore in Ireland, Unionist) readers.

The important lesson to take from this is that the effectiveness of Wilde's prose is dependent not upon its "truth," but upon its artifice, its self-conscious manipulation of certain sorts of discourse. Then the most important question becomes whether that manipulation is appropriate to Wilde's purposes. And this is not a question which can be answered by appealing to biography, but by making literary-critical judgments.

Notes

1. A more detailed description of Wilde's prison manuscript, and of the different phases of composition which it appears to exhibit, can be found in Ian Small, ed., *The Complete Works of Oscar Wilde. Volume II. De Profundis. "Epistola: In Carcere et Vinculis"* (Oxford: Oxford University Press, 2005), 6–11. The text of Ross's 1905 edition (collated with his 1908 edition) and the prefaces to both works are all reprinted in that volume.

2. For an account of Ross's actions, see Maureen Borland, *Wilde's Devoted Friend: A Life of Robert Ross, 1869–1918* (Oxford: Lennard Publishing, 1990).

3. There are similarities here with some of Wilde's other works published only after his death. Most notable is his Oxford essay "The Rise of Historical Criticism"; the manuscript of that essay (which takes the form of three notebooks currently held at the Clark Library) was significantly tidied up by Ross when he published it in his *Collected Edition*. We discuss "The Rise of Historical Criticism" in more detail in chapter four.

4. For the sake of consistency all quotations from the prison manuscript are tied to the *Complete Works*, II. It should be noted, however, that Small does not print the prison manuscript as copy-text, although it can be fully reconstructed from information in his textual notes. In our quotations we give the text as it appears in Wilde's manuscript, and as a consequence include indications of Wilde's deletions, crossings out, insertions, and so forth, using the following sigla: < > indicates material that is scored through; / \ indicates material that has been inserted, either above or below the line; the abbreviation *illeg. words* indicates illegible words.

Works Cited & Consulted

Beckson, Karl. *The Oscar Wilde Encyclopedia.* New York: AMS Press, 1998.

Borland, Maureen. *Wilde's Devoted Friend: A Life of Robert Ross, 1869–1918.* Oxford: Lennard Publishing, 1990.

Bowers, Fredson. *Essays in Bibliography, Text, and Editing.* Charlottesville: University Press of Virginia, 1975.

Brown, Julia Prewitt. *Cosmopolitan Criticism: Oscar Wilde's Philosophy of Art.* Charlottesville: University Press of Virginia, 1997.

The Complete Letters of Oscar Wilde. Merlin Holland and Rupert Hart-Davis, eds. London: Fourth Estate, 2000.

The Complete Prose Works of Matthew Arnold. 11 vols. R. H. Super, ed. Ann Arbor: University of Michigan Press, 1960–1977.

The Complete Works of Oscar Wilde. Volume II. De Profundis. "Epistola: In Carcere et Vinculis." Ian Small, ed. Oxford: Oxford University Press, 2005.

Douglas, Alfred. *The Autobiography of Lord Alfred Douglas.* 1929; London: Martin Secker, 1931.

Ellmann, Richard. *Oscar Wilde.* London: Hamish Hamilton, 1987.

Greg, W. W. "The Rationale of Copy-Text," in Greg, *Collected Papers*, J. C. Maxwell, ed. Oxford: Oxford University Press, 1966, 374–91.

Holland, Merlin. *Irish Peacock and Scarlet Marquess: The Real Trial of Oscar Wilde.* London: Fourth Estate, 2003.

The Letters of Oscar Wilde. Ruper Hart-Davis, ed. London: Hart-Davis, 1962.

Murray, Douglas. *Bosie: A Biography of Lord Alfred Douglas.* London: Hodder and Stoughton, 2001.

Pater, Walter. *Imaginary Portraits*. London: Macmillan, 1887; 1919.

Stevenson, Robert Louis. *The Works of Robert Louis Stevenson. Tusitala Edition*. 35 vols. London: William Heinemann, 1923–1924.

Wilde, Oscar. *De Profundis*. Robert Ross, ed. London: Methuen, 1905.

_____. *De Profundis*. Robert Ross, ed. London: Methuen, 1908.

_____. *De Profundis: A Facsimile*. Merlin Holland, ed. London: The British Library, 2000.

_____. *Intentions and The Soul of Man*. Robert Ross, ed. London: Methuen, 1908.

_____. *Reviews*. Robert Ross, ed. London: Methuen, 1908.

_____. *The Soul of Man and Prison Writings*, Isobel Murray, ed. Oxford: Oxford University Press, 1990.

_____. *A Woman of No Importance*. Robert Ross, ed. London: Methuen, 1908.

| IV | *Intentions*: A Serious Writer for Trivial Readers; Or, A Trivial Writer for Serious Readers?

EARLIER we noted the discrepancy between academic interest in Wilde and his perennial popularity with the general reading public. In fact Wilde's popular reputation today—as the author of four stylishly subversive comedies, a couple of touching short stories, and the macabre *Dorian Gray*—is not that different from the one which he enjoyed in the 1890s. Generally speaking, late-nineteenth- and twenty-first-century readers seem to make the same sorts of judgments about Wilde's *oeuvre*: works which were relatively little read in Wilde's time are still relatively little read today. His standing among academics, though, is different, and this state of affairs has come about because the grounds for the academic recuperation of Wilde's reputation have little in common with the values of general readers who typically prize Wilde's work for its capacity to entertain.

Concerned to establish Wilde's place in a literary canon, one which encompasses contemporaries such as Henry James, Walter Pater, or Joseph Conrad, academics have often considered it important to establish his credentials as an original and "serious" thinker in tune with the intellectual currents associated with modernist thought and art. The occasional critic has even been tempted to see in Wilde's wit a "profound philosophical seriousness" rather than just humour (Brown, xvi). As far back as the 1970s it was not unusual to identify Wilde as a key theorist of the *fin de siècle*, and to compare his influence with that of Friedrich Nietzsche (see, for example, Fletcher and Stokes, 114). Some years later this idea developed in such a way that Wilde's writing—particularly his critique of nature and his interest in linguistic instability—was seen as an anticipation of the epistemological and moral relativism associated with late-twentieth-century postmodernism. Viewed from both positions, Wilde is avant-garde: he is outside or ahead of his time, and aligned with modes of writing or philosophical inquiry which fall well beyond the interests of most general readers.

A different avenue for understanding the intellectual fabric of Wilde's work was explored by Philip E. Smith II and Michael S. Helfand in their 1989 edition of his *Oxford Notebooks* which, they claimed, revealed a hitherto unrealized depth and complexity in his undergraduate education. Jottings in the notebooks seemed to show that Wilde had read not only the main texts of Greek and Roman literature and philosophy expected from a nineteenth-century classics student, but also some contemporary German philosophy (particularly Friedrich Hegel), some French social theory (such as Auguste Comte), as well as works by recent British historians, scientists, and anthropologists (including Henry Buckle, Charles Darwin, and Edward Tylor). This description of what we might term Wilde's intellectual development—derived from details of the curriculum he studied as an undergraduate at Trinity College, Dublin and then at Magdalen College, Oxford—in turn enabled critics such as Linda Dowling to revalue Wilde's engagement with Greek and Roman culture in such a way that it became central to his life. For her that engagement represented an intrinsic part of his understanding of his own sexual identity because it provided a discourse that permitted the articulation of, as well as an intellectual validation for, male-male desire. The originality of this argument was that it removed the issue of Wilde's homosexuality from his biography (from an account of actual sexual practices and perhaps partners), and as a consequence allowed it to be reified: that is, it made homosexuality principally a matter of discourse. Dowling's interest in the way classical references functioned to intellectualize male-male desire was thus an exclusively textual one. Although details of his sexual practices were obviously important in suggesting some reasons for the nature of Wilde's concerns, her evaluation of his writing ultimately rests on its contribution to a particular area of cultural and intellectual debate, many of the details of which (once again) clearly lie outside the interests of the general reader (both in the nineteenth century and today).

The third and oldest way of recuperating Wilde's reputation as a serious thinker began with the work of George Woodcock in the late 1940s. He attempted to see Wilde as an important political theorist. For Woodcock, Wilde's most significant work was "The Soul of Man Under Socialism" which Woodcock read in the context of the history of anarchy, setting it alongside works by figures such as the contemporary exiled Russian anarchist Prince Peter Kropotkin and the mid-nineteenth-century French philosopher and social theorist Pierre-Joseph Proudhon. Later critics would extend this line of argument to address Wilde's engagement with other strands of late-nineteenth-century political debate, such as socialism and individualism (both of which were contested concepts at the time Wilde was writing). Isobel Murray's reading of what she called Wilde's "prison writing" presented Wilde as both an original theorist of liberty, who synthesized such divergent sources as Ralph Waldo Emerson and the fourth-century BC Chinese mystic Chuang Tzû, as well as a political activist who campaigned for prison reform (evidenced in the letters he wrote on this topic to the *Morning Chronicle* after his release from prison). More recently still—and in implicit opposition to Woodcock and Murray—critics interested in Wilde's Irish nationality have claimed to find in some of his works a critique of British colonialism and an articulation of a form of republicanism, political positions that again enable him to be described as a literary innovator, either (in Declan Kiberd's view) heading up the "Irish risorgimento" or (in Richard Pine's argument) as an originator of a modernist tradition later and separately inherited by W. B. Yeats, Jorge Luis Borges, Jean Genet, and Roland Barthes. What is common to all these arguments about the political nature of Wilde's writings is the (by now) familiar idea of him writing "against the grain"—that is, against the expectations and values of middle- and upper-class Victorian readers and theatregoers. Once again we are given an interpretation of Wilde's writings that is in stark contrast to the way in which they were read by most of his contemporaries and continue to be read by the majority of readers today.

The most recent and ambitious attempt to cast Wilde as a serious intellectual is Julia Prewitt Brown's *Cosmopolitan Criticism*, a work that incorporates elements of all three of the arguments we have outlined above. Placing Wilde in what she sees as a tradition of continental philosophy, originating with Immanuel Kant and Friedrich Schiller, strengthened by Søren Kierkegaard and Nietzsche, and culminating in the work of Walter Benjamin and Theodor Adorno, Brown sees Wilde articulating a cosmopolitan aesthetic, one which translates politically into an openness to other cultures, and which has elements in common with the cosmopolitanism advocated by some recent political thinkers in the United States. More significantly, perhaps, she charts Wilde's working through of this idea as a "thirty-year" process, dating from his days as a schoolboy at Portora Royal School to the writing of *De Profundis*, and encompassing most of his *oeuvre*. It becomes, in effect, the defining purpose of his life and art, giving unity and coherence to what might otherwise seem an eclectic and uneven career. We might note in passing that no nineteenth-century reader could possibly have shared this perspective on Wilde, for none would have been in a position to view the *oeuvre* in this way; in point of fact there can only have been a small handful of readers who could claim to have known (or owned) much more than half of Wilde's published writings, for they had been directed at such different sorts of audiences, and had sold in small numbers. The price Brown pays for intellectualizing Wilde, then, is to estrange him from his own time, as well as from many modern readers, few of whom will approach his individual works as elements to be understood in terms of some larger "philosophy of art."[1]

What is common to all these ways of recuperating Wilde as a serious thinker (rather than an entertaining writer) is that an appreciation of that intellectual or philosophical seriousness seems to require lengthy elucidation by academic critics. Wilde, that is, is made out to be a difficult writer, one inaccessible to the common reader. It is also noticeable that many of the studies we have mentioned (including Brown's) place considerable emphasis on parts of the *oeuvre* least read by that common reader—particularly Wilde's critical writings, a category that includes his graduate essay "The Rise of Historical Criticism" (never published in his lifetime), and the four essays which make up *Intentions*. Although many modern readers might be able to quote aphorisms from those critical essays, probably only a few could summarize accurately their arguments, and it was not until 2001 that his critical writings became available on their own in a modern paperback edition. Here, then, we seem to have a particularly striking example of that contrast between the writer of popular entertainments and the writer constructed by academics whom we mentioned in our introduction. Brown's Wilde, grappling with the complexities of Kant's *Critique of Pure Reason*, would be virtually unrecognizable to the general reader, aware of Wilde's engagement with things German only through slighting references to that country's language and music in the plays.

Our challenge in this chapter is not to inquire whether both these "Wildes" can coexist—of course they can, and obviously already do so; it is rather to investigate whether it is necessary for them to continue to inhabit such distinctly separate cultural worlds. In trying to come to terms with this question, there are a number of topics that we need to explore. First (and fundamental-

---

The Title of "The Rise of Historical Criticism"   Like the title *De Profundis*, which was given by Robert Ross to his abridged versions of Wilde's prison manuscript, the title "The Rise of Historical Criticism" was also the invention of a later editor. Wilde's own name for his essay (the manuscript of which, in three morocco-bound notebooks, is held in the Clark Library) was simply "Historical Criticism: Αλήθεια." The Greek subtitle—which translates as "Truth"—was almost certainly an allusion to an anecdote in Aelian's *Varia Historia*, 14. 34, which describes how ancient Egyptian priests were also judges, and in that capacity had to be "exceptionally honest and rigorous," qualities which were symbolized by a statuette of lapis lazuli, worn around the neck, which was called "Truth" (Αλήθεια). The story of how Wilde's essay lost its subtitle and gained a new, longer main title is an intriguing one, and it shows how often expediency, rather than accuracy, has played a significant role in the transmission of Wilde's texts.

According to Stuart Mason, the manuscript of Wilde's essay was one of many that disappeared (or were sold) following the sale of his effects at Tite Street on 24 April 1895. It first resurfaced in 1905 when part of it (the material in the first notebook) was privately printed under the title "The Rise of Historical Criticism" in New York in an edition of 225 numbered copies by the Sherwood Press. This first notebook was subsequently offered for sale in July 1905 (a description of it appeared in the sale catalogue of S. B. Luyster, Jun., of 35 John Street, New York).

ly) we will reexamine the grounds upon which Wilde has been understood as
a serious writer. This in turn will lead us to reexamine the nature of his learning, and the ways in which he deploys it in his *oeuvre*, particularly in his critical writings. Then we will investigate whether providing for the general reader
information about the full range of Wilde's reading—as an editor does when
he or she annotates his work—necessarily turns him into a difficult writer. The
question we want to address is a straightforward one: what is that scholarly erudition for? We will argue that the presence of what (to the modern reader in
particular) may appear to be esoteric references or allusions is not necessarily
an indication of intellectual sophistication or philosophical complexity; it may
just reflect the different educational backgrounds that separate the average late-
nineteenth- from the average twenty-first-century reader. What matters more
are the ends to which these references and allusions are put, and the manner in
which they are signalled to the reader. At this point in our argument we will
draw some comparisons with near-contemporary authors—Walter Pater and T.
S. Eliot—who also conspicuously parade their learning, and who have also often
been considered to be difficult for general readers. Finally we shall try to come
to some conclusions about the nature of Wilde's learning in relation to his place
in literary history: that is, whether it operates in such a way to align him with,
say, modernist writers or even with postmodernists. Before we begin, though,
it will be useful to return briefly to the issue of Wilde's popularity in his own

---

continued   Mason does not record who bought the first notebook. We know, however,
that it was not purchased by Robert Ross, for when he published the first portion of Wilde's
essay in volume VII of his *Collected Edition* in 1908, he used the text and title of the 1905
Sherwood Press edition. In a note appended to the edition of that volume printed on Jap-
anese vellum, Ross recorded his gratitude to a "Mr Charles Glidder Osborne, who has examined the original manuscript, now in America." When Osborne (who may have been the
purchaser of the first notebook when it was sold in July 1905) checked the manuscript for
Ross he must have neglected to tell him that the Sherwood Press title was erroneous. Mason
notes, somewhat cryptically, that some time after he had published the first part of Wilde's
essay Ross "found" the remainder of the piece "in two quarto exercise books" (Mason, 470).
These were reproduced in volume XIV of the *Collected Edition*. When he consulted these
last two notebooks Ross would have clearly seen for himself that Wilde's choice of title was
"Historical Criticism: Αλήθεια," for it is repeated at the front of each notebook. Yet Ross did
not make this correction: instead he retained the Sherwood Press title, which has been reproduced in every edition of the essay since. Editorial quibbling over titles may seem a trivial matter until we recall how significant they can be in determining the ways in which we
approach a piece of writing as well as, in this particular case, how central the concept of
truth would become in Wilde's later writing.

time, as it turns out to have an important bearing on how academic critics have approached the whole topic of his intellectual seriousness.

Wilde's Popularity in His Time

When we use the term "popularity" of a writer in the late nineteenth century we usually take as our measure the sales of particular works, or—in the case of a play—where it was performed, the length of its run, and its box office receipts. By any criterion, Wilde's society comedies certainly were popular successes, although they had nothing like the popularity of the plays of some of his contemporaries—particularly Arthur Wing Pinero and Henry Arthur Jones. Judged in terms of sales they achieved during his life, Wilde's prose works appear to have been much less popular. According to Mason's figures, the sales of the book version of *Dorian Gray* and of the three volumes of short stories barely reached four figures apiece. *Intentions* sold in similar numbers, but the poetry sold only in hundreds. The only exception was *The Ballad of Reading Gaol*; this work went through seven editions in Wilde's lifetime, but the total sale still ran only to thousands (Mason, 332, 360, 364, 355, 282, 407–23). These figures do seem poor compared to audiences for the plays, but they were about average for their time, particularly in the case of criticism and poetry, genres acknowledged by several publishers in the late nineteenth century to be difficult to sell. Of course there were authors who did very much better than Wilde; and there were "best sellers," usually long novels, a genre which did not interest him, but which could sometimes sell in tens or occasionally hundreds of thousands. Wilde's sales figures should not therefore be taken as evidence that some of his prose was too difficult or too learned for late-nineteenth-century general readers. In fact contemporary reviewers tended to note the opposite, frequently complaining about the facile nature of his learning. This judgment contrasts oddly with the views of some of those modern critics whose work we have just surveyed. Whose judgment should we trust, that of Wilde's contemporaries, most of whom shared his education, or that of modern critics, many of whom have not?

The Depth of Wilde's Learning

So what do we know about Wilde's learning? The story which we are most usually told about it dwells, as we hinted above, on his success as an undergraduate at Trinity College, which in turn won him a classical demyship to Magdalen. The demyship (or scholarship at Magdalen) did represent real academic distinction, but we should remember that the award was a closed one (that is, one restricted to students at Trinity) and that Wilde was therefore competing against a relatively small group—those well-educated and able Irish Protestants who wanted to continue their studies in England. The Oxford double first was a considerable achievement as well; but once more we should bear in mind the fact the syllabus was not as extensive nor the examination system nearly as rigorous as they later became. (It was for this reason that contemporary commentators complained so often about the influence of private tutors and cramming schools, which, it was claimed, could achieve in a few months what was supposed to require several years of study at university.) Moreover, Wilde's achievements—although apparently, in Wilde's own words, astonishing "the dons"—did not earn him that fellowship at Oxford that he so desired. Wilde entered two prize competitions at Oxford: in 1878 the Newdigate Prize for poetry and in 1879 the Chancellor's English Essay prize. He won the Newdigate, but the essay now known as "The Rise of Historical Criticism" failed to win the Chancellor's prize. In fact the prize was not awarded to anyone in 1879. This was strange, for the same group of individuals judged both competitions, and so it is difficult to believe that Wilde's failure in the essay prize, the one in which he so assiduously exhibited his learning and thus his credentials for an Oxford fellowship, was due to prejudice. Awards of fellowships were based on wider grounds than mere success in examinations, and it is quite possible that Wilde's learning, though impressive enough to earn him a double first, was perceived to be too facile compared with the qualities expected of a potential fellow. Here it is perhaps worth noting that a decade or so earlier one of Wilde's mentors at Oxford, Walter Pater, was reported to have been given a fellowship at Brasenose College because of his extracurricular knowledge of German philosophy (moreover he had graduated with only a second-class honours degree).

It might be tempting to think that "The Rise of Historical Criticism"—that critical work which is so central to Brown's and to Smith and Helfand's claims about the development of Wilde's intellectual concerns—articulated a thesis of such startling originality or iconoclasm that it fell outside the boundaries of what was then acceptable academic discourse. In this view, it would not be shortcomings in Wilde's learning which had excluded him from an academic career, but rather the fact that his intellectual reach exceeded his grasp. Unfortunately, though, a close reading of the essay does not bear out this argument: by far the largest part of it is translation or paraphrase of well-known texts from the Oxford Greats curriculum. Moreover some of the textual examples singled out by Wilde appeared in such standard contemporary textbooks as John Addington Symonds's *Studies of the Greek Poets* and John Grote's ten-volume *History of Greece*. In a similar vein, many of what appear to be the more esoteric references in the essay—to, say, ancient Chinese annals, or the Indian King Chandragupta, or the statue of Memnon, or the Minyan Treasure-House at Orchomenus—almost certainly derived from a relatively small number of well-known secondary sources, in these cases from Hegel's *Lectures on the Philosophy of History* (which had been translated into English by J. Sibree in 1872).

Even what appear to be Wilde's own judgments on certain aspects of Greek and Roman history—on, for example, the Catiline conspiracy or the role of the Roman pontifical colleges in fostering historical composition—can also often be traced back to standard undergraduate textbooks that we know he had studied—works as famous as Mommsen's *History of Rome*. Occasionally Wilde is original: so his attempt to draw analogies between Greek historians (such as Polybius) and certain currents in modern thinking (notably the evolutionary view of society put forward by Herbert Spencer) may indeed have seemed novel to the essay's first readers. At the same time, though, we ought to be aware of the fact that the nature of those comparisons tended to derive from scholarship that was quite dated by the time he was writing. For example, on several occasions in his essay Wilde alludes to Henry Buckle's *History of Civilization in England* (1857–1861), a work which seems to have appealed to him because it argued that human behaviour, like the operation of the physical world generally, was governed by regular principles or laws, the existence of which permitted the writing of history to attain, or aspire to, the status of a science. This proposition, in its turn, had certain analogies—according to Wilde—with the concept of causation that could be found in the work of a number of ancient Greek historians, particularly Herodotus, Thucydides, and Polybius. What is relevant here is not so much the validity or otherwise of Wilde's comparison, but the fact that by the time he was writing Buckle's (originally controversial) history was nearly twenty years old, and its propositions concerning the scientific basis of history were already out of date. In other words, Wilde's attempt in his essay to point out the modernity of Greek authors by comparing them with what he called the "most scientific of modern methods" was based on a concept of historiography that in the eyes of many contemporaries was not just dated, but was sim-

---

"The Rise of Historical Criticism" & Wilde's Scholarship   The fact that Wilde's graduate essay was written for an academic audience, and that its main purpose was to gain an academic post, gives us a useful insight into Wilde's—and possibly also his contemporaries'—attitudes towards scholarship. If she were to glance at Wilde's manuscript (as opposed to the "tidied up" version printed by Ross and subsequent editors) the modern graduate student would be struck by how careless Wilde seems in the way he registers his source materials. Citations are only rarely given for quoted material; quoted material itself is only rarely indented, and when it occurs within the main text, it is hardly ever properly marked off with quotation marks. When Wilde does mark the beginning of a quotation, he generally omits the closing quote marks, so it is difficult to tell where quotations end, a practice found later in many of his reviews for the *Pall Mall Gazette*. He also includes within his quotations material that would normally be excluded, such as "he said." In addition the essay contains numerous spelling and grammatical errors as well as an idiosyncratic (and often confusing) method of punctuation. So, for example, em-dashes are used where the modern reader would normally expect a full stop, and sentences following full stops do not always begin with capital letters.

ply incorrect: not promising material for an aspiring fellow in what was then Britain's most distinguished university. Far from being radical, by 1879 Wilde's thesis, which stressed the role of the "speculative faculty" in historical research, may have struck his academic judges as old-fashioned.

To stress the lack of originality of Wilde's thinking in "The Rise of Historical Criticism" and his use of familiar academic sources is not as pejorative as it seems. It is rather to recognize the essay for what it is: a conscientious exhibition of undergraduate learning, occasionally spiced with a dash of originality. Compared with the later published work, what is absent from the essay is that rhetorical *élan*, that confidence and ease in the handling of complex source materials which allowed for a nonchalantly relaxed and witty display of learning. "The Rise of Historical Criticism" is not an elegant piece of prose, nor one that makes for easy reading. But that difficulty is not because it is particularly erudite, its sources esoteric, nor its argument complex; rather the opposite: often the writing is merely laboured. Indeed one modern editor has quite fittingly described it as "longwinded" and something of a "dumpling" (Holland, ed., *Works*, 908). In some places in the manuscript paragraphs end mid-sentence and lines are skipped before the next paragraph begins, as if Wilde could not quite work out how to link his thoughts together. There are also places where gaps have been left with just a series of notes or jottings which presumably Wilde intended to amplify later. (Evidence of these shortcomings was erased when the essay was published by Robert Ross posthumously.) At its best "The Rise of Historical Criticism" has a journeyman quality to it, so that it reads more like an anticipation of the modestly successful anonymous journalism which occu-

---

continued   When compiling his *Bibliography of Oscar Wilde* in the early decades of the twentieth century, Stuart Mason commissioned J. W. Mackail, Professor of Poetry at Oxford (from 1906–1911), to read Wilde's essay in order to gain some insight into how it might have been received by its original intended audience. Mackail's comments, as reported by Mason, are intriguing, for he does not make any reference to what—to modern eyes—looks like slipshod scholarship, noting simply: "The essay, young as it is, is quite up to the general level of that sort of thing and I do not know why the prize was not awarded" (Mason, 470).

It is not easy to interpret Mackail's comments. It is possible, although unlikely, that scholarship was not particularly important in Oxford examinations at the time; it is also possible that Mackail did not read the essay closely, or was simply being polite. A third possibility is that modern concepts of scholarly rigour, those associated with larger developments in the social organization of knowledge, such as the twin processes of specialization and professionalization, became established only in a piecemeal fashion. Thus writing that looks "unscholarly" to modern eyes might have been quite acceptable in its own time.

pied Wilde for most of the mid-1880s than those flamboyant *tours de force* that make up *Intentions*.

The logic of these details is to suggest that there may be an alternative way of understanding the significance of Wilde's undergraduate career and the importance of the knowledge he acquired during it for the writer he later became. Wilde was undoubtedly a clever and diligent student, with a particular facility for Greek translation, an excellent memory, and catholic reading habits; but he does not seem to have been intellectually precocious or scholarly, particularly in terms of his engagement with contemporary classical and historical knowledge. This observation might appear negative, but it is not necessarily the case that scholarship alone makes for either a good, or even an entertaining writer. Often the opposite: there were many erudite Victorian critics, such as John Churton Collins, who were tedious writers and whose criticism is virtually forgotten today.

What other evidence do we have for the development of Wilde's intellectual interests? As we have noted, there are a number of surviving notebooks, mostly dating from his undergraduate years, which appear to record some of his thoughts on the books he read, and which may have been used for some of his later writing (the clearest link between them and later work is the piece most contemporary with them, "The Rise of Historical Criticism"). There are two very early notebooks (in the Clark Library) which date from Wilde's time at Trinity and which contain jottings on philosophy and particularly on Aristotle's *Ethics*. There is another early notebook, now at Yale University, which contains extensive jottings on Theodor Mommsen's *History of Rome*. There is a further such book (currently in a private collection, but described in the Prescott Catalogue at entry 441) which also contains notes on Greek and Roman history and philosophy. And finally there are the two notebooks (again held in the Clark Library) published by Smith and Helfand in their *Oscar Wilde's Oxford Notebooks*.

Taken together these extant books have a complex story to tell us about Wilde's early intellectual development beyond the dictates of the Oxford undergraduate curriculum; indeed, as we have noted, the record of his reading in them extends well beyond what would have been works set for examinations. The story they tell is also necessarily a fragmentary one, partly because of the way in which Wilde took notes. Many of his entries—particularly those in the two notebooks published by Smith and Helfand—have a shorthand quality to them; Wilde typically used these notebooks to copy out phrases or quotations that struck him as being particularly memorable and worthy of record. However, they do not, taken on their own, constitute evidence for a sustained encounter with any of the books he read. Nor can we know whether the evidence they provide for his reading is exhaustive or even representative; nor, indeed, whether a couple of sentences copied out from one chapter of a multivolume work are proof that he read all of it, read it thoroughly, or even admired it.[2] We should also bear in mind that Wilde's notebooks were private documents, and we cannot be sure of their precise use. They may have been *aide-memoires*, revision tools, or some kind of reading diary. Moreover, the jottings in them that have not been traced to contemporary published sources may have derived from comments made in lectures to which Wilde listened, or they may have been records of observations made in tutorials or casually by some of his friends. All this is to suggest that they are not necessarily always original reflections.

To interpret those jottings, then, as evidence of Wilde developing some "serious" philosophical position—whether that "synthesis of Hegelian idealism and Spencerian evolutionary theory" posited by Smith and Helfand (Smith and Helfand, vii), or what Brown describes as the development of "the philosophical taxonomy by which [Wilde] would later come to treat the problem of art" (Brown, xv)—requires many gaps to be filled and often great leaps of faith. Certainly, such an interpretation places a weight on the evidence that in truth it cannot really bear. There is, moreover, a quite different way of interpreting the jottings in the notebooks. Instead of trying to fill in the gaps to produce a coherent narrative, we could equally well remark on the relative autonomy of each note, and see in them a quality remarkably similar to the aphorisms with which Wilde was reported to have peppered his conversation and which occur in his published works—that facility for summing up "all systems in a phrase and all existence in an epigram" which he recollected in *De Profundis*. In this argument the importance of the evidence contained in the notebooks is not to do with matters of intellectual development, with detecting the emergence of a philosophy, but rather with the development of a style, of a singular, and not necessarily scholarly, engagement with source material.

The point here is not whether one of these interpretations is more "correct" than the other, but simply that both are possible or plausible, because the evidence from the notebooks never speaks for itself. This in turn should alert us to the difficulties of using materials written at a very early stage in Wilde's career to explain what happened later. Such analyses are always *post hoc*, in the sense that it is the later work (or rather, a particular interpretation of the later work, such as assumptions about its difficulty, seriousness, or erudition) which draws the critic back to the juvenilia. We can see the force of this observation if for a moment we reverse its terms: so, if the Oxford notebooks or "The Rise of Historical Criticism" were the only pieces of Wilde's critical writings that we had in front of us, would any feature of them be striking enough to make us want to read more, to find out if there was any later criticism? Would those scattered jottings and that rambling essay announce themselves as evidence of an original creative mind at work? The answer is of course a resounding "No."

There is another caveat to be applied to this use of Wilde's early writing: most readers rarely try to understand a later work by making comparisons with something written years earlier (and for a very different purpose) or suspend judgments about a work written by a young man in anticipation that better works will emerge later. The unwritten assumption is that we cannot understand a single work until we understand the *oeuvre*, a dilemma that recalls a classic hermeneutic catch-22—we cannot understand the parts until we understand the whole, but we cannot understand the whole until we understand the parts. The logic of all this is that we should perhaps look more closely at Wilde's learning in the particular contexts in which it is exhibited, and this means taking account of the concept of audience for which the critical essays in works like *Intentions* were directed. What observations can we make about Wilde's learning as it appears in such pieces?

The Character of Wilde's Learning

When we talk about how Wilde's learning is exhibited in *Intentions* we obviously have a fairly secure notion of his intended audience, and therefore a firmer sense of what particular textual or intertextual effects he may have had in mind. Nonetheless there is an important if subtle distinction to be made between reading a work like *Intentions* for evidence of philosophical seriousness and examining the ways in which the volume displays its knowledge. In the first case, the work is being identified fairly closely with the author; but in the second there is a possible discrepancy between knowledge and the methods by which it is exhibited. This in turn opens up the space in which irony operates; it allows us to see that the ways in which knowledge is displayed—the particular use of, say, allusion and citation—can be as significant as that knowledge itself. The best way to understand these distinctions is probably by some examples, beginning with those passages that appear to be the most difficult because the learning in them—certainly upon a first reading—seems to be so dense.

With Wilde that learning frequently takes on the character of a kind of list. It occurs in most of the nondramatic works, but most particularly in *Intentions*. The following passage from "The Decay of Lying" is a good example:

> It was not always thus. We need not say anything about the poets, for they, with the unfortunate exception of Mr. Wordsworth, have been really faithful to their high mission, and are universally recognized as being absolutely unreliable. But in the works of Herodotus, who, in spite of the shallow and ungenerous attempts of modern sciolists to verify his history, may justly be called the 'Father of Lies'; in the published speeches of Cicero and the biographies of Suetonius; in Tacitus at his best; in Pliny's *Natural History*; in Hanno's *Periplus*; in all the early chronicles; in the Lives of the Saints; in Froissart and Sir Thomas Malory; in the travels of Marco Polo; in Olaus Magnus, and Aldrovandus, and Conrad Lycosthenes, with his magnificent *Prodigiorum et Ostentorum Chronicon*; in the autobiography of Benvenuto Cellini; in the memoirs of Casanuova; in Defoe's *History of the Plague*; in Boswell's *Life of Johnson*; in Napoleon's despatches, and in the works

of our own Carlyle, whose *French Revolution* is one of the most fascinating historical novels ever written, facts are either kept in their proper subordinate position, or else entirely excluded on the general ground of dulness. (Ross, ed., *Intentions*, 27)

At this point in his argument Vivian is attempting to provide Cyril (and thus the reader) with a vivid illustration of his apparently counterintuitive argument that the most valuable and memorable kind of writing, paradoxically including history, is that which is "absolutely indifferent to fact." And of course he is also in a sense showing off, trying to overwhelm Cyril's rather halfhearted objections ("I think that view might be questioned") with a flood of increasingly esoteric examples.

Most modern readers' initial impressions of this "list" will probably centre on its length and eclecticism; most, too, will be familiar with only a few of the authors whom Wilde mentions. So Wordsworth needs little or no introduction (although a modern as well as a nineteenth-century reader might wonder why so many years after his death Wilde still calls him "Mr."). But while Defoe's, Boswell's, Carlyle's, and Malory's writings will also probably be known (at least in part), Casanova, Napoleon, Cellini, and Marco Polo will principally be just names. The same is true of Wilde's list of classical authors. Modern readers may at least have heard of Tacitus, Pliny, Herodotus, and Cicero, but unless they have enjoyed (or endured) a classical education are unlikely to be familiar with anything those Greek and Roman worthies actually wrote. And what about Olaus Magnus, Aldrovandus, and Conrad Lycosthenes? These will almost certainly be completely unknown to our general reader. Would late-nineteenth-century readers have been less ignorant? Some would certainly have been better informed about the classical references, and some may also have been familiar with the writings of Casanova, Napoleon, Cellini, and Marco Polo. (For example, a new edition of Napoleon's letters had been published in 1884, Marco Polo's writings had appeared in a list of "books to read" in an 1886 review for the *Pall Mall Gazette*, and Benvenuto Cellini's autobiography had been translated into English in 1888.) But the Swedish historian Olaus Magnus (1490–1558), the Italian naturalist Ulisse Aldrovandi (1522–1605), and Swiss philologist Conrad Lycosthenes (1518–1561), would probably have been as remote for the reader then as now. The important question thus becomes whether these different levels of knowledge actually matter? Or, put another way, does a full acquaintance with all the references in Vivian's list make any difference to how we interpret it, and thus to our acceptance of Vivian's proposition about the role of facts in history? Are the specificities of the particular references significant?

The answer to this last question is both "yes" and "no" in the sense that the specificity of a particular reference seems to become less important the more esoteric it is. To put this another way: a reader will have "got the point"—not in fact a difficult one to get—after understanding only a few of the references, because that point does not change as we move through the list. So the function of the increasing impenetrability of Wilde's list is precisely to out-manoeuvre the reader in a game of intellectual one-upmanship, to go beyond what he or she is able to verify. Precisely where and when this occurs will of course vary from reader to reader, but once again this variability does not really matter. For example, nearly all readers (then and now) will see that in referring to Wordsworth, Wilde/Vivian is not deriding Romantic poetry in general, but rather Wordsworth in particular, precisely because of his claims in the Preface to the *Lyrical Ballads* about sincerity of poetic expression and the poet's fidelity to nature. Similarly, the reference to Boswell's biography works because he was known to have made up many of the details of his volume (a topic which received a great deal of publicity in the late nineteenth century following the revelations of Charles Rogers's *Boswelliana: The Commonplace Book of James Boswell*, 1874).

Even if we allow for the fact that historically separate groups of readers will have different kinds of education, the ways in which Wilde's rhetoric operates remain virtually unchanged. As we have said, many nineteenth-century readers would certainly have appreciated the specificity of the classical references—the fact that in his *Histories* Herodotus scathingly dismissed sources which claimed

---

Parading Knowledge in "Pen, Pencil, and Poison"   "Pen, Pencil, and Poison" may strike many modern readers as the most "learned" of Wilde's pieces in *Intentions*, not in the sense of it being necessarily the most abstruse or wide-ranging in its references or allusions, but rather in the way it appears to draw on a very detailed body of research about the life and works of a figure who will be largely unfamiliar to them, that of the Victorian poisoner Thomas Griffiths Wainewright. Knowledge about Wainewright comes to the reader in two forms. First, there are the details of his biography, about which Wilde appears to be impressively well-informed: so we are given precise descriptions of Wainewright's parents (including an account of the epitaph printed in the *Gentleman's Magazine* following the death of his mother), his upbringing in his uncle's "fine Georgian mansion" with its "lovely gardens and well-timbered park," his education at "Charles Burney's academy at Hammersmith," and so forth (Ross, ed., *Intentions*, 63). Second, there are the very lengthy lists of paintings, engravings, books, jewellery, and furniture which Wilde uses in order to convey to the reader the breadth and refinement of Wainewright's taste. Thus, for example, we are told that in his library Wainewright has "an engraving of the 'Delphic Sibyl' of Michael Angelo," "the 'Pastoral' of Giorgione," as well as some "Florentine majolica," "a rude lamp from some old Roman tomb," "a book of Hours," some of "Tassie's gems," a "tiny Louis-Quatorze *bonbonnière* with a miniature by Petitot," a "fine collection of Marc Antonios," "Turner's 'Liber Studiorum,'" "the head of Alexander on an onyx of two strata," and a "superb *altissimo relievo* on cornelian" of "Jupiter Ægiochus" (Ross, ed., *Intentions*, 69).

that people such as the "Neuri" turned into wolves, or that those inhabiting the mountains north of Scythia had "goat's feet." They would also have known that—these caveats notwithstanding—Herodotus could also confidently attribute the deaths of two Spartan envoys at the hands of the Athenians to "the venting of the rage of Talthybius" (a mythical figure worshipped as a hero at Sparta and Argos) and as a "sure sign of heaven's handiwork." Some of those selfsame readers would also have known that Cicero's versions of his own speeches in the senate (on, for example, the Catiline conspiracy) appeared quite differently in reports of them made by writers such as Sallust in his *Bellum Catilinae*. A few might conceivably have known too that one of the most famous speeches reported by Tacitus (in his *Annals*)—that by the emperor Claudius when he gave freedom to the Gauls—was later proved to have been significantly rewritten, rearranged, and reordered when fragments of Claudius's actual speech, inscribed on bronze tablets, were discovered at Fourière near the modern city of Lyons in 1524. But the fact that modern readers (and of course many nineteenth-century readers) do not know these particular details does not really matter—they will still have understood the general thrust of Vivian's argument much earlier. Moreover, as we said, the main point of that long list is that some of it should *not* be understood: its ultimate incomprehensibility is an intrinsic part of the joke.

---

continued   However, this apparent "research" becomes much less striking when we realize that nearly all of it was taken from a single book, W. Carew Hazlitt's *Essays and Criticisms by Thomas Griffiths Wainewright* (1880). That volume brought together a collection of Wainewright's critical writings (mainly from the *London Magazine*), and prefaced them with a long introductory essay that attempted to separate fact from fiction in Wainewright's extraordinary life. Wilde's grudging acknowledgment of Hazlitt's volume towards the end of "Pen, Pencil, and Poison"—he refers to it condescendingly as "quite invaluable in its way" (Ross, ed., *Intentions*, 92)—seems designed to disguise the fact that his whole piece was constructed more or less of paraphrases and quotations from the essays that Hazlitt had anthologized, together with many borrowings from Hazlitt's own introduction (Wilde even repeats Hazlitt's mistakes). So what exactly was Wilde's game here? Did he assume that most readers would be unfamiliar with Hazlitt's volume and therefore would not realize the extent of his indebtedness? And what of those who did? In "The Critic as Artist" Wilde seems to have had the perfect answer: when discussing the topic of originality, Gilbert claims that "treatment is the test" (Ross, ed., *Intentions*, 143)—that is, the source or originator of an idea is less important than what the critic is able to do with it. In such a view the acknowledgment of source materials—the whole paraphernalia of modern scholarship—is conveniently rendered redundant.

It follows from this that a modern reader should not be dismayed or over-whelmed by a parade of recondite knowledge—this is precisely Wilde's point. Moreover research into the individual references, although perhaps of some interest in itself, will not significantly alter their understanding of what Wilde/Vivian is trying to do. A second observation to make is that Wilde's references are not functioning in the way that scholarly allusion normally does—that is, when full knowledge of an allusion is a precondition of a reader's full under-standing of a work's argument. At one level, then, Wilde seems to be poking fun at varieties of useless scholarly knowledge, while at the same time fully exploit-ing an opportunity to display the width of his own catholic reading. And this in turn explains exactly why some contemporary reviewers could acknowledge what they saw as a certain cleverness in Wilde's argument but also disapprove of its apparent lack of serious purpose.

Not all Wilde's allusions in *Intentions* are as densely packed as those in the pas-sage that we quoted above; nevertheless the listing effect—the quick succession of name after name—does reappear surprisingly often, and generally works in a similar way, in the sense that the absence of specific knowledge about a name being mentioned barely detracts from an understanding of the point being made. Take, for example, the following passage from "The Critic as Artist" which begins (again) with the relatively familiar but then proceeds to the recondite:

> Who, as Mr. Pater suggests somewhere, would exchange the curve of a single rose-leaf for that formless intangible Being which Plato rates so high? What to us is the Illumina-tion of Philo, the Abyss of Eckhart, the Vision of Böhme, the monstrous Heaven itself that was revealed to Swedenborg's blinded eyes? Such things are less than the yellow trumpet of one daffodil of the field, far less than the meanest of the visible arts; for, just as Nature is matter struggling into mind, so Art is mind expressing itself under the conditions of matter, and thus, even in the lowliest of her manifestations, she speaks to both sense and soul alike. (Ross, ed., *Intentions*, 177–78)

Nineteenth-century readers (and some modern ones) would certainly have heard of the first two names, and be alert to the fact that the first was a near-contemporary of Wilde. However, relatively few readers (either then or now) would necessarily have known—or have been able to recall immediately—the exact work by Pater to which Wilde was alluding. It was in fact a line in an essay entitled "Coleridge" which was first published in the *Westminster Review* in 1865 and then reprinted in 1889 in Pater's essay collection *Appreciations*: "Who would change the colour or curve of a rose-leaf for that οὐσία ἀχρώμαος, ἀσχημάτιστος, ἀναφὴς—that colourless, formless, intangible, being—Pla-to put so high?" (Pater, *Appreciations*, 68). Once more the main questions are: how important is this piece of information; does the reader *need* to know Pat-er's exact words, and where they come from, in order to appreciate Wilde's (or Gilbert's) point?

We can encounter the rather casual formula Wilde uses—"as Mr. Pater suggests somewhere"—fairly often in nineteenth-century prose; it serves to indicate that a detailed familiarity with a source is not an absolute requirement for comprehension. We are told the words are from Pater, that Pater is referring to a comment from Plato, and we can easily understand (even without having read any Plato) that a contrast is being made between the tangible beauty of a rose leaf, present to our senses in the here and now, and some kind of rarefied, abstract, spiritual ideal that inhabits only Plato's world of ideas. To be informed that Pater originally made this observation in the context of a discussion of Coleridge, or that he had reinforced his argument by using the example of "the Hindoo mystic" (rather than Wilde's Philo, Eckhart, and the rest) does not fundamentally change our understanding of the point in question; nor indeed does it make that much difference if we have the Greek words in front of us, or know where exactly they occur in Plato's works. And this is because Gilbert is not inviting a scholarly engagement with either Plato's or Pater's texts: he is simply and casually invoking their names as authorities, or mentioning them as "serious" representatives of alternative ways of understanding beauty.

Of course for the reader who was (and is) familiar with the writings of these two figures, then there are other layers of meaning to be unravelled. For example, that Wilde should single out Pater's comments on a rose leaf might call to mind the waspish parody of Paterian aestheticism in the satirical novel *The New Republic* (first published in 1876–1877, when Wilde was at Oxford) by the young conservative writer, W. H. Mallock. There Pater appears under the name of "Mr. Rose," a character whose devotion to sensual beauty includes an excited interest in young page boys and erotica. That association in turn might also call to mind, for the same reader, the controversies that had surrounded Pater's earlier exposition of his ideas about beauty in his first book, *Studies in the History of the Renaissance* (1873). The conclusion of that work had been withdrawn from the second edition (which appeared in 1877) because of accusations, fuelled by rumours about Pater's homosexuality, that it advertised an amoral hedonism. The reader in possession of all this knowledge might thus infer that in endorsing Paterian sensuality, as opposed to Platonic intangibles, Wilde/Gilbert is slyly advocating a precise kind of sensual pleasure; and that the "us" he so casually invokes is actually a coded reference to a particular interest group.

It is exactly these chains of association that academic critics (and editors) will typically feel obliged to lay before modern readers—that, after all, is their job; and in so doing they bring into the open a range of meanings that permit one to construe a subversive sexual politics underlying Wilde's criticism. This in turn can allow such works to become grist to the mill of writers like Neil McKenna, who claim that everything Wilde wrote was in the service of "his commitment to 'the Cause.'" What we need to remember, though, is that this level of allusion—whether or not actively intended by Wilde—would only have been available to a very small group of readers, to those who had been contemporaries of Wilde and Pater at Oxford in the mid-1870s (that is, nearly fifteen years before "The Critic as Artist" was first published), and who had been close enough to events there to have known about the homosexual scandal in which Pater had been involved. It is worth reminding ourselves that the rumours about Pater's homosexuality, although occasionally hinted at in the national press, circulated principally in the closed world of Oxford colleges. Moreover, although Mallock's *The New Republic* was obviously exploiting this rumour mill, it is an open question whether or not his portrait of "Mr. Rose" was sufficiently pointed, or indeed sufficiently accessible, to do Pater any real damage in the eyes of those readers living outside Oxford.

More importantly, perhaps, we also need to realize that recognition of this sort of joke depended primarily upon what we might term private, as opposed to public and scholarly, knowledge: that is, the potential connotations conjured up by the term "rose leaf" do not require of the reader any complex intellectual engagement with Wilde's text. The joke—if appreciated—is not fundamentally a literary one and does not depend on any form of textual difficulty. Further-

---

Wilde, Pater, & the Pleasure of the "in-joke"   A number of modern critics have detected in Wilde's account of the Victorian art critic and poisoner Thomas Griffiths Wainewright, in his essay "Pen, Pencil, and Poison," a series of coded allusions to Walter Pater. Some of these are reasonably obvious: for example, several of the literary and art works that Wilde dwells upon in order to trope Wainewright's taste might just as easily stand in for Pater's connoisseurship. So Wainewright's love of "La Gioconda, and early French poets and the Italian Renaissance" reads suspiciously like part of the contents list of the essays in Pater's *The Renaissance*; his "grand dish with the marriage of Cupid and Psyche" is reminiscent of chapter five of *Marius the Epicurean* (1885) where Pater gives a shortened and, at the time, much admired translation of Apuleius's second-century account in Latin of the Cupid and Psyche myth in his *Metamorphoses*. Other links between Pater and Wainewright, however, seem more private and also more cruel. Thus Wainewright's "tall copy of the *Hypnerotomachia*"—an account of the erotic adventures of the protagonist, Poliphili, in the pursuit of his beloved, Poilia—would have called to mind for some readers W. H. Mallock's satirical portrait of Pater in the guise of the fictional Mr. Rose, in which the tastes of the Pater/Rose figure include pornographic books. Likewise Wainewright's "fondness," like Baudelaire's, for "cats" associated Pater, who was also reputed to have been very fond of those animals, with the most controversial of French Decadent writers. Finally, there is Wainewright's "love of green" which would remind those readers who knew Pater intimately of his rooms at Brasenose College which were panelled in what some of his contemporaries later described as "a pale green tint" which gave off a peculiar "greenish light."

more we might also notice that Wilde's use of Plato (as an authority to be set in opposition to Pater) is entirely orthodox. The appropriation of Platonic views of male-male love in order to legitimate a homosexual identity—that intellectual activity which Dowling sees as so central to Wilde's interest in Greek philosophy—is not at issue here. Rather, that set of associations cannot logically be brought into play for those readers wishing to see sexual connotations in the allusion to rose leaves, because if they are, then the distinction between Platonic and Paterian ideas of beauty collapses, and Gilbert's argument falls apart. Another way to put this might be to say that the literary effect of the allusion—Gilbert's use of two eminent writers (one contemporary and one ancient) to trope two different views of beauty (one concrete and immediate, one spiritual and abstract)—actually requires "personal" knowledge to be set aside.

And what of the "list" that follows the mention of Pater and Plato: the "Illumination of Philo, the Abyss of Eckhart, the Vision of Böhme, the monstrous Heaven itself that was revealed to Swedenborg's blinded eyes"? It is hard to know how many of these references would have been known to the average late-nineteenth-century reader, but probably only a few. Philo Judaeus, an important scholar of Hellenic Judaism born around 25BC, and the German mystic

---

continued   Green, of course, was not a neutral colour in English culture of the 1880s and 1890s: in his *English Poems* (1892), the poet and critic Richard Le Gallienne (1866–1947) commented on the "popular vogue which green has enjoyed for the last ten or fifteen years," observing that in its "more complex forms," the colour implied something "not quite good, something almost sinister" (Beckson, 122–23)—an association which Wilde later exploited in *Salome* when he used "a little green flower" as a symbol of Salome's perverse desire. It recalls, too, how on the opening night of *Lady Windermere's Fan* Wilde and (it is alleged) all the gay members of the audience wore green carnations in their buttonholes. The association between the colour green and a Decadent sexuality was fixed in the popular imagination by the publication in 1894 of Robert Hichens's first novel, *The Green Carnation*, a witty satire on Decadence in general and Wilde in particular, which contained distinct homoerotic suggestions. We need to remember here that at the moment when "Pen, Pencil, and Poison" was first published in the *Fortnightly Review* in January 1889, Pater's reputation was on a firmly upward trajectory, following the successes of *Marius* (1885), *Imaginary Portraits* (1887), and the third edition of *The Renaissance* (1888). Seen in this light Wilde's use of Wainewright to recall, to those "in the know," the sexual scandal that had threatened to blight Pater's career in the 1870s looks rather vindictive—an attempt, perhaps, to disparage a figure who was always a rival to Wilde's own claims to critical preeminence (Pater's essay "Style," in which he applied his aesthetic criticism to works of literature, had been published just a month earlier in December 1888 in the same periodical, the *Fortnightly Review*).

Jacob Boehme (1572–1624), would probably have been little more than names recalled but vaguely; the Swedish scientist, philosopher, and theologian Emanuel Swedenborg (1688–1772) and the German Dominican Johannes (Meister) Eckhart (c. 1260–1327) might possibly have been slightly better known, since new editions of their work had appeared in the 1870s and 1880s respectively. It is still unlikely that many of Wilde's readers would have had a detailed knowledge of them. But, as with the references to Olaus Magnus, Aldrovandus, and Conrad Lycosthenes in the passage quoted earlier, this does not matter much: we still get the point, because Gilbert (who, like Ernest and Wilde, enjoys parading his knowledge) gives us quite enough clues. "Illumination," "Abyss," "Vision," "Heaven"—these terms are sufficient to indicate that with these authorities (as with Plato) we are again in the realm of abstraction, rather than that of tangible, physical beauty. Moreover, there is little sense that looking up the details of any of these authors' works—reading, say, Swedenborg's description of his encounter with the spiritual world in his *De Coelo et ejus mirabilibus* (or *A Treatise Concerning Heaven and Hell, Containing A Relation of Many Wonderful Things Therein*)—will be time well spent: rather the opposite. The whole pleasure of reading this passage—encapsulated by Gilbert's elegantly casual phrase "What to us...?"—lies in the realization that the learning being exhibited (which of course most of us don't share, as Gilbert well knows) is as redundant as it is impressive. The reader does not need to be a scholar to understand a joke about scholarship.

Much the same sort of effect can be seen in the following passage, also from "The Critic as Artist":

> But I see that the moon is hiding behind a sulphur-coloured cloud. Out of a tawny mane of drift she gleams like a lion's eye. She is afraid that I will talk to you of Lucian and Longinus, of Quinctilian and Dionysus, of Pliny and Fronto and Pausanias, of all those who in the antique world wrote or lectured upon art-matters. She need not be afraid. I am tired of my expedition into the dim, dull abyss of facts. There is nothing left for me now but the divine μονόχρονος ἡδονή of another cigarette. Cigarettes have at least the charm of leaving one unsatisfied. (Ross, ed., *Intentions*, 124)

Here, again, the reader does not need to know the precise details of who these classical authors were or what they wrote: all that matters—and this we can pick up from Gilbert's bored tone—is that they were authorities, and there were many of them. The significance of the list thus resides as much as anything in the way that it is structured: those three pairings followed by "and Pausanius" are designed rhetorically to give the impression of that prized Decadent quality, *ennui* or utter weariness. The reader does not have to have studied Greats at Oxford to get the joke (though it might have been all the more pointed had he done so). And what of the Greek phrase? Do we need to know that "μονόχρονος ἡδονή" ("momentary pleasure") had been quoted by Pater in chapter nine of his novel *Marius the Epicurean*, where it was attributed to the Greek philosopher Aristippus (born c. 435BC,), who founded the Cyrenaic school which argued that the sovereign good consisted in pleasure, a precept which anticipated Epicureanism? Undoubtedly there would have been some nineteenth-century readers who would have understood this allusion, and who would no doubt have appreciated a joke against Paterian seriousness. (As we explain below, Pater invoked this phrase in the service of a complex scholarly exploration of the philosophical differences between spiritual pleasure and simple hedonism.) And those selfsame readers may also have been alert to the connotations underlying Wilde's allusion to Pater's comments on the beauty of a rose leaf which we noted above.

What needs stressing, though, is that these personal asides at Pater's reputation, directed, as we said, to only a select few, are once again not relevant to Gilbert's intellectual argument. On the contrary: recognizing the personal politics underlying these allusions tends to undermine Gilbert's invocation of Pater as an authority on sensual pleasure to be set against idealists such as Plato. In other words, in order to get Gilbert's joke—what we might term the rhetorical effect of his comments—we should not investigate the origins of the Greek allusion too closely. The most the reader needs is the ability to translate the phrase, and perhaps identify it with Aristippus, and thus with a philosophical justification of pleasure; but even if he or she can do none of these things, there is still a joke to be seen, that something as apparently banal as smoking a cigarette can be dignified by a Greek epithet. Learning, once again, is being exhibited for the reader's admiration at the same time as it is being trivialized.

"For mine own part, it was all Greek to me" (*Julius Caesar*)

It is worth interrupting our larger argument to consider in more detail Wilde's use of Greek in *Intentions*. For a writer who, as we noted above, was so at ease with ancient Greek texts, and who so liberally scatters his critical prose with the names of Greek authors (particularly Plato, Aristotle, Aeschylus, and Euripides), it is perhaps surprising to learn that there are only four occasions in the whole of *Intentions* where he actually quotes directly in Greek, and even then the quotations are brief, just a word or phrase. In addition to the example given above, the others are: "we find the delicate fictile vase of the Greek, with its exquisitely painted figures and the faint *ΚΑΛΟΣ* [beauty] finely traced upon its side" (from "Pen, Pencil, and Poison"); "To-night it may fill one with that *ΕΡΩΣ ΤΩΝ ΑΔΥΝΑΤΩΝ* [love of the impossible], that *Amour de l'Impossible*, which falls like a madness on many who think they live securely and out of reach of harm, so that they sicken suddenly with the poison of unlimited desire, and, in the infinite pursuit of what they may not obtain, grow faint and swoon or stumble"; and "To us, at any rate, the *ΒΙΟΣ ΘΕΩΡΗΤΙΚΟΣ* [contemplative life] is the true ideal. From the high tower of Thought we can look out at the world. Calm, and self-centred, and complete, the aesthetic critic contemplates life" (both from "The Critic as Artist") (Ross, ed., *Intentions*, 69, 149, 182–83).

For nineteenth-century readers these would not have been difficult terms or phrases to translate (schoolboy Greek would have been, and is still, adequate); and even for the reader who knows no Greek at all, the general sense of what is being said is made clear enough from the context of the rest of the sentence. Some readers might have recognized in the second example an allusion to a line in Euripides's *Heracles* where Amphitryon, the father of Hercules, is pleading for the lives of his grandchildren who have been sentenced to death: "ἄλλως δ' ἀδυνάτων ἔοικ' ἐρᾶν" ("Yet it seems I am foolishly in love with the impossible"). But once again, even for those unable to identify this source, Wilde's paraphrase supplies enough information to allow them to understand the nature of the love which is described.

The lightness of Wilde's touch here and the lack of any real demand being made of the reader are significant: the chief function of these Greek quotations is (again) rhetorical, to show that the speaker (Gilbert in "The Critic as Artist") or the narrator (in "Pen, Pencil, and Poison") has enjoyed a certain sort of education—that Greek phrases come to him as naturally and fluently as English ones (or indeed French ones). The modern reader does not, then, need to dwell too long on the precise significance of these Greek terms or their sources (recognizing the allusion to *Heracles* does not lead us into thinking more deeply about the Greek quotation or its relevance to Wilde's argument). That this tactic was by no means the only (or even, perhaps, the most usual) way of alluding to classical works in late-nineteenth-century criticism can be seen, as we will explain below, by comparing Wilde's prose to that of Pater. But Wilde's use of Greek sources in some of his other works—such as "The Rise of Historical Criticism"

Wilde and the Art of Smoking Smoking, in Wilde's *oeuvre*, is almost always associated with the dandy for whom it signals refinement, sophistication, and of course leisure: a cigarette is one of the dandy's key cultural accessories. "The Decay of Lying" opens with Cyril associating relaxation with "smoking cigarettes" and it is made clear by his request midway through the dialogue for "Another cigarette, please," that smoking and talking go hand in hand (Ross, ed., *Intentions*, 31). In *The Picture of Dorian Gray* Lord Henry opines to Dorian through the "thin blue wreaths of smoke that curled up in such fanciful whorls from his heavy opium-tainted cigarette" (*Complete Works*, III: 4). In Act I of *A Woman of No Importance*, Lady Stutfield admires Lord Alfred's "very charming … gold-tipped cigarettes" which, as Lord Alfred airily explains, "are awfully expensive" (Ross, ed., *A Woman of No Importance*, 30). The most famous use of this Wildean prop is of course to be found in *The Importance of Being Earnest* where a cigarette case left in the smoking-room is crucial to the plot.

and *De Profundis*, both of which were written for different occasions and audiences compared to those of *Intentions*—also stands as a useful contrast.

Take, for example, the following passage in "The Rise of Historical Criticism," one which to the reader unfamiliar with ancient Greek would make almost no sense:

> The various manifestations of this law, as shown in the normal, regular, revolutions and evolutions of the different forms of government ... are expounded with great clearness by Polybius, who claiming for his theory in the Thucydidean spirit, that it is a κτῆμα ἐς ἀεί, not a mere ἀγώνισμα ἐς τὸ παραχρῆμα, and that a knowledge of it will enable the impartial observer ... to discover at any time to what period of its constitutional evolution any particular state has already reached and into what form it will be next differentiated: though possibly the exact time of the changes may be more or less uncertain. (Ross, ed., *Miscellanies*, 193)

Here we need to know both the precise translation of these Greek terms and the exact context in which they occur. Otherwise we cannot appreciate how Polybius's "theory" (about which we also need quite detailed knowledge) can be "Thucydidean in spirit."[3]

The phrases that Wilde quotes may be translated as a "possession of all time" and "a prize to be heard for the moment," and the passage in full (which is an explanation of Thucydides's historical method) reads in translation as follows: "And it may well be that the absence of the fabulous from my narrative will seem less pleasing to the ear; but whoever shall wish to have a clear view both of the events which have happened and of those which will some day, in all human probability, happen again in the same or a similar manner—for these to adjudge my history profitable will be enough for me. And, indeed, it has been composed, not as a prize-essay to be heard for the moment, but as a possession for all time."[4] The passage in Polybius's work to which these comments (accord-

---

continued   In that play, however, Wilde typically subverts the association between smoking and bohemianism when Lady Bracknell responds to Jack's admission that he smokes: "I am glad to hear it. A man should always have an occupation of some kind" (Ross, ed., *The Importance of Being Earnest*, 40). Wilde himself also seems to have been a heavy smoker. When he stepped out to address the audience on the first night of *Lady Windermere's Fan* he was described by the *Sunday Times* reporter as having a cigarette in his hand. A cartoon from 1895, entitled *Biter Bit: the arrest of Oscar*, draws him lounging nonchalantly in an easy chair with a lighted cigarette, as detectives burst in to arrest him. In many photographs, too, including the famous poses with Douglas and the post-prison pictures of a portly Wilde posing at Naples, he has a lighted cigarette dangling from the fingers of his right hand.

ing to Wilde) apply occurs in his account of revolutions in the *Histories* (VI. 9.
10 ff.). More particularly, Wilde seems to have in mind some lines (in VI. 9. 14),
which he quotes in Greek in the margins of the manuscript version of his essay,
in which Polybius describes how a state that "has been formed and has grown
naturally ... will undergo a natural decline and change into its contrary."[5] We
can see that here Wilde is attempting to engage his reader in an area of scholarly debate, one that assumes a specialist knowledge of Greek literature (which
of course the essay's intended readers—distinguished Oxford academics—possessed, and who were probably, as we noted earlier, far better educated than Wilde). By contrast, the allusions to Greek literature in *Intentions* do not require
anything approaching this level of intellectual work. In that volume, learning is
an altogether more casual and witty affair.

Before moving on to compare Wilde with writers whose scholarship is used
for markedly different purposes, there is one final example from *Intentions*—from
one of Gilbert's speeches in "The Critic as Artist"—that is worth examining:

> But we who are born at the close of this wonderful age, are at once too cultured and
> too critical, too intellectually subtle and too curious of exquisite pleasures, to accept
> any speculations about life in exchange for life itself. To us the *citta divina* is colourless,
> and the *fruitio Dei* without meaning. Metaphysics do not satisfy our temperaments, and
> religious ecstasy is out of date. The world through which the Academic philosopher
> becomes "the spectator of all time and of all existence" is not really an ideal world, but
> simply a world of abstract ideas. (Ross, ed., *Intentions*, 177)

At first glance, the use of allusion in this passage appears rather different from
the other examples we have examined: so there are no lists and no translations
of the terms in foreign languages; and rather than a named individual, the quotation is attributed simply to "the Academic philosopher." How difficult, then,
is this passage to decipher? What level of knowledge does it require of the reader? The first clue is provided by the mention (in the final sentence) of a world
of "abstract ideas." This passage occurs just before Gilbert's contrast between
Pater's and Plato's notions of beauty which have been discussed above. So the
reader who is unsure of the identity of the Academic philosopher would find
out soon enough (although we need to acknowledge that the phrase "Academic philosopher" would have been familiar to Wilde's contemporaries, most
of whom would have known enough about Plato to know also of his famous
Academy).[6] But what of those first two phrases that translate (as most can easily guess) as "the divine city" and "enjoyment of God"?

Here is it perhaps relevant to note that Wilde had used the phrase "*citta divina*" at least twice before, and on both occasions when he was addressing a popular audience. So in his 1882 lecture "The English Renaissance of Art"—written
for his American lecture tour—he referred to "that *città divina* [with the correct accent], as the old Italian heresy called it, the divine city where one can

stand, though only for a brief moment, apart from the division and terror of the world and the choice of the world too" (Ross, ed., *Miscellanies*, 271); and then some years later he also used it in a review for the *Pall Mall Gazette* in June 1889, commenting that "Mr Austin's vision of the *citta divina* of the future is not very inspiring" (Ross, ed., *Reviews*, 514). These examples suggest that the allusion probably operated, and was intended so to operate, at a fairly general level, referring to any imagined ideal city or life—or as Gilbert helpfully explains, any form of "metaphysics"—as opposed to a particular literary one (such as, for example, the one imagined in the heretical poem *La Città di Vita* [1455–1464] by the Florentine writer Matteo Palimieri, and to which Pater alluded in *The Renaissance*[7]). "*Fruitio Dei*" works in a similar way. Wilde himself may possibly have derived the phrase from a line in Benjamin Jowett's introduction to Plato's *Symposium* (in the second volume of his *Dialogues of Plato*) which he had copied into his *Commonplace Book*: "ερως [love] … is like the fruitio Dei of the mediaeval saint, or Dante's love for Beatrice, or the hunger and thirst after righteousness" (Smith and Helfand, 149). It seems highly unlikely, though, that Wilde required the reader of *Intentions* to make exactly this connection. Knowing that Jowett had used the phrase when discussing the topic of abstract love makes, perhaps, for a witty joke against his scholarship and his particular use of Plato. Significantly, though, it does not materially add to the reader's understanding of Gilbert's argument. In order to grasp his main point we only need to know that—as he himself explains—he is referring to the valorization of any form of religious or spiritual ecstasy.

We see in this passage, then, that Wilde's allusions can operate with varying levels of knowledge, and that a detailed acquaintance with some of his sources can provide some readers (those in the know, as it were) with an extra joke. However, such jokes tend to be personal in the sense that they are directed against contemporary figures whose authority Wilde had private reasons to challenge. For example, it has been suggested by some critics that Wilde's personal hostility towards Pater may have had something to do with a feeling of resentment, or even contempt, at the way in which Pater had dealt with his own sexuality—by withdrawal and conformity—when threatened with scandal and public exposure. Another way to put this might be to say that this level of reference directs us towards thinking more about writers and personalities than about the specificities of their texts. More importantly, perhaps, the general reader (whether today, or in the late nineteenth century) who misses such references does not as a consequence misunderstand the logic of Wilde's argument, nor, indeed, the general target of his satire. So we can appreciate Gilbert's witty dismissal of spiritual and idealized love, as it is celebrated by Greek authors such as Plato, without necessarily having to know the details of a late-nineteenth-century scholarly debate about Hellenism and homosexuality, nor indeed about the power of Benjamin Jowett in deciding careers both in Oxford and in the real world beyond it. When modern academics point these sorts of details out to us, it may add an extra layer of meaning and allow us to see aspects of *Intentions* as more politically charged than we might hitherto have thought. But it is unclear whether such information contributes very much to our enjoyment of the volume's rhetorical strategies, as opposed to illuminating some of the personal circumstances of Wilde's own life. On the contrary: it could be argued that the continued relevance of Wilde's critical writings is precisely because they work, and were in fact designed to work, without such specialist or personal knowledge.

We also need to be aware of the fact that there are often inconsistencies in the learning that Wilde places on display. A striking example can be seen in his allusions in *Intentions* to French Impressionism. In both "The Decay of Lying" and "The Critic as Artist" the superior aesthetic sensibilities of Vivian and Gilbert (in contrast to those of their respective interlocutors, Cyril and Ernest) are troped by reference to their tastes in pictorial art. So in the view of Vivian, Monet, and Pissarro (both of whom had recently exhibited works in London) represent the height of artistic sophistication and modernity, exemplifying, so Vivian claims, one of his (and Wilde's) central critical precepts—that it is life which imitates art, rather than (as the realists proposed) art imitating life:

> And so, let us be humane, and invite Art to turn her wonderful eyes elsewhere. She has done so already, indeed. The white quivering sunlight that one sees now in France, with its strange blotches of mauve, and its restless violet shadows, is her latest fancy, and, on the whole, Nature reproduces it quite admirably. Where she used to give us Corots and Daubignys, she gives us now exquisite Monets and entrancing Pissaros. (Ross, ed., *Intentions*, 42–43)

In "The Critic as Artist" Gilbert also comments on the use of colour by French Impressionists, although he is rather more condemning than Vivian of their treatment of nature:

> But even the Impressionists, earnest and industrious as they are, will not do. I like them. Their white keynote, with its variations in lilac, was an era in colour....Yet they will insist on treating painting as if it were a mode of autobiography invented for the use of the illiterate, and are always prating to us on their coarse gritty canvases of their unnecessary selves and their unnecessary opinions, and spoiling by a vulgar over-emphasis that fine contempt of nature which is the best and only modest thing about them. One tires, at the end, of the work of individuals whose individuality is always noisy, and generally uninteresting. There is far more to be said in favour of that newer school at Paris, the *Archaicistes*, as they call themselves, who, refusing to leave the artist entirely at the mercy of the weather, do not find the ideal of art in mere atmospheric effect, but seek rather for the imaginative beauty of design and the loveliness of fair colour, and rejecting the tedious realism of those who merely paint what they see, try to see something worth seeing, and to see it not merely with actual and physical vision, but with that nobler vision of the soul which is as far wider in spiritual scope as it is far more splendid in artistic purpose. They ... have sufficient aesthetic instinct to regret those sordid and stu-

pid limitations of absolute modernity of form which have proved the ruin of so many of the Impressionists. (Ross, ed., *Intentions*, 204–206)

In Gilbert's view, Impressionism, far from being "the latest" fancy, is somewhat *passé*, having been superseded by a different artistic movement, that of the Archaicistes. In fact, the careers of the so-called Archaicistes (that is, artists such as Gustave Moreau, Odilion Redon, and Rodolphe Bresdin) more or less overlapped with those of the Impressionists (Moreau died five years earlier than Pissarro, and was one year his junior). Moreover the most celebrated appraisal of their exotic and intense style had appeared in a work that predated Wilde's *Intentions* by several years, Joris-Karl Huysmans's *A Rebours* (1884)—it may indeed have been Wilde's source for the observation. There Huysmans's protagonist Des Esseintes gives a voluptuous description of these "disconcerting," "fantastic," and "frenzied" works which leave the viewer "amazed and pensive."[8] To claim that the Archaicistes were the "newer" school in Paris was thus debatable, but for an English reader (both in the late nineteenth century and today), they were certainly the lesser-known movement. A preference for the Archaicistes over the Impressionists might thus be taken as an indication of Gilbert's more refined (and possibly more Decadent) connoisseurship.

But what is the reader of *Intentions* in its entirety to think? Can we reconcile the differing evaluations of Impressionism which these allusions seem to gesture towards? Can Monet's mauves and lilacs be both "exquisite" and "earnest" (a loaded term if ever there was one in Wilde's vocabulary)? Can Impressionism be both the "latest fancy" and yet less novel than the "newest school"? Can it both be an exemplification of the superiority of art over life while at the same time tending to spoil "by a vulgar over-emphasis that fine contempt of nature"? What, according to *Intentions*, constitutes true modernity in art? Is it the symbolic and archaic subjects chosen by the Archaicistes, or is it the Impressionists' radical revisioning of landscape? If we try to press Wilde for answers to these questions we only involve ourselves in further imponderables, such as, for example, the problems of ascertaining the relationship between the expertise of Vivian and that of Gilbert, and of how both of their knowledge of contemporary art relates to Wilde's own.[9]

Vivian's extolling of the modernity of Monet is perfectly understandable as an illustration of his comments about the way art sets visual patterns which nature then copies: thus, he claims, we now see the world in terms of Monet's mauves as opposed to what Wilde had elsewhere termed "the grey mists" of Corot and "opal mornings" of Daubigny, artists who belonged to the earlier, Barbizon school (*Complete Letters*, 211). In a similar way, Gilbert's weariness of Impressionism's effects, of what he sees as its slavish adherence to "absolute modernity of form," is comprehensible in terms of his attempt to persuade Ernest of the value of the "decorative arts" in which artistic inspiration always comes "from form, and from form purely," not from being left at the "mercy of the weather" or painting *en plein air*. Difficulties arise only if we try to put these comments together and extrapolate from them a canon of artworks which can illustrate a consistent aesthetic. The problem is not that Vivian and Gilbert are working with different criteria of aesthetic value (both, for example, deplore realism); it is rather that their appreciation of the works they choose to illustrate their aesthetic principles is subordinate to their larger argument. So for Vivian, Impressionism can be usefully invoked as testimony to the creativity of art in its rejection of mere imitation; for Gilbert, however, the same movement's mode of seeing can be used to illustrate a lack of inventiveness, not because it is in any way indebted to realism, but because seeing with "actual and physical vision" is inferior to "that nobler vision of the soul." Although these statements do not contradict each other—clearly there can be more than one kind of nonmimetic art—they produce different evaluations of Impressionism, and this in turn makes it difficult to derive from *Intentions* a reliable "map" of Wilde's own artistic taste.

The question of the ultimate value of Impressionism in Wilde's *oeuvre* remains elusive. Moreover, providing the reader—as scholars will inevitably be tempted to do—with ever more detailed "background" information about French Impressionists, useful and interesting though it might be, does not resolve the issue. It will not magically bring into a line those contradictory or errant judgments (although it might explain why and how they could coexist within a culture). And this is because making sense of *Intentions* does not require the reader to join up, as it were, all the intellectual dots. Rather the opposite: searching too hard for coherence in that work, trying to trace a pattern in the range of allusions and reference, and to derive from it an intellectual or artistic canon, will lead only to frustration. As Wilde himself warned at the end of the final piece in that volume: "Not that I agree with everything that I have said.... There is much with which I entirely disagree. The essay simply represents an artistic standpoint, and in aesthetic criticism attitude is everything" (Ross, ed., *Intentions*, 269). To this we might add that the appropriate attitude to adopt when reading aesthetic criticism, at least that practised by Wilde, is to remain, as we said, on the surface of things.

Wilde & Intertextual Authority

As we might expect, however, many of Wilde's contemporaries were not content with what Henry James called mere surfaces. If we compare the use of sources and references in a range of late-nineteenth- and early-twentieth-century works, we will be in a position to have a clearer understanding of what is involved when we label a work as intellectually difficult rather than (as in *Intentions*) simply using knowledge which seems intended principally to perplex readers. Good examples of these writers are, as we have said, Pater—Wilde's near contemporary—and T. S. Eliot, perhaps the most distinguished poet of the generation which followed that of Wilde.

Pater is a writer whose works are mainly known today in academic circles or to a small group of *aficionados*. It may come as something of a surprise, then, to learn that in his own lifetime Pater's critical writings and fiction consistently outsold those of Wilde. Moreover, with the possible exception of his first book, *The Renaissance* (1873), they were also consistently better received by critics and academics. This in turn might explain why Pater is so often a personal target for Wilde. Part of Pater's reputation in the late nineteenth century might have had to do with the fact that he possessed a more astute sense of his readership, and as a consequence of the kind of writer he wished to be, than Wilde ever did. Pater demands that the reader follow him on an intellectual odyssey through the byways of classical culture, and his contemporary readers (there were many well educated enough to embark on that journey) realized that if they were prepared to take up his challenge they would not be disappointed. In other words, Pater announces the "literariness," the high culture, and the scholarly basis of his work from the outset.

We can see this exemplified in the very title of his only novel, *Marius the Epicurean: His Sensations and Ideas*, published in 1885, two or three years before Wilde began work on his criticism. Before they even turn to the first chapter of Pater's novel, readers have quite a lot of information to make sense of: to know what Epicureanism is; to understand nineteenth-century critiques of it as mere hedonism (as opposed to a serious philosophy); to realize the Latin significance of the name "Marius"; and—a little later—to recognize, read, and identify the epigraph on the title page, given only in Greek. All this announces the novel's "difference." And the reader who, despite all this, expected the usual Victorian plot, characterization, and entertainment would certainly have been disappointed. Unlike in *The Picture of Dorian Gray*, learning is not sweetened by the melodramatic thrill of thwarted love, murder, and revenge. Pater, from the beginning, takes no hostages. For him and his readers, scholarship, learning, and knowledge were an entirely serious business. This is not to say that there are no jokes in the novel, but they are not at the expense of scholarship, as with Wilde; rather they work almost as a celebration of it. Moreover they require of the reader a level of knowledge at least equal to Pater's own.

The novel contains numerous quotations, some submerged, from a variety of classical sources. Several of these are the same as those often invoked by Wilde: Virgil, Ovid, Plato, Livy, the letters of Pliny and of the Stoic philosopher Cornelius Fronto. However, the function of all these works in Pater's story goes well beyond providing a simple historical texture or background for a novel (which is set in second-century Rome); nor—as with Wilde—are they cited just as authorities to endorse or complicate a particular line of argument.

They are rather used as part of a complex intertextual game, understanding the rules of which requires a precise recall of the specific pieces of text to which Pater alludes. Moreover, the narrative itself often gives little clue to the uninitiated about the nature of the game being played, or indeed whether there is a game at all. For example, on several occasions Pater quotes from (or translates) the correspondence between Cornelius Fronto and the Roman emperor Marcus Aurelius Antoninus, the existence of which was discovered in 1815. Thus we find passages such as:

> And at least his success was unmistakable as to the precise literary effect he had intended, including a certain tincture of "neology" in expression—*nonnihil interdum elocutione novella parum signatum*—in the language of Cornelius Fronto, the contemporary prince of rhetoricians. (Pater, *Marius*, I: 61)

Or:

> Like the modern visitor to the Capitoline and some other museums, Fronto had been struck, pleasantly struck, by the family likeness among the Antonines; and it was part of his friendship to make much of it, in the case of the children of Faustina. "Well! I have seen the little ones," he writes to Aurelius, then, apparently absent from them: "I have seen the little ones—the pleasantest sight of my life; for they are as like yourself as could possibly be....Ah! I heard too their pretty voices, so sweet that in the childish prattle of one and the other I seemed somehow to be listening—yes! In the chirping of your pretty chickens—to the limpid and harmonious notes of your own oratory." (Pater, *Marius*, I: 245)

Or:

> And here Cornelius Fronto was to pronounce a discourse on the *Nature of Morals*.... And he did this earnestly, with an outlay of all his science of mind, and that eloquence of which he was a master....Certainly there was rhetoric enough: a wealth of imagery: illustrations from painting, music, mythology, the experiences of love: a management, by which subtle, unexpected meaning was brought out of familiar terms, like flies from morsels under amber, to use Fronto's own figure. (Pater, *Marius*, II: 3–4)

In these instances we have three different ways of representing Fronto's words to the reader: in the first passage we are only given the Latin (which translates as "some parts here and there were not marked with sufficient novelty of expression"). In the second (and apparently most straightforward) example Pater translates the Latin for us, though in a manner which in its colloquial charm and immediacy changes the tone of the original. In the third, he appears to be giving a sort of *précis* of a speech by Fronto (although in this instance, and unlike the letters to Marcus Aurelius, neither the document itself, nor any mention of it in other authors, has survived, and so there was nothing for Pater to quote from, to translate, or to paraphrase). These choices—of a Latin quote, then an English translation rendered into direct speech, and then a paraphrase of a speech which has been "imagined" or "ventriloquized" by Pater—suggest that he may be indulging in some form of textual play, for they explicitly call to the reader's attention a variety of interpretative and hermeneutic questions to do with the nature and status of his Latin source material.

Do Fronto's and Marcus Aurelius's letters rehearse or reveal the personal thoughts of each man (as their presence in a novel might demand)? Can we reconstruct from them a sense of their characters? Were those letters, as the narrative voice confidently asserts, "certainly sincere," despite the apparently formal and often formulaic way in which they conducted their literary conversation? Or, are those letters merely a species of intellectual display, an arena in which each man could exercise his rhetorical skills, particularly as at the time one of the correspondents was absolute ruler of the European world? And if they are display, how far is Pater's "fictionalization" of an oration by Fronto legitimate, insofar as it is employed in the service of an intellectual goal—better to weigh up the merits of Stoic philosophy? It is worth noting that Pater also significantly reorders and rewrites, through his translations, many of his other Latin and Greek sources, most significantly Aurelius's *Meditations*. Again the effect is to allow him to present Stoicism in a particular light, to draw attention to its nobility while at the same time emphasizing some of its shortcomings, such as its inability to come to terms with the rich variety of human experience, and especially human suffering.

To engage with these issues obviously requires an intimate acquaintance with the documents Pater was using and a knowledge of which ones he invented. To put matters another way, the reader must work hard to make sense of Pater's strategies. An inability to appreciate the differences between those Latin sources which have been faithfully quoted and those which have been slightly reordered and reinterpreted, as well as the differences between both these and those "sources" which have been "made up," excludes the reader from fully understanding (or entering into) the novel's complex debates about Roman ethics. And this is because those debates are conducted via a subtle interrogation of the source materials of Roman history and historiography, an interrogation that asks some penetrating questions about the authority, reliability, and status of texts. Pater's textual "games"—if that is the right term for them—are thus not a kind of "added extra," designed to engage the attention of the well-educated reader: they are the substance from which the novel is crafted, its rationale, as it were. In "The Critic as Artist," as we saw, Fronto was just another name in a long list of classical bores; but in *Marius the Epicurean*, Fronto is, essentially, a textual construct, and the invoking of his name draws us inexorably into textual debates and the niceties of late-nineteenth-century classical scholarship. This in turn may explain why even the best of editorial apparatuses is unlikely to transform *Marius* into a modern best seller. Because the novel has only a rudimentary narrative, little characterization, and no dramatic events, there is nothing else to engage the reader's attention beyond this intellectual game.

And what about *The Waste Land*, a poem that can seem at first glance to many readers (especially students) to be as impenetrable, as intimidating in its use of sources, as *Marius the Epicurean*, but which, unlike that novel, has had a significant afterlife beyond scholarship? We have observed that in *Marius the Epicurean* textual difficulty occurs only in part because its references are recondite; much more alienating for the modern reader is the fact that the textual issues which they point the reader towards are themselves complex (and not to everyone's taste). In Wilde's prose writing, as we have argued, although some of his textual references are equally recondite, the appreciation of the points of his argument does not require a full or detailed knowledge of them. *The Waste Land* uses references often as esoteric as those to be found in Pater, and—again as with Pater—the reader does need to know their origins, and to be able to make sense of them, in order to appreciate the poem. But with Eliot, the purposes and ends of erudition are quite different: we are not led outside the text into debates about scholarship, textual authority, and epistemology. Rather the allusions beyond the text push us back towards it. Pater's intertextuality is centrifugal; Eliot's, by contrast, is centripetal. Wilde's moves us neither to or from his text. These distinctions are again made clearer if we examine some examples.

Early drafts of *The Waste Land* reveal its original epigraph to have been some lines from Joseph Conrad's novella *Heart of Darkness*, a work published recently enough to have been in the minds of many of Eliot's original readers. That epigraph read as follows:

> Did he live his life again in every detail of desire, temptation, and surrender during that supreme moment of complete knowledge? He cried in a whisper at some image, at some vision,—he cried out twice, a cry that was no more than a breath—
>
> "The horror! The horror!" (*The Waste Land*, 3)

Valerie Eliot's edition of the drafts and manuscripts of the poem reveals a handwritten addition to the typed quotation identifying its source as "CONRAD." The notes to her edition also register the reservations of Ezra Pound, Eliot's first "editor," about the use of the epigraph, that Conrad was not "weighty" enough. By the time the Boni and Liveright first edition of the poem appeared in New York in 1922, Conrad had been displaced by the altogether more heavy Petronius and a quotation from the *Satyricon*:

> Nam Sybillam quidem Cumis ego ipse oculis meis vidi in ampulla pendere, et cum illi pueri dicerunt: Εἰβυλλα τί θέλεις; respondebat illa: ἀποθανεῖν θέλω.

[For indeed I myself saw the Sybil of Cumae with my own eyes suspended in a basket, and when the boys said to her: "What do you want," she replied "I want to die."] (*The Waste Land*, 133)

As with the epigraph to *Marius the Epicurean*, these lines stand unidentified and untranslated. (Even the notes that Eliot added to his poem do not identify or translate them.) Like Pater, then, Eliot and/or Pound is assuming a reader with a fairly detailed classical education. Of course Petronius's Latin and Greek are not nearly as accessible for the general reader—neither in the early twentieth century nor today—as the passage from Conrad is or would have been. That inaccessibility, however, is not simply to do with one's facility in translating Greek or Latin (actually the lines are not particularly difficult linguistically) but because they come from a source which, as Rod Boroughs pointed out some years ago, was slightly *risqué* and esoteric.[10] The *Satyricon* would not have been part of the typical or "official" Latin curriculum either at school or university. It was considered to be disreputable, not a work for polite reading, a reputation which Wilde had exploited earlier in *Dorian Gray*.

To understand the significance of Eliot's or Pound's use of this allusion, and its relation to the poem as a whole, requires a quite detailed knowledge of both sources and their cultural currency. We need to know, for example, that in classical mythology the Cumaean Sybil possessed the ability to read the future and that her prophecies were often misinterpreted. We also need to know that she had asked from Apollo the gift of eternal life, a boon which the god had granted. But she failed to ask for the accompanying gift of eternal youth, and so in the *Satyricon* she is a figure shrivelled by an eternity of old age: she becomes, like Eliot's Tiresias, a spectator of the absurdity of human life. At first sight we may seem now to be in Paterian country, deep among the intricacies of classical knowledge and how it is to be interpreted. However, this is not really the case, for Eliot is not asking us to consider the variety and status of classical figurings of the Sybil, nor recent scholarly debates about her significance in Roman culture, nor the textual issues involved in reading Petronius's *Satyricon*. He is not, like Pater, pointing us towards the different translations of classical literature, nor contemporary controversies about the forged fragments of the *Satyricon*; rather the classical reference serves principally as a striking image to propel the reader into some of the central themes of the poem itself—its sense of the sordidness of human sexuality, and the relationship between knowledge and age.

The same can be said of some of the allusions within the poem. In "The Fire Sermon" section the following quotations are juxtaposed with no textual signposts whatever—titles, authors, or quotation marks, and so on:

By the water of Leman I sat down and wept ...
Sweet Thames, run softly till I end my song,
Sweet Thames, run softly, for I speak not loud or long.

> But at my back in a cold blast I hear
> The rattle of the bones, and chuckle spread from ear to ear. (lines 182–186)

Eliot's notes to "The Fire Sermon" gloss two of these references (although not specifically in relation to these lines) as an allusion to Edmund Spenser's *Prothalamion* and Andrew Marvell's "To His Coy Mistress." What is omitted from those notes is a reminder that line 182 is taken, with significant changes, from Psalm 137.1 (in the Authorized Version: "By the rivers of Babylon, there we sat down, yea, we wept, when we remembered Zion"). Nor is the reader informed that the quotation from Spenser has been slightly modified, and that lines 185–186 contain only echoes of Marvell's famous final stanza. This is why, as many critics have noted and many readers have discovered, the notes which Eliot included at the end of the poem are of such limited use. They tell us only of an origin; they don't even attempt to gloss an allusion's significance. And this may not have been because Eliot was being in some way obtuse or elitist, as John Carey has maintained. Rather it is as if Eliot wants the reader to keep her mind on the poem and not on the erudition that went into its making. Eliot is not merely exhibiting cultural knowledge: he is requiring the reader to engage in some form of cocreative activity, and it is this feature of *The Waste Land*, rather than the simple number and range of allusions, which makes it difficult, even for those readers who share Eliot's cultural background. The difficulties arise from reading the poem as a *poem*, from seeing the place of the poem's allusions in the structure of the work as a whole.

How Difficult Is Wilde's Critical Writing?

The term "difficulty" is relative; it is one which philosophers might label a double predicate—difficult in what ways, and difficult for what sort of reader with what sorts of expectations, we might want to ask? In this chapter we have

---

The *Satyricon* of Petronius The *Satyricon* of Petronius was a common reference point for numerous *fin-de-siècle* writers on both sides of the English Channel. It forms part of Dorian's reading habits in *The Picture of Dorian Gray*, and there are also borrowings from and allusions to it in works by the French writers Marcel Schwob and Pierre Louÿs (both of whom were friends of Wilde), as well as Anatole France, Jean Lorrain, and Joris-Karl Huysmans. The protagonist of Huysmans's *A Rebours* memorably describes the *Satyricon* as a novel with "no plot or action ... simply relating the erotic adventures of certain sons of Sodom" (Huysmans, 43). The *Satyricon* was also an important source for a number of late-nineteenth-century studies of sexuality, including Richard Burton's account of pederasty in the essay appended to his 1885–1888 translation of the *Arabian Nights*, Marc-André Raffalovich's *Uranisme et Unisexualité* (1896), and the various writings on homosexuality in the 1860s by the German scholar Karl Heinrich Ulrichs.

tried to draw a distinction between the difficulties which arise when readers do not share the same kinds of cultural knowledge as the author, and therefore fail to recognize textual references and allusions; and the difficulties which are a consequence of the complexity of the issues which certain kinds of allusions point the reader towards. It is only in the latter case that allusions, once identified, continue to create interpretative problems for the reader. Wilde's critical prose, we have argued, is generally free from this second sort of difficulty. Despite the range of erudition which he displays, his arguments, though provocative and striking, are not particularly hard to understand, and he does not require from his reader very much intellectual effort. In fact too much effort can actually spoil the effect, either by revealing a debt (for example in his use of Hazlitt in "Pen, Pencil, and Poison") which detracts from Wilde's originality, or by compromising an essay's coherence. And this may be one reason why contemporary reviewers of *Intentions* were perplexed and disappointed by it: the "cleverness" which they observed did not lead them in the directions they expected to go.

What is most striking about Wilde's criticism, compared to that of a number of his contemporaries, is how lightly and irreverently he wears his learning; even for readers who are not familiar with his range of source materials there is invariably a good joke to be had, often at the expense of scholarship. Paradoxically, then, encouraging modern readers to stay—as Wilde put it—on "the surface of things" may be the best way to keep his critical prose alive and relevant. This is not to deny that a serious point may be being made via irreverence—a point, perhaps, about the standards of the scholarly community from which Wilde himself may have felt excluded when he failed to gain an Oxford fellowship. There may also be a vein of seriousness—nastiness might be a better term— behind some of the personal allusions. The jibes at the reputations of Pater and Jowett in particular look like a continuation of some form of Oxford in-fight-

---

continued Little wonder, then, that the *Satyricon* gained a reputation, as Rod Boroughs puts it, as "a particularly unwholesome piece of literature." It survives only in an incomplete and fragmentary form, and has consequently been the subject of a number of forgeries as various hoaxers have claimed to have found other missing fragments. (In the mid-seventeenth century, however, a genuine manuscript of one of the work's central episodes was discovered in Dalmatia.) By the end of the nineteenth century the most readily available translation was that by Walter K. Kelly; the titles given to the English and American editions of his work give a sense of how the text was typically being marketed: *Erotica: The Elegies of Propertius, The Satyricon of Petronius Arbiter, and the Kisses of Johannes Secundus* (1854); and *The Satyricon; or, Trebly Voluptuous. By Petronius Arbiter, Minister of Pleasure to the Emperor Nero* (1866). The names of both Oscar Wilde and Algernon Swinburne were also linked with translations, neither of which materialized.

ing. Moreover by looking at these aspects of Wilde's criticism it is possible to politicize his writing, to affiliate him to, say, postmodernist critiques of textual authority, or to see in his anti-institutionalism an impertinence cherished by an exiled Irish nationalist. Yet these are not the only ways to read Wilde; nor, perhaps, are they the most rewarding or entertaining. In the next chapter we will continue this discussion of Wilde's "seriousness," but by concentrating on what, at first glance, seem to be his least serious works: the society comedies.

Notes

1. Such an all-inclusive approach to Wilde's *oeuvre* has other pitfalls, and these can be glimpsed in a startling error in Brown's first sentence, when she describes Portora Royal School as being located "in Dublin" when it was in fact in Enniskillen (in what is now Northern Ireland); given the centrality of geography in defining Irish identities and politics, this is an odd slip to make, but perhaps a convenient one for an argument in favour of a cosmopolitanism that overrides national boundaries.

2. Here we might make a comparison with what is probably the most ambitious attempt to establish the intellectual foundations of a nineteenth-century writer's work—Billie Andrew Inman's exhaustive reconstruction of Walter Pater's reading from records of his library borrowings at Oxford. The list of books she compiled is indeed extensive, but it in no way can be assumed to represent the contents of Pater's mind, nor the extent of his reading, nor how he reacted to what he read. See Inman, *Pater and His Reading, 1874–1877, with a Bibliography of His Literary Borrowings, 1878–94* (New York: Garland Publishing, 1990).

3. For those who are interested in such matters, Wilde is referring to a passage in Thucydides's *History of the Peloponnesian War*, I. 22. 4.

4. This (and all other Greek translations) are taken from the Loeb Classical Library: see *Thucydides*, Charles Forster Smith, trans. (London: William Heinemann, 1919, 1969), I: 39–41.

5. Polybius, *The Histories*, W. R. Paton, trans. (London: William Heinemann, 1923, 1977), III: 289.

6. The quotation is a translation of a phrase in Plato's discussion of the true philosopher in *The Republic*, 474c–486a; it is translated, more literally, in the Loeb Classical Library as: "Do you think that a mind habituated to thoughts of grandeur and the contemplation of all time and all existence can deem this life of man a thing of great concern?" (Plato, *The Republic*, P. Shorey, trans. [London: William Heinemann, 1937, 1969], I: 9–11.) Wilde often quoted the phrase—it appeared in "The Rise of Historical Criticism," his 1882 lecture "The English Renaissance of Art," and in the revised version of "The Portrait of W.H."

7. For details, see Hill, ed., *Walter Pater: The Renaissance*, 218.

8. J.-K. Huysmans, *A Rebours*, Robert Baldick, trans. (Harmondsworth: Penguin, 1959), 72–74. The description occurs in chapter five of the novel.

9. It might be tempting to explain these inconsistencies in the representation of French Impressionism in terms of the fact that "The Decay of Lying" and "The Critic as Artist" were initially composed separately for publication in different issues of the *Nineteenth Century*. However, neither of the passages on Impressionist art actually appeared in the periodical versions of the two essays, although manuscript evidence suggests that they had been present in early drafts of both pieces.

10. Boroughs comments: "the *Satyricon* had long been regarded as one of the naughtier classics because of its sexual, most especially its homosexual, subject-matter"; see Boroughs, "Oscar Wilde's Translation of Petronius: The Story of a Literary Hoax," *English Literature in Transition*, 38.1 (1995), 17–18.

Works Cited & Consulted

Brown, Julia Prewitt. *Cosmopolitan Criticism: Oscar Wilde's Philosophy of Art*. Charlottesville: University Press of Virginia, 1997.

Carey, John. *The Intellectuals and the Masses*. London: Faber and Faber, 1992.

The Complete Letters of Oscar Wilde. Merlin Holland and Rupert Hart-Davis, eds. London: Fourth Estate, 2000.

The Complete Works of Oscar Wilde. Merlin Holland, ed. London: Collins, 1994.

Dowling, Linda. *Hellenism and Homosexuality in Victorian Oxford*. Ithaca: Cornell University Press, 1994.

Eliot, T. S. *The Waste Land: A Facsimile and Transcript of the Original Drafts*, Valerie Eliot, ed. London: Faber and Faber, 1971.

Fletcher, Ian, and John Stokes. "Oscar Wilde," in *Anglo-Irish Literature: A Review of Research*, Richard J. Finneran, ed. New York: MLA, 1976.

Hichens, Robert. *The Green Carnation*. London: William Heinemann, 1894.

Huysmans, J.-K. *A Rebours*, Robert Baldick, trans. Harmondsworth: Penguin, 1959.

Inman, Billie Andrew. *Pater and His Reading, 1874–1877, with a Bibliography of His Literary Borrowings, 1878–94*. New York: Garland Publishing, 1990.

Kiberd, Declan. *Inventing Ireland*. London: Jonathan Cape, 1995.

Mason, Stuart. *A Bibliography of Oscar Wilde*. London: T. Werner Laurie Ltd., 1914.

Oscar Wilde's Oxford Notebooks. Philip E. Smith II and Michael S. Helfand, eds. New York: Oxford University Press, 1989.

Pater, Walter. *Appreciations, With an Essay on Style*. 1889; London: Macmillan, 1912.

_____. *Marius the Epicurean*. 1885; 3rd. ed. 2 vols. London: Macmillan, 1892.

_____. *The Renaissance*, Donald Hill, ed. Berkeley: University of California Press, 1980.

Pine, Richard. *The Thief of Reason: Oscar Wilde and Modern Ireland*. Dublin: Gill and Macmillan, 1995.

Wilde, Oscar. *Intentions and The Soul of Man*. Robert Ross, ed. London: Methuen, 1908.

_____. *Miscellanies*. Robert Ross, ed. London: Methuen, 1908.

_____. *The Soul of Man and Prison Writings*. Isobel Murray, ed. Oxford: Oxford University Press, 1990.

_____. *Reviews*. Robert Ross, ed. London: Methuen, 1908.

Woodcock, George. *The Paradox of Oscar Wilde*. London: T.V. Boardman, 1949.

| v | The Plays:
The Public & Private Worlds
of Oscar Wilde

The Public World of the Society Comedies

WE ARGUED in chapter two that it is possible to find in some of Wilde's works two distinct kinds of allusions: the private and biographical on the one hand, and the intellectual and the literary on the other. Wilde's four society comedies—*Lady Windermere's Fan* (1892), *A Woman of No Importance* (1893), *An Ideal Husband* (1895), and *The Importance of Being Earnest* (1895)—complicate this simple dualism by offering many examples of a third kind of reference, that of the social and cultural contexts against which and for which they were written, a subject more often called their topicality. (As we have seen, an analogous, but not really similar kind of reference is to be found in *De Profundis*, in the sense that Wilde's account of his and Douglas's private relationship is set against a background of complex social mores, such as the aristocratic practice of self-imposed exile in British colonies to avoid scandal or embarrassment at home.)

As far as the society comedies are concerned, academic critics have usually understood what we have described as the private and biographical in terms of a series of coded (or as we labelled them earlier, subtextual) references to homosexuality and the various subcultures in which it thrived in the 1890s. For example, a subject typically alluded to in Wilde's comedies is that of a man taking a mistress or lover, or leading a double life in general, together with the consequent threat of exposure and scandal in the press. This theme has been seen to possess a particular resonance with the contemporary criminalization of homosexuality as much as its overt relevance to heterosexual adultery, which is of course its primary meaning in the plays. At a more local level some critics have claimed to find a whole range of subtextual meanings in single lexical items. These often amount to what we might call a double language and have been perceived in phrases such as Bunburying (which we also mentioned in chapter one), in Wilde's own name and its homophone (wild), and in that of Ernest. Attention has also been drawn to the topic of male beauty (as it is discussed, for

114

example, by the female characters in Act II of *A Woman of No Importance*), and to the dramatic investment in male–male, as opposed to male–female, relationships. So some critics have found the dynamic between, say, Algernon and Jack, or between Gerald Arbuthnot and Lord Illingworth to be much more compelling than the relationships which any of those men have with female characters in the plays.

By contrast, the intellectual and literary references in the society comedies tend to have been understood in terms of Wilde's dramatic sources or literary analogues. Thus numerous critics have commented on Wilde's adaptations of the structure of the contemporary French *pièce bien faite* (or the "well-made play"), or of particular devices taken from contemporary British theatre, or of patterns of dialogue derived from British and Irish Restoration comedy. In keeping with this general view there have also been a number of critics who argue that we can see in Wilde's plays some thematic and structural debts to specific contemporary works, such as the suggestion that the plot of *The Importance of Being Earnest* was based on W. S. Gilbert's *Engaged*.[1] Critics who are predisposed to see such "borrowings" as indicative of a lack of originality or inventiveness on Wilde's part—at least in terms of plotting and theme—could find corroboration for their view in another body of research that has drawn attention to what might be described neutrally as Wilde's reuse of his own material, the moving of lines

---

Performance and "reading texts"   One reason why we are able to study Wilde's society comedies so easily is because he decided to publish them; the vast majority of late-nineteenth-century dramatic works were never made available to the general reading public, and can only be studied today by those readers patient enough to work though the mountains of material in the Lord Chamberlain's Collection in the British Library, which contains the licensing copies of all plays performed on the public stage. (Whether these copies were an entirely accurate record of what was actually performed on stage is not always easy to determine.) The idea of a "reading text" of a play—a version quite distinct from the texts that would be typed or printed (usually privately) for use by actors—was relatively novel in the 1890s, particularly for the work of contemporary dramatists. Moreover the market for such books was uncertain, making them a risky investment for any publisher. Even very successful dramatists, such as Henry Arthur Jones, rarely made any money out of the published versions of their plays. It is unsurprising therefore that Wilde's society comedies were published only in limited editions: the first two, *Lady Windermere's Fan* and *A Woman of No Importance*, were brought out in editions of just 500 copies by a small, specialist 1890s publisher called the Bodley Head which had a reputation for coterie publishing. The last two, *An Ideal Husband* and *The Importance of Being Earnest*, both of which appeared after Wilde's release from prison, were published in editions of 1,000 copies each by an even smaller enterprise—the one-man firm of Leonard Smithers who was chiefly known as a publisher of pornography and who soon afterwards went bankrupt.

or blocks of dialogue between the plays (from *An Ideal Husband* to *Earnest*, for example) or from nondramatic works, such as the fiction, into the plays (most obviously seen in the reuse of aphorisms and witty repartee from *The Picture of Dorian Gray* in *Lady Windermere's Fan* and *A Woman of No Importance*).

This interest in the manner in which the plays were composed has become a focus of attention only relatively recently, and dates from the first variorum editions of them produced some twenty-five years ago. Since then their construction has been systematically scrutinized by text editors, such as Joseph Donohue, and by a small number of critics, principally perhaps Sos Eltis. In terms of critical judgments or literary evaluation, Wilde's writing practices, as we see them exhibited in the plays' stemmata, have tended to produce divergent opinions. As we suggested, for some they are further evidence of a lack of originality, or even a kind of plagiarism or cheating. Other critics, though, have seen Wilde's reuse of material more positively: for them it becomes a form of self-quotation and irony, a version of Wilde the proto-postmodernist, the writer who plays with his readers and typically with how they expect to find qualities such as originality in dramatic works. Then there is a further group who have viewed Wilde's writing practices pragmatically, as the economical use of resources by a hard-pressed professional dramatist eager to make the most of his material, often

---

continued   Because early typescripts and licensing copies have survived for the society comedies, it is possible to see how Wilde changed his plays when presenting them as reading rather than performance texts. In *An Ideal Husband* he added more and more detailed stage directions, as well as lengthy descriptions of each of the "persons of the play"; these could include ironic commentaries on the characters. For example, near the beginning of Act I Sir Robert Chiltern is described as having "*a nervous temperament, with a tired look. The firmly-chiselled mouth and chin contrast strikingly with the romantic expression in the deep-set eyes. The variance is suggestive of an almost complete separation of passion and intellect.... It would be inaccurate to call him picturesque. Picturesqueness cannot survive in the House of Commons. But Vandyck would have liked to have painted his head*" (Ross, ed., *An Ideal Husband*, 11). Here Wilde, like his contemporary George Bernard Shaw, is writing more like a novelist than a playwright, appealing to the reader's visual imagination. In his reading texts Wilde also tended to lengthen his plays by adding minor (and sometimes nonspeaking) characters and extending speeches; in *Lady Windermere's Fan*, for example, some speeches are more than doubled in length and are also generally more impassioned and self-consciously rhetorical. Again it is as if Wilde is trying to present his dramatic world as fully as possible, but on the page rather than on the stage. Paradoxically, though, Wilde did not follow this pattern in every case: so his published edition of *The Importance of Being Earnest* actually omitted various stage directions (although these were mainly to do with "blocking" or the positioning of characters on the stage space).

prepared to repeat a winning formula. This last kind of explanation has found particular favour with cultural historians who have studied the changing conditions for writers in the late nineteenth century, and who have isolated what they see as the effects of a nascent but increasingly important consumerism on the commercial theatre and the culture industry in general.

It is worth stressing, though, that none of these features of Wilde's writing—neither his use of dramatic traditions nor his borrowings from his own, earlier works—seems to have troubled successive theatre audiences, who seem content to see them merely as a Wildean trademark, a brand they are happy to come back to. For individuals interested solely in modern theatre and the pleasure of attending particular performances, information about what Wilde "did" with the sources from which he borrowed (whether he subverts, satirizes, improves, or merely slavishly copies from them) is largely irrelevant, certainly to an enjoyment of the plays. And this in turn may explain why the concern with originality and intertextuality figures more strongly in accounts of literary rather than dramatic history. Intertextuality is an issue mainly for those critics who study the versions of his plays that Wilde published and who treat them—as the process of publication explicitly invites them to do—as polished artifacts which have a life and value beyond the particularities of specific performances.

The Topicality of the Society Comedies

These are, as we have said, the usual ways of dealing with the plays either in terms of their place within the Wilde canon or in terms of literary and dramatic history. What of our third category, that of the plays' social and cultural contexts, or what we have called their topicality? This particular quality is again most easily glimpsed, albeit in a piecemeal way, in modern scholarly editions, some of which seem to vie with each other to produce what are virtually encyclopaedic accounts of late-nineteenth-century British social mores. We are invited, either explicitly or implicitly, to see Wilde's plays as elaborate late-nineteenth-century comedies of manners, and Wilde himself as a writer caught up in, and playing with, the minutiae of late-nineteenth-century etiquette.

Here the justification, rarely made fully or openly, is of the following sort. Nineteenth-century Britain was subject to immense and rapid social changes. Certainties about status and hierarchy were disappearing as the result of a number of large and irresistible historical and economic forces, principally the rapid growth in the population, the equally rapid growth in its wealth, and a movement in the ownership of that wealth away from established interests, such as the aristocracy, to the new industrial and financial entrepreneurs who emerged at the end of the eighteenth and during the first half of the nineteenth centuries, and then to the burgeoning middle and lower-middle classes. This process led to anxieties about status, which led in turn to the development of various forms of rigid social practice intended to permit traditional centres of power to differentiate themselves from social newcomers (the *parvenu* or outsider is a repeated motif in Wilde's works). The codification of what was seen as acceptable behaviour was known formally as social etiquette. Wilde's society comedies take as their principal themes the actions of a leisured aristocratic or upper class, and were aimed at an audience who either aspired to the lifestyle of that class or (and this is more likely) were fascinated by, perhaps resentful of, the "goings-on" of their "betters," happy to see representations of them as flawed or immoral individuals. These plays, together with the production qualities brought to them by their various West End managers, would presuppose in the audience a detailed knowledge of that social system, of the class values it exhibited, and of the etiquette, social customs, and manners that defined it.

Those dramatic critics and historians who have seen fit to excavate this level of historical reference invariably feel obliged to give details of the nature and social significance of practices and habits that have now virtually disappeared from British life. These include phenomena such as calling cards, different sorts of meals and their basis in class distinctions (for example, the contrasts between a "high" or "meat" tea and dinner, or the connoisseurship of some French and German wines as a mark of social distinction), dress codes (such as dressing for dinner or the wearing of "mourning" dress), courtship rituals (for example, the chaperoning of young women), the social geography of London, and semi-public events in the London Season. The assumption underlying this kind of research is that theatre is fundamentally a social institution and cannot be fully understood without a knowledge of the society (and particularly the audiences) for which it was written and performed. A related insight is that the politics of late-nineteenth-century British theatre were deeply topical yet simultaneously circumscribed by its fundamentally conservative commercial interests. So a knowledge of London society of the 1890s has also to take account of the whole structure of contemporary theatrical institutions, from the bricks and mortar of the actual theatre buildings, to the individual characters of their managers and their companies, as well as to larger issues such as the economics of the theatre and to details (and occasionally reconstructions) of particular notable performances.

This body of scholarly material—an attention to the biographical, literary, and social reference of Wilde's plays—has been produced at the expense of enormous effort and is often very valuable to the academic community, interested as it has recently been in issues such as canonicity, originality, and the politics both of texts and of the literary institutions that produced them. It is also a useful resource for theatre historians who have of late become increasingly preoccupied with the study of performance practice and the difficulties involved in reconstructing the details of particular performances, especially when they took place before the advent of the technology for modern visual recording. At the same time, however, and as we have already hinted, that knowledge, taken in its entirety, has tended to produce a range of judgments about Wilde's society comedies that do not sit easily with each other. More importantly for our overall argument, they do not seem to have any particular relevance to the experiences of modern audiences or readers of the plays, or the theatrical equivalent of the Amazon.com reader we mentioned in chapter one.

For example, by looking closely at submerged biographical references some critics have turned the plays into subversive, almost revolutionary works that fundamentally challenged the political and social status quo. Some have examined what they perceive to be Wilde's sense of exclusion, either because of his nationality or his sexual orientation. For an Irish writer such as Terence Brown, this sense of exclusion is a consequence of Wilde being an Irishman working in the colonizer's country; for others that sense derives from his status as a gay outsider. Such observations as these lend a political dimension to the plays' satire on English aristocratic manners; they become the revenge of the marginalized subject on his oppressor. By contrast, other critics, attentive to aspects of the plays' social context, have found virtually the opposite politics at work in them. For example, Sheila Stowell and Joel Kaplan's discussion of the use of fashion houses and *haute couture* in the first productions of the plays has shown how the society comedies could be staged in such a manner that they flattered their audiences, making the works (and by implication the author of them) complicit in the very bourgeois and high capitalist values which other commentators have claimed they subvert. Although there is an obvious tension between these two views, they are not necessarily incompatible. It is possible to claim that the texts of the plays are subversive, but that a particular kind of staging could have made that politics invisible. In order to substantiate such an argument we would need to investigate the nature and extent of Wilde's agency in the production process. Unfortunately, however, investigations of this sort have produced only further conundrums.

Discussions of Wilde's relations with the theatre industry of the 1890s have produced a line of argument which holds that his initial intentions were indeed radical but were compromised by the cultural and financial power of the actor-managers with whom he worked. Thus critics like Sos Eltis have interpreted Wilde's revisions to his plays as a movement towards conformity, a concession that was forced upon him and is made visible textually as the critic traces a work's stemma.[2] Here it is worth remembering that the fine details of Wilde's plays were often worked out during the rehearsal process and in consultation with the actor-managers—George Alexander and Herbert Beerbohm Tree—with whom he worked; there are late drafts of his plays in which revisions are marked up by hands other than those of Wilde. Moreover there is plenty of evidence to suggest that figures such as Alexander were on occasions capable of being overbearing and manipulative. In a revealing study Joel Kaplan has shown that following a dispute with Wilde over the ending of *Lady Windermere's Fan*, Alexander enlisted the help of Clement Scott, one of the most eminent theatre critics of the time, to articulate in a first-night review what was in effect his (Alexander's) own dissatisfaction with the play's structure. This course of action immediately persuaded Wilde to agree to revise the ending in the way Alexander had proposed during rehearsal. As a result the revelation of Mrs. Erlynne's identity as the mother of Lady Windermere was moved from Act IV to the end of Act II, a change which (in the eyes of some modern critics) makes her a more conventional figure whose actions (in Acts III and IV) can be understood via the familiar melodramatic trope of the wronged victim, rather than that of the scheming female adventuress.

On the other hand, however, studies of Wilde's financial situation in the early 1890s suggest that he had as much investment, both financial and cultural, in his plays as those managers who were staging them, and that it would not have been in his interest to see their dramatic success undermined in any way. So rather than seeing the plays' first productions in terms of a betrayal of Wilde's political intentions, in this argument they can be understood as the culmination of a long process of textual and dramatic refinement designed to ensure their success. Viewed from this perspective, Wilde's movement towards conformity was a process with which he was actively complicit, and so his relationships with his actor-managers can be seen more in terms of cocreativity than coercion. This line of argument, too, has plenty of evidence to support it; for example, details that highlight the fraught nature of Wilde's relationship with Alexander can be countered with other evidence pointing to their closeness and to the latter's generosity. On several occasions Wilde approached Alexander to ask him to lend him money, and almost certainly offered him the first refusal of *The Importance of Being Earnest* in anticipation that their friendship would result in Alexander giving him the best terms. Wilde's relationship with Tree, who was certainly involved in some of the revisions made in final rehearsals to *A Woman of No Importance*, was also long-standing and seems to have gone well beyond the level of the mere professional courtesy expected of a manager dealing with a writer. More significant, though, is the fact that when, often many years later, Wilde came to publish his plays, in every case he kept faith with the large-scale structural changes allegedly "imposed" upon him (although he did make numerous small verbal and stylistic revisions). Moreover, in the case of the publication of *The Importance of Being Earnest* and *An Ideal Husband* these decisions were made at a time when one might have thought that Wilde would have been most politicized, when (following his imprisonment and exile) he had most reason to be resentful of the British establishment.

The Concept of Context

At this point we might want to ask what is at issue in the tensions between these different ways of understanding the relationships between the plays and their "contexts"—whether we understand this last term to refer to staging, composition, biography, nationality, gender politics, or whatever. Is it simply a local disagreement among Wilde scholars about how to read the society come-dies? As a way of answering this question we can begin by noting that contra-dictions seem to be arising because what is being defined as a context is being used to support what is to all intents and purposes a preexisting reading of the plays or a preexisting concept of Wilde's intentions in writing them. Once we grasp the implications of this situation, the tensions between various critical positions become easier to understand. If a critic has a preconceived view that Wilde's nationality is the dominant aspect of his character, then information which appears to support Wilde's complicity with British commercial inter-ests will be relegated in importance or ignored altogether. In such a view, for example, Alexander will be more likely to be seen as a bully than a cocreator, even though biographies of him do not really confirm such a view. Converse-ly, if one is predisposed to see Wilde as a willing exile from Ireland, eager to acquire for himself the trappings of British aristocratic success (that is, literally as well as metaphorically "sleeping with the enemy"), then his interest in mak-ing money, even at the price of artistic and political compromise, is easier to understand, and the commercial nature of the West End theatre will seem more like an opportunity than a constraint. From these observations we can see that context never speaks neutrally to the critic. Actually, contexts are quite mute—they don't "speak" at all. If one wished to be argumentative one might suggest that the critic is constructing the context he or she needs to find. For this rea-son any appeal to context alone—social, economic, political, biographical, and so forth—cannot reconcile interpretative differences.

Put this way, arguments about the manner in which Wilde's plays are to be interpreted seem to have a ring of familiarity to them. They are reminiscent of a controversy that took place over half a century ago and that informed a debate conducted in the first numbers of the Oxford academic literary period-ical, *Essays in Criticism*, founded under the guidance of F. W. Bateson in order explicitly to counter the unapologetically evaluative Cambridge literary peri-odical, *Scrutiny*, then edited by F. R. Leavis. *Essays in Criticism* carried a series of exchanges between Leavis and Bateson over the role of what was then called the "social context" of literary works. Bateson's proposition was that an "essen-tial requirement" of judgments about a work's literary value—about whether, in his words, we are "able to use it, to live ourselves into it"—was "an understand-ing" of its "original social context," for it was only in relation to that context that "the values implied [in the work] become explicit, and its relative goodness or badness declares itself" (Bateson, 19).

To modern eyes, Bateson's idea of a social context was a fairly restricted one: it meant mainly an economic and then perhaps a political context, when politics was defined in terms of class. It ignored, that is, modern contextual interests to be found in issues of gender, book history, the rise of consumerism, theatre history, and so forth. That narrowness, though, was a consideration that was largely irrelevant to Leavis. He took issue with the whole proposition that context could ever form part of an initial *literary* response: for Leavis, context, however defined, was always a construction, one perceived in, or—more likely—one placed upon, the past by the historian. More importantly, for the modern reader it was a prior judgment about a work's literariness which determined the limits and relevance of the historical information that the reader brought to bear on it. It was not, as Bateson implied, the other way around. By recasting this argument in terms more relevant to understanding Wilde's works, we can see that what is being contested is the nature of the relationship between a knowledge of the historical circumstances (however those circumstances are defined) surrounding a work and the prior attribution of literary identity and literary value to it.

It should be clear from the examples which we have cited that information of the kind being brought to our attention by literary or theatre historians about the context or contexts of Wilde's works is reminiscent of the logical flaw that Leavis detected in Bateson's argument. Too often a description of the conditions under which a work by Wilde was produced is used as a reason to justify why it has been read, why it should continue to be read, why literary value accrues to it, and how one should understand that literary value. Although it can certainly be interesting to locate Wilde's plays within a social history of taste, or within a history of changes in class values, such an ambition will never provide compelling grounds for reading or performing them today.

This distinction is an important one, for it goes to the heart of why much academic research on Wilde strikes the common reader or the average theatregoer as irrelevant. This irrelevance becomes more obvious if we examine the contrast between what we can for convenience call (borrowing a phrase which was first used by Jan Kott apropos of Shakespeare) "Wilde our contemporary" and the historicized (and almost archaic) Wilde of much scholarly research. It is striking how few modern revivals of the plays—certainly in Britain—ever attempt to reconstruct the late-nineteenth-century social world so painstakingly uncovered by academics. For most modern directors that world is too remote for audiences today to understand. For example, Philip Prowse, who directed and designed several successful productions of Wilde's society comedies in the 1980s and early 1990s, has commented on the difficulties some modern actors have in understanding the precise social niceties in the plays, where class dis-

tinctions are to do with much more than just money. Prowse, like other directors, found it necessary to find equivalents of Wilde's themes in modern class
and gender politics, so in his 1991 staging of *A Woman of No Importance* at London's Barbican Theatre he cast a black actress in the role of the American heiress,
Hester; and in his 1986 production of *An Ideal Husband* he took various liber-
ties with the text, cutting some of Lady Chiltern's more melodramatic lines and
allowing Mrs. Cheveley a rather modern "fuck" when she finds herself unable
to remove an incriminating piece of jewellery.

Likewise, Bill Alexander's production of *Lady Windermere's Fan* at the Bir-
mingham Repertory Theatre in the mid-1990s virtually rewrote the character of Dumby. In Wilde's text Dumby is a slightly raffish but witty "masher,"
or man-about-town, a foil to another witty, slightly decadent minor character,
Cecil Graham. Thematically Dumby's function is twofold. It is first to point to
the verbal deceptions and inconsequentialities that oil much of the day-to-day
intercourse of London "polite society." As he knows that society to be economical with the truth, so he tailors his social chitchat to please what he anticipates will be the opinions of his interlocutors. But he has a second important
thematic function: his flirtation with the "woman with a past," Mrs. Erlynne,
arouses jealousy in Lady Plymdale, with whom, we can infer, he has an unex-
plained but presumably illicitly intimate and obviously heterosexual relationship. In Bill Alexander's production, this hint of sexually illicit behaviour and
the threats it poses were maintained, but by some changes that had no textual warrant. Dumby, made up with lipstick and eyeshadow, was now seen to be
a camp figure, ominously leering at the young men at Lady Windermere's ball,
something which of course could never have happened on the London stage
in the 1890s.

Bill Alexander was using a historically decontextualized adaptation of the role
of a minor character in the play in order to remain faithful to the spirit of the
original, and thus to ensure the continued appeal of "Wilde our contemporary."
To give a sense of the sexual danger that Dumby posed Alexander presumably
felt it necessary to ratchet up Dumby's transgression so that it was more appropriate to behaviour that modern audiences might find outrageous. We might
note generally here that the tendency of modern productions to "uncover"
homosexual rather than heterosexual tensions in the plays might have its origins
in an attempt to recapture the sense of shock which revelations about adultery
and children born out of wedlock would have provoked in late-nineteenth-
century theatregoers. Similarly, the production of *An Ideal Husband* at Chich-
ester at around the same time, with Paul Eddington as Lord Goring, exploited
the modern resonances of some of the play's political comments, particularly
the widespread feelings of disenchantment with all British political parties and

political processes felt by many Britons during the last years of Margaret Thatcher's administration and virtually all of John Major's.

If these observations are correct, then we seem to have arrived at something of an *impasse*. If Wilde's society comedies are as adaptable or as open as many modern productions suggest, and if context, too, is an unstable concept, its boundaries shifting to accommodate particular critics' preoccupations, do modern readers or students of Wilde's plays really need to bother themselves with that mountain of scholarly material that academics produce? After all, it will not, as we have said, fix the meanings of the plays; on the contrary, it seems to have produced more dissent than agreement—academics are probably as divided in their views about Wilde's dramatic achievements today as they have ever been. Of course to expect scholars to agree with one another is probably wishful thinking; but equally utopian is the expectation that scholarship alone can determine an interpretation of a literary work. This caveat, however, does not make scholarship redundant or irrelevant. On the contrary, if we investigate the tensions which exist between various forms of scholarly knowledge—in Wilde's case between the biographical, literary, and social references of the plays—we can see how it is that readers are able to arrive at such different interpretations of the same plays and why, too, some interpretations can be considered more correct or plausible than others, when "correctness" and "plausibility" are defined in terms of freedom from contradiction and incoherence. We will begin this investigation by examining how different kinds of scholarship bear upon possible readings of a single scene, the famous opening of *The Importance of Being Earnest*, and then broaden the argument to include some significant dramatic moments in Wilde's other society comedies.

Music, Manners, Food, & Class

The opening lines of *The Importance of Being Earnest* give a textbook illustration of the ways in which the three kinds of reference we have described can operate. The first published (1899) version of the play begins in Algernon Moncrieff's flat in Half Moon Street, which runs between Curzon Street and Piccadilly in London. The Licensing Copy of the play, that version of it which was submitted to the Lord Chamberlain's Office for official approval, places it simply in Piccadilly. Joseph Donohue's reconstruction of the text of the first performance notes that the fashionable areas of Piccadilly and Mayfair—then as now—denoted wealth and leisure, and that Half Moon Street was an entirely appropriate address for a wealthy young man about town in the 1890s. A separate group of critics have observed that other addresses in the play, particularly those to be found in the earlier four-act version, are more pointed in their social reference, a detail which we examine below.

Thereafter the stage directions indicate that Lane, Algernon's manservant, is found arranging afternoon tea. Algernon, who is heard playing music off, enters:

ALGERNON
Did you hear what I was playing, Lane?

LANE
I didn't think it polite to listen, sir.

ALGERNON
I'm sorry for that, for your sake. I don't play accurately—anyone can play accurately—but I play with wonderful expression. As far as the piano is concerned, sentiment is my forte. I keep science for Life.

LANE
Yes, sir.

ALGERNON
And, speaking of the science of Life, have you got the cucumber sandwiches cut for Lady Bracknell?

LANE
Yes, sir.   *Hands them on a salver*

ALGERNON (*Inspects them, takes two, and sits down on the sofa*)
Oh!—by the way, Lane, I see from your book that on Thursday night, when Lord Shoreham and Mr Worthing were dining with me, eight bottles of champagne are entered as having been consumed.

LANE
Yes, sir; eight bottles and a pint.

ALGERNON
Why is it that at a bachelor's establishment the servants invariably drink the champagne? I ask merely for information.

LANE
I attribute it to the superior quality of the wine. I have often observed that in married households the champagne is rarely of a first-rate brand.

ALGERNON
Good heavens! Is marriage so demoralizing as that?

LANE
I believe it is a very pleasant state, sir. I have had very little experience of it myself up to the present. I have only been married once. That was in consequence of a misunderstanding between myself and a young person.

ALGERNON (*Languidly*)
I don't know that I am much interested in your family life, Lane.

LANE

No, sir; it is not a very interesting subject. I never think of it myself.

ALGERNON

Very natural, I am sure. That will do, Lane, thank you.

LANE

Thank you, sir.   *Lane goes out*

ALGERNON

Lane's views on marriage seem somewhat lax. Really, if the lower orders don't set us a good example, what on earth is the use of them? They seem, as a class, to have absolutely no sense of moral responsibility.

(Ross, ed., *The Importance of Being Earnest*, 1–4)

Dramatically these short exchanges serve to introduce a number of the main themes of the piece, but they are also extraordinarily rich in the variety and forms of their reference and allusion. The easiest and most available way of understanding the opening speeches is in terms of the familiar literary trope of the wise servant and the gullible master. This was to become the staple of writers such as P. G. Wodehouse (in the characters of Bertie Wooster and his manservant Jeeves) some years after Wilde's death, but it has a pedigree that goes back to Plautus, via the works of writers as well known as Ben Jonson and Cervantes. Unlike the servants in Wilde's first two society comedies (who are simply mechanisms for stage business and for furthering the action of the plot), Lane, and earlier Phipps (in *An Ideal Husband*), are scrupulously polite and observant of their positions, but they verbally negate that sense of class inferiority by asserting an equality of wit and intelligence. It is clear, then, that our appreciation of this archetypal power relation, and the comedy to be derived from it, can transcend the specifics of any particular social and historical setting. Interestingly many modern comedies continue to employ this same basic dramatic structure. On the other hand, an outline knowledge of the specificities of the plays' social and historical settings does serve to introduce us into the strongly demarcated world of nineteenth-century taste and class, and consequently scholarship into that world of taste can reveal extra layers or nuances of comedy.

The first local reference is to a familiar nineteenth-century debate about musical performance, more particularly about the relationship between technical virtuosity and artistic expressivity, issues which can, for example, be found in late-nineteenth-century reactions to the performances of the great Russian pianist Anton Rubinstein. (Wilde attended one of Rubinstein's concerts in Dublin in 1877, and Rubinstein made a farewell tour of England in 1886–1887.) Musical expressivity in turn had become a topic of general cultural discussion because of the popularity of the piano as an instrument for amateur drawing-room recitals in middle- as well as upper-class homes. In *An Ideal Husband* Mabel

Chiltern complains to Lady Chiltern of being proposed to when trapped in the "music-room" with "an elaborate trio going on": "'I didn't dare to make the smallest repartee,'" she explains. "'If I had, it would have stopped the music at once. Musical people are so absurdly unreasonable. They always want one to be perfectly dumb at the very moment when one is longing to be absolutely deaf'" (Ross, ed., *An Ideal Husband*, 106).

In *The Importance of Being Earnest* the primary function of the exchange about Algernon's piano playing is, as we have noted, to establish the tone of the relationship between master and servant. Lane's refusal to flatter Algernon's ego through an excess of deference, to offer up to him the uncritical approbation that an employer clearly expects from an employee, introduces an anxiety that will continue to motivate the play's interrogation of class relations—that a character's moral or intellectual authority cannot be mapped on to his social and economic status. Lane is a servant with attitude, with a mind of his own, one who needs no lessons (either on wine, or on aesthetics, or on marriage, as it will turn out) from the aristocracy or the upper-middle classes. But why make piano playing the occasion for this exhibition of independent judgment? Presumably because it was an area of expertise in which so many West End theatregoers could claim some degree of competence. (Here it is hard to think of a modern equivalent, certainly in the realm of music, where technology provides much of our primary experience of performance, and where musical taste tends to be defined in terms other than that of class.) The play, then, is exposing the class-

The Signifying Power of Food   Meals and foodstuffs are rarely used neutrally in literary works. From Eve's tasting of the fruit of the Tree of Knowledge in Eden, food has been used as a means of troping other concerns than simple alimentation. Often it is used as a means to denote appetite, and particularly sexual appetites. Indeed Wilde uses precisely this tradition to describe Douglas's excesses—both culinary and carnal—in *De Profundis*. Equally often, however, food and meals are a means of representing class and power relationships. So in Dickens's early fiction meals, usually feasts and presided over by a patriarchal figure, are used to denote familial, and therefore (for Dickens) social, harmony. In later novels mealtimes are also used to signal social pretension. Novelists contemporary with Dickens, such as Elizabeth Gaskell, use food or its absence to intimate class antagonisms. The wealthy and powerful gorge themselves while the poor starve; but the willingness of the poor to share their last crust is indicative of a community spirit absent among the selfish rich. The class values revealed in what particular foods are consumed, and in the manner of their consumption, are also exploited by writers more contemporary with Wilde, such as George Gissing who uses a preference for tinned food to denote lower-class values. Wilde, too, frequently uses cheap or mass-produced foods to indicate an unsubtle palate and therefore an unsophisticated taste.

based assumptions about the intelligence of the "lower orders" while simultaneously satirizing the audience's own pretensions to cultural sophistication. (The
added implication of Lane's silence is that his master is playing so badly that he
cannot possibly make a polite comment about it.)

Then there are references to food, specifically to cucumber sandwiches and
champagne. The most important function of these comestibles as signifiers is
that they denote luxury; and the principal anxiety which Wilde's jokes draw
upon is that both (like musical expertise) were markers of class taste that were
rapidly losing their exclusivity. So some commentators have remarked upon the
popularity of champagne as a wine served at dinner parties in the 1890s, and
have noted the regret felt by contemporary wine connoisseurs that cheap champagne was taking the place of what Wilde calls here "first-rate brands," those
produced by the most famous houses of Epernay, such as Perrier-Jouet (which
he frequently drank in the company of Douglas and which he mentions in *De
Profundis*). Throughout his *oeuvre* Wilde typically associates the appreciation of
fine wines with upper-class (and particularly a refined male) taste; so the hero
of "Lord Arthur Savile's Crime" is immediately put at his ease by "the genial
little German," Herr Winckelkopf, when offered "the most delicious Marco-
brünner" which he sips in a "pale yellow hock glass marked with the Imperial
monogram" (Ross, ed., *Lord Arthur Savile's Crime*, 46).

As Donohue has noted, the class-based nature of champagne drinking was
also an issue in Wilde's cross-examination by Carson in his action for crimi-

---

continued   In *Lady Windermere's Fan*, for example, the Duchess of Berwick disparagingly
refers to the nouveau-riche Mr. Hopper, a suitor for her daughter, by commenting that his
"father made a great fortune by selling some kind of food in circular tins—most palatable, I
believe—I fancy it is the thing servants always refuse to eat" (Ross, ed., *Lady Windermere's
Fan*, 31). Likewise in "Lord Arthur Savile's Crime" the relative sophistication of Herr Winckelkopf in matters of wine is immediately undercut by its absence in matters of food—he offers Lord Arthur a "meat tea" (at a time when, for the British aristocracy, an evening meal
was always a more elaborate repast, taken later, and was called "dinner"). In both cases the
superiority of English tastes over those of foreigners is being stressed.

There is ample evidence that Wilde himself saw lavish entertainment as an opportunity
to exhibit his own fine tastes, and dining at expensive restaurants was a feature of his life in
the 1890s, a habit he attributes to characters most closely identified with himself. So in "The
Critic as Artist" Gilbert talks of discussing "some Chambertin and a few ortolans" (Ross, ed.,
Intentions, 154). In letters written to the *Morning Chronicle* after his release from prison,
Wilde complained of how the prison diet was inedible and degrading for inmates (even
though Home Office doctors had found no evidence of his being malnourished).

nal libel against the Marquess of Queensberry. Wilde was questioned by Carson about his habit of entertaining young men, and particularly Alfred Taylor (who ran a male brothel), and who in turn introduced Wilde to two other young men, Charles Parker and a friend, whom Carson later identified as "a gentleman's valet" and "a groom." All three had dined with Wilde in some luxury at the Savoy Hotel on the Thames Embankment in Victoria. Asked whether their meals included "plenty of champagne," Wilde replied: "they had whatever they wanted," adding "What gentleman would stint his guests?" To this comment Carson retorted: "What gentleman would stint his valet?" Unwilling to let the matter drop, Carson then asked whether Wilde had served "small bottles of iced champagne" to the young men, and asked further: "Was it a favourite drink—iced champagne?" Wilde replied: "Is it a favourite drink—iced champagne?"—"Yes."—"Yes, strongly against my doctor's orders."—"Never mind the doctor's orders."—"I don't. It has all the more flavour if you discard the doctor's orders" (Holland, 168–70).[3] The implication of Carson's questions—which Wilde had attempted to diffuse with a witty retort—was that there could be no social occasion where a servant and a gentleman would drink champagne together; and that therefore the relationship between Wilde and his guests had to be an "improper" one, of a sexual nature, with champagne being offered as some form of payment for sexual favours.

What about the significance of Lane's omission of a pint of the wine from his cellar-book, a detail also implicit in Carson's questioning, which includes a specific reference to "small bottles" of the wine? Until the 1960s pints of champagne were quantities regularly bottled by many champagne houses specifically for the British market. A pint (the British or imperial measure of liquid of 56.5 cl., not the American one of 47.5 cl.) is larger than the standard French half-bottle of wine but smaller than a full bottle (75 cl.); consequently it was the ideal size for a young man to consume on his own before he went out to dinner or to seek other entertainments, such as (in Algernon's later words to Jack) "trotting" "round to the Empire at ten." In other words, the implication is that the pint of champagne was drunk by Lane on his own in his butler's pantry. And it is precisely because such consumption is private—Lane may be drinking with his master's approval, but he is not drinking in his master's company—that Algernon offers no objection to it (he asks about the details of Lane's cellar-book "merely for information"). A familiarity with the etiquette surrounding the consumption of champagne, like that to do with piano recitals, allows us to see that Wilde is blurring class distinctions, although in a manner which, in keeping with the comic tone of the play, is entirely safe. Lane may have knowledge and experience which equals or exceeds that of his master (Lane, too, knows a "superior" wine when he tastes one), but he does not share that knowledge with Algernon, nor does he place it on public display: it does not form the basis of any kind of intimacy. Lane's relation to Algernon is thus quite different from that which

Carson imputed to Taylor's and Parker's friendship with Wilde, where the public consumption of wine together did indeed signal a transgressive or socially unacceptable friendship.

The drinking of champagne is the social reference which has detained most critics, but why, we might ask, the specificity of cucumber as a sandwich filling? Here scholarly commentary is slight (to the point of nonexistence), yet textually and dramatically speaking the term "cucumber" is as strongly foregrounded as champagne is—more so perhaps, as it is picked up later in the scene when the cucumber sandwiches run out. Gardening manuals from the late nineteenth century testify to the premium placed on the cucumber as a salad vegetable, that it was "everywhere valued" and as a result "much spirit [was] shown in its production." This is because rather than being imported into Britain for most of the year (as today), in the 1890s virtually all cucumbers were homegrown, often at considerable expense and with considerable difficulty in heated greenhouses. As a consequence, ensuring "an abundant and continuous supply" for "all seasons" was a complex and expensive undertaking (Sutton and Sons, 50–51);[4] hence the connection in Algernon's mind between cucumbers and what he calls "the science of Life."

Moreover, by the late decades of the century cucumbers (like champagne) were becoming increasingly prized by the middle classes; and again like champagne, the middle classes could generally only afford inferior specimens, or what were then called "summer" cucumbers, the more hardy ridge varieties, which were grown for a limited season, without heat, and which had a less subtle taste. The best cucumbers (known then as "frame cucumbers") required a constant minimum nighttime temperature of 60°F (15°C) and could therefore only be grown professionally or "in the gardens of the wealthy" (Sutton and Sons, 51). And this is why Wilde's text draws attention to the extravagance of purchasing cucumbers and, later, to their rarity. (Lane reports that he has been unable to buy more cucumbers in the market despite going there twice with "ready money.") Understood in this way, the plan to serve his Aunt Augusta with what we may presume are the finest kind of cucumber sandwiches (she asks pointedly for one of those "nice cucumber sandwiches you promised me") functions primarily to signal Algernon's recognition of her social superiority. And Algernon's (and Jack's) preemptive consumption of those sandwiches in turn introduces what will become a central comic theme in the play: the struggle between aristocratic men and dowager duchesses for power and status in the marriage market.

Today such is the influence of Wilde's play that the eating of cucumber sandwiches for afternoon tea as a marker of social refinement has become something of a cliché; and modern theatregoers seeking to understand the pointedness of Wilde's joke are quite likely to read into the references to cucumbers (and particularly the attempted purchase of them for "ready money") some kind of cheap sexual innuendo, one suggested by a knowledge of Wilde's biography. So here it may seem significant that cucumbers turn out to be circulated only between men: they are provided by Lane and consumed by Algernon and Jack (Algernon only ever plans to offer the youthfully attractive Gwendolen plain "bread and butter"). Thus we might be tempted to generalize and conclude that the "real" issue of the play is a contest between men and women over the possession of the male body. Certainly Wilde does use food as a means of troping sexual appetites, both in *The Importance of Being Earnest* and in *An Ideal Husband*. For example, in Act I of *An Ideal Husband* the sexual propriety of the female characters is signalled by their attitudes towards "supper"; so although the risqué Mrs. Marchmont and Lady Basildon admit to each other that they are "dying" for something to eat, when the latter woman is questioned by a man, the Vicomte de Nanjac, she stiffly claims "I never take supper" (Ross, ed., *An Ideal Husband*, 34–35). But for the late-nineteenth-century audience the principal comic potential of cucumbers, as a specific sort of food, almost certainly resided in their implicit class value, the social nuances of which are easily lost on modern audiences, for whom cucumber eating (like wine drinking) has become thoroughly democratized.

Grasping the signifying power of particular foods in the 1890s can thus serve to remind us that the most overt jokes in Wilde's plays were also those which were often the most safe, exploiting as they did generic and largely conventional reversals in the power relations between the classes and the sexes. Although Lane's drinking of champagne and attempted purchase of cucumbers may seem to gesture towards the more dangerous (and private) ground of male–male desire—particularly those elements of it suggested by details of Wilde's biography—they do not have to be explained in this way, and it is unlikely that they were so interpreted by the majority of the play's original audiences.

The Domains of Public & Private Knowledge

We can see here how studying the social or topical references in *The Importance of Being Earnest*—what we might more usefully call the public knowledge which the play draws upon—gives a rather different sense of its politics than one brought about by a concentration on its private or biographical allusions. Public knowledge, that is, tends to anchor the play more firmly in a heterosexual world; this in turn helps us to understand why it was so successful with contemporary audiences. Of course one of the difficulties of reading *The Importance of Being Earnest* today is that it is nearly always the private references which come most readily to mind: modern readers and theatregoers tend to know more about Wilde's biography than they do about, say, the precise social values attached to particular late-nineteenth-century foods and drinks, and they are in this sense alerted in advance to look for a homosocial or homoerotic context. If we recognize the truth of this situation, the appropriate critical question becomes whether such a biographically informed reading actually makes more sense than any other, and whether (as we put it earlier) it can contribute to a coherent interpretation of the work. Another way of posing this question is to ask how the private or biographical allusions that have been found by recent critics can be integrated with the public knowledge which the play more obviously and more conventionally draws upon.

The relationship between certain details of Wilde's life and elements of *The Importance of Being Earnest* was mooted by Lord Alfred Douglas well over half a century ago. In his *Autobiography* Douglas observed that much of the dialogue between Jack and Algernon was based upon what he remembered of his banter with Wilde when the play was being written on the English south coast, so much so that he suggested that it was to all intents and purposes a collaborative venture. It is impossible to corroborate Douglas's claim now (and that claim anyway may have been no more than an attempt to capitalize upon Wilde's fame), but there are a number of details that suggest how aspects of Wilde's personal life might indeed have "leaked" into the work. A little later on in the first act of *The Importance of Being Earnest* we are told that Algernon has taken possession of a cigarette case inadvertently left behind by Jack on an earlier visit. The case bears an inscription from Cecily, whom Jack identifies as his aunt. However the inscription is made to him as "Jack" when, as Algernon points out, his calling card identifies him quite differently, as a certain "Mr *Ernest* Worthing" living in an apartment in "The Albany" off Piccadilly (Ross, ed., *The Importance of Being Earnest*, 14–15). That address, as several critics have noted, was associated with some of the more prominent members of London's homosexual circles. This association is in turn reinforced by the knowledge that in Queensberry's trial Wilde admitted that he had given cigarette cases as presents to young male friends, in particular to Alfred Taylor and Sidney Mavor. The relationship between deception and a double life on the one hand, and gifts of cigarette cases on the other, has thus been interpreted as yet another coded signal to the audience (or to select members of it) that Wilde was in part writing about himself, and that the illicitness of "Bunburying" was because it involved secret male-male relationships, rather than secret heterosexual adulterous ones. How justified are we in reading the cigarette case episode in this way? And is it anything more than an isolated reference?

As Alan Sinfield has pointed out, when he wrote *The Importance of Being Earnest* Wilde could not possibly have known that he was later to face detailed cross-examination in three trials and that cigarette cases would "prove embarrassing" (Sinfield, 35). Moreover the use of personal possessions as plot devices that can reveal secrets in characters' lives was common both in Wilde's other society comedies and in the well-made play generally. (Good examples are to be seen in the use of a fan and the brooch/bracelet in *Lady Windermere's Fan* and

An Ideal Husband respectively, or of a pen in Henry Arthur Jones's *The Case of Rebellious Susan*.) Like those references to cucumbers and champagne, then, the most readily available (or public) meaning of cigarette cases was a wholly uncontroversial one. We should also notice how swiftly *The Importance of Being Earnest* moves us on from the exclusively male environment with which it opens, and which has prompted the search for those homosexual and homosocial allusions, to the altogether more conventional ground of heterosexual courtship rituals (the entrances of Lady Bracknell and Gwendolen, and the subsequent establishing of those themes, occur less than three hundred lines into the play). As the dramatic action unfolds the comic tensions arise not from the juxtaposition of what might be taken as an authentic male-male world with a trivial male-female one, but from the mirroring of upper-class male-female desire in the passions of individuals from the lower orders. Like Lane, Miss Prism and the Revd. Canon Chasuble—Laetitia and Frederick—also turn out to have been leading a kind of double life, propriety having dictated that their courtship rituals were conducted "metaphorically" through the coded language of bees and horticulture. The secret—or otherness—which the plotting of the play works most consistently and coherently to expose is thus not about sexual identity or sexual preferences, but about class differences. The ending, then, echoes the themes of class and power established in the opening scene. And here again we are on familiar comedic territory, reminded by the socially inclusive ending that (as in Shakespearean comedies) the young and the old, the rich and the poor, men and women, are all subject to the selfsame human desires, and to the vanities and hypocrisies which accompany them.

Bunburying Like cucumber sandwiches, Wilde's term "Bunburying" as a euphemism for living a double life has passed beyond his play into the English language generally. Unsurprisingly many critics have been intrigued by the possible origin of the word. Some have pointed to the punning association of "bun" and "bum," one which does not work so well in modern U.S. usage. Another has claimed that "Bunburying" was British slang for a male brothel; yet another that it was a term for a homosexual pickup. These explanations rest on the assumption that "bun" is slang for buttock (although attempts to find such usage in late-nineteenth-century dictionaries of slang have proved unsuccessful). Other critics have noted that Wilde had a friend from Trinity College, Dublin called Henry S. Bunbury. Yet others still have observed that Bunbury was the name of a character in an unpublished play, the name of a village in Cheshire, and an entry in the army lists of 1894. A more recent commentator has noted that the name could have been found in the obituary columns of the two main daily papers of the time, the *Times* and the *Morning Post*. Bunburying, then, could have had a range of meanings for nineteenth-century readers and audiences, from the overtly sexual to the innocently geographical.

If we are disposed to see the opening exchanges in the play as alluding to a homosocial world, one where "family life" (as Algernon and Lane agree) is "not a very interesting subject," then, as we have noted, the critical question we need to consider is how such private or coded references interact with the more obvious public jokes about class and age. We should remember that in Wilde's and Queensberry's trials, the social distinction between Wilde and the young male companions he entertained at the Savoy was consistently invoked as evidence that the friendships were "unnatural," and that the intimacy which Wilde claimed to exist between them could only have been purchased. The unequal class basis of those relationships was further emphasized in the attention Carson gave to the attempt by two of the young men concerned to blackmail Wilde (the 1885 Labouchere Amendment, under which Wilde was tried for gross indecency, had come to be popularly known as the "blackmailer's charter"). The effect of Carson's questioning, then, was to present Wilde's sexuality in exploitative terms, as one dependent on (rather than, as Wilde wished to present it, as transcending) his class and financial power over his young male "friends." If we wish to pursue those hints in the opening few hundred lines of *The Importance of Being Earnest* and understand the whole of the play biographically—as about male-male desire—then we need to acknowledge that it in no way broaches any of the issues exposed by Carson's cross-examination, and which were manifestly part of Wilde's and Douglas's own sexual life from their first meeting onwards. As we observed in chapter two, in *De Profundis* Wilde repeatedly drew attention to the need to extricate Douglas from threatened scandals and potential blackmailing by "renters" or male prostitutes.

At first sight the easy banter and camaraderie in the opening exchanges between Lane and Algernon look more like an escape from these realities; that is, they seem to gesture towards an idealized homosocial world, one where male servants willingly collude with their male masters in order to resist the prejudices of a coercive heterosexual society, and where loyalty comes about through mutual self-interest. The difficulty here is that there is little comic or dramatic potential in such idealized relationships, and thus, theatrically (as well as socially), the world of male-male desire, so conceived, can only ever exist offstage as an unexamined other against which we view the power struggles of a flawed heterosexual world. One reason why Lane disappears so quickly from the action of the play (he only figures in the opening exchanges) may be because there is no space for his character to be developed except, perhaps, in terms of the theme of betrayal; but such a theme would have turned *The Importance of Being Earnest* into a very different play—a much more personal one, perhaps, but certainly not a comedy.

It is also worth remembering that where "real life" is allowed to intrude into the action, in the scene deleted by George Alexander that has come to be known as the "Gribsby episode," it is in terms of the nonpayment of debts, a gentle-manly and thus entirely class-bound misdemeanour that can be understood in thoroughly conventional terms. The penniless but well-born and well-man-nered gentleman is, after all, a staple theme of eighteenth- and nineteenth-cen-tury fiction; moreover, a detachment from the vulgar world of ready money is a definition of aristocratic and dandaical privilege to which we have already been introduced very early in the play.

None of this is to deny, however, that such an incident does once again have many resonances with some details of Wilde's own life for, as he later testified, he was technically bankrupt when he wrote *The Importance of Being Earnest*. Moreover, this situation had come about in part because (as he later bitterly complained in *De Profundis*) he had spent so much of his income on funding his and Douglas's secret life, specifically on the latter's extravagant hotel and restau-rant bills. If we pursue this biographical allusion, the most obvious way to read Gribsby's claim that he has "arrested in the course of his duties nearly all the younger sons of the aristocracy" is in terms of a personal jibe against Douglas's "reckless extravagance" (to borrow Jack's phrase). Rather than Wilde rehears-ing anxieties about the possible consequences of his own lack of restraint—as

---

The Three Versions of *The Importance of Being Earnest*   Modern readers of *The Impor-tance of Being Earnest* can choose three different versions of it. First, there is the three-act "reading version" that Wilde published in 1899 with Leonard Smithers and that is repro-duced in most modern editions. Then there are some modern editions—notably the Collins *Complete Works*—that print an earlier, four-act version of the play that has undergone some reconstruction from surviving manuscript and typescript drafts. To be precise, these consist of a series of exercise books containing what look to be the earliest drafts of the play set out in a four-act version; some slightly later typescripts of Acts I, III, and IV with Wilde's notes and alterations and that are variously dated September and November 1894; and a full type-script of a four-act version of the play that is dated 31 October 1894 (a transcription of which was first published in 1956). Third and finally, Joseph Donohue (with the help of Ruth Berg-gren) has attempted to reconstruct the text of the first performance of the play—that is, the three-act play that George Alexander staged at the St. James Theatre in 1895 and that dif-fered in several respects from the three-act play that Wilde published in 1899 (the licensing copy of *The Importance of Being Earnest* in the Lord Chamberlain's Collection in the Brit-ish Library is also in three acts).

Each of these three texts of *The Importance of Being Earnest* has a different kind of au-thority and thus possesses a different claim on our attention: none, however, can be said to be entirely the product of Wilde's own hand. When he worked on the 1899 edition, Wilde was living in hotel rooms in a self-imposed exile and did not have any of his papers—in-cluding earlier drafts of *The Importance of Being Earnest*—to hand (most had been sold or stolen from his Tite Street home).

some critics have assumed—the scene looks much more like the articulation of a simmering resentment against his lover's financial carelessness, a frustration that despite the wealth and privilege into which Douglas had been born (he was, significantly, the youngest of four sons), it was always Wilde who was responsible for picking up the tab, for funding the appetites of a "young man who eats so much, and so often."

Such personally motivated anger makes little sense in terms of the comic logic of the play, for bitterness and resentment towards aristocratic profligacy tends to place Wilde on the side of the law and of the play's *raisonneurs*, those puritans (like the Revd. Chasuble), or the newly censorious Jack, who would call to heel "the disgraceful luxury of the age." In other words, if details of Wilde's and Douglas's life had indeed "leaked" into *The Importance of Being Earnest*, then it may have happened more by accident than design, for the implications of the biographical allusions in the Gribsby episode seem to run counter to those we have identified in the opening scene and which point to champagne drinking as coding idealized and mutually satisfying male–male relationships, where the amount and cost of alcohol consumed does not belong to Wilde's actual world, but is a matter for "information only." If we do wish to read Algernon and Jack as "versions" of Douglas and Wilde (as Douglas suggested) then we need to acknowledge that the exploration of male–male desire which the play gives us is hardly a consistent one, nor does it have much to do with the social or polit-

---

continued   He thus based his text on a typescript sent to him by Smithers which had formerly belonged to George Alexander and which incorporated Alexander's own suggestions and changes to the play, including of course Alexander's decision to cut it from four to three acts. Although Wilde revised this typescript—he added words and phrases, struck out some stage directions, and marked passages for omission—there is little evidence of any attempt to revert to his original intentions. Moreover, it is difficult to know whether such a decision was pragmatic (that Wilde was no longer able to reconstruct the longer version from memory), or creative (that he now saw that Alexander's version was superior as a piece of theatre). The four-act version of the play may seem the most authentic, in that it was in this form that he originally submitted the work to Alexander. On the other hand, though, we do not have Wilde's final four-act play: the most complete typescript, that dated 31 October 1894, unfortunately does not carry the latest revisions. So all modern "four-act" versions are editorial reconstructions which combine early and late drafts, and thus incorporate judgments other than those of Wilde. Donohue's performance text is probably the furthest from Wilde, for we know that Wilde had little involvement in the rehearsal process when many changes to the text would have been made (he was in Algiers with Douglas at the time). But it is the best social text we have—the best record of what contemporary audiences actually witnessed and heard.

ical realities of homosexual life at that time. Those allusions make most sense as expressions of the tensions underlying Wilde's and Douglas's own particular situation, as Wilde's simultaneous obsession with and resentment of Douglas's youthful beauty; yet it is also that very particularity and privacy which guarantee their invisibility to (and irrelevance for) the vast majority of theatre audiences.

Are the Society Comedies Homoerotic or Homophobic?

The logic of our argument so far is that it is not that one cannot find plausible allusions to gay lifestyles in *The Importance of Being Earnest*, but those which scholars have detected are not consistent, nor developed in the course of the play; nor do they seem capable of sustained development, even in the service of the most radical rereadings. So if a director were to stage the opening of *The Importance of Being Earnest* by emphasizing a sexual intimacy between Algernon and Jack (one moreover witnessed by Lane), it is difficult to see how this revelation could be meaningfully sustained for the entire play, nor the relevance it would have to the sorts of secrets exposed in the work's denouement, whether of the three- or four-act versions of the play. The same can be said of some of Wilde's other society comedies. As we will show, both *An Ideal Husband* and *A Woman of No Importance* also seem to have distinct homoerotic elements to them. Moreover, and unlike the comic world of *The Importance of Being Earnest*, they use the devices of melodrama to hint at a complex power relation underlying male-male desire. At the same time, though, in neither work can a homosexual thematic provide a coherent reading of the entire play, nor (and this is more surprising) does the recognition of it make either play any less conventional in its politics. Once more we will find that the apparently biographical elements of the work (what we have called its "private knowledge") and its social or topical references (its "public knowledge") seem to be pushing us in contradictory directions; but being alert to those tensions does allow us to see both the strengths and weaknesses of the plays' structures.

Shortly after the opening of Act II of *An Ideal Husband* Sir Robert Chiltern relates to his friend Lord Goring the power exerted over him by Baron Arnheim and the reasons he was seduced into betraying state secrets for money:

> SIR ROBERT CHILTERN *(Throws himself into a chair by the writing-table.)*
> One night after dinner at Lord Radley's the Baron began talking about success in modern life as something that one could reduce to an absolutely definite science. With that wonderfully fascinating quiet voice of his he expounded to us the most terrible of all philosophies, the philosophy of power, preached to us the most marvellous of all gospels, the gospel of gold. I think he saw the effect he had produced on me, for some days afterwards he wrote and asked me to come and see him. He was living then in Park Lane, in the house Lord Woolcomb has now. I remember so well how, with a strange smile on his pale, curved lips, he led me through his wonderful picture gallery, showed me his tapestries, his enamels, his jewels, his carved ivories, made me wonder at the strange loveliness of the luxury in which he lived; and then told me that luxury

was nothing but a background, a painted scene in a play, and that power, power over other men, power over the world, was the one thing worth having, the one supreme pleasure worth knowing, the one joy one never tired of, and that in our century only the rich possessed it.

LORD GORING *(With great deliberation.)*
A thoroughly shallow creed.

(Ross, ed., *An Ideal Husband*, 80–81)

In his introduction to his revised edition of *An Ideal Husband*, Russell Jackson points out how this passage can be construed as containing layers of reference that gesture towards a world well beyond the drawing rooms and ballrooms in which nearly all of the action of the society comedies is contained. It is, for Jackson, redolent of a "secret life more profound than Chiltern's wife ever suspects or discovers, a seduction with deeper implications than an offer of the means to worldly success" (Jackson, ed., *An Ideal Husband*, xxix). That "secret life" is an exclusively male one and is characterized by extreme wealth, by power, and by exquisitely sophisticated tastes. In this sense it is reminiscent of the male-male world so consistently evoked in *The Picture of Dorian Gray* and in some of the dialogues in *Intentions* (although, typically for Wilde, it is simultaneously satirized by the use of ridiculous and completely improbable aristocratic names—so Arnheim was "living in the house of Lord Woolcomb").

Moreover the language of Chiltern's speech, with its emphasis on objects such as the "wonderful picture gallery," "his tapestries, his enamels, his jewels, his carved ivories," is evocative of the aesthete's tastes and reminds us of Wilde's own fascination with *A Rebours* and French Decadence. But like Wainewright's artistic connoisseurship in "Pen, Pencil, and Poison," or that of Lord Henry Wotton in *The Picture of Dorian Gray*, it carries with it overtones of danger, of what Wilde in *De Profundis* called the fruit of the trees in the "other half of the garden." Thus Chiltern's vocabulary also reminds us of some of Wilde's correspondence to his male friends in which he describes the pleasures of this life of refinement—in collocations such as "strange loveliness," "wonderfully fascinating," "most terrible," and particularly in "pale curved lips," a phrase which Wilde frequently used to describe the physical beauty of Alfred Douglas. Jackson goes on to point out that it is possible to see the revisions that Wilde made to the play for its book publication in 1899—"the removal of circumstantial details of Mrs. Cheveley's involvement with Arnheim"—as being "intended to make the Baron a more mysterious, less clearly heterosexual figure" (Jackson, ed., *An Ideal Husband*, xxix). It is only a short step from here, then, to infer that the power that Arnheim has, that "power over other men," is one associated with homoeroticism.

However the later exchange with Goring, the dandy figure in the play, serves as a critique of such a lifestyle. Goring peremptorily dismisses it as a "thoroughly shallow creed." Thereafter Chiltern explains his relationship with Arnheim as a purely financial one, and so his actions, while morally reprehensible, are made safe, at least in sexual terms. This changed atmosphere is emphasized by Goring's joke about Chiltern's attempt at atonement:

SIR ROBERT CHILTERN
I don't say that I suffered any remorse. I didn't. Not remorse in the ordinary, rather silly sense of the word. But I have paid conscience money many times. I had a wild hope that I might disarm destiny. The sum Baron Arnheim gave me I have distributed twice over in public charities since then.

LORD GORING (Looking up.)
In public charities? Dear me! what a lot of harm you must have done, Robert!

(Ross, ed., *An Ideal Husband*, 84–85)

This sense that the play is moving quickly back to the familiar and unthreatening ground of a comedy of manners is reflected in the stage directions for Goring. While Chiltern makes his confession, Goring speaks "*with great deliberation*" and keeps "*his eyes steadily fixed on the carpet*." But when he makes his joke about charity he is "*looking up*," and is soon confident enough to be "*leaning back with his hands in his pockets*," and eventually, like all of Wilde's dandies, "*arranging his necktie*" and "*settling his buttonhole*." Once more, Russell Jackson makes clear the stereotyped character which Wilde is invoking: "Wilde makes Goring the play's *raisonneur*, the familiar stage figure of the experienced man of the world who provides the wisdom of the world and helps to resolve the difficulties of the principal couple. Such parts occur in many plays of the time, and especially fine examples were written for Charles Wyndham by Henry Arthur Jones" (Jackson, ed., *An Ideal Husband*, xxxi). The *raisonneur* knows well the realities of the life to which Chiltern has alluded; consequently he acts to dismiss the threat of that life, and as the scene progresses he is able to revert back to the languid, nonchalant dandy, whose social *raison d'être* is of course to take nothing seriously.

We should remember that in the 1899 edition of the play the stage directions are Wilde's and are thus free from interventions from players, theatre manager, or the demands of the office of the Lord Chamberlain. They were made for a reading text, two years after his release from prison, and four years after the play's first production. If Wilde is on the one hand hinting that Arnheim is a more dangerous and sexually ambivalent figure, he is simultaneously limiting what we can do with those hints. This raising but immediate closing down of dangerous topics might look like a loss of nerve but, exiled in France and far removed from British prudishness as he was in 1899, it is hard to see why such a course of action would have appealed to Wilde. It is much more plausible that

Wilde's directions were included for their overall dramatic effect to reassure us that his play is after all a comedy of manners.

As Jackson also suggests, it is possible, even tempting, to understand Chiltern's secrets in sexual terms and thus to connect the play's theme of public exposure to the anxieties that were then animating Wilde's own life. However, the deliberate curtailing of this line of interpretation, which we have just described, in the reactions Wilde gives to Goring (who is finally to marry Chiltern's sister, Mabel) suggests that if he was aware of such a subtext, Wilde did not want it to dominate the action. Indeed the play concludes with the conventional melodramatic language of heterosexual love and self-sacrifice, a language far removed from the world of *The Picture of Dorian Gray*, where such values exist only in Sibyl Vane's life of theatrical make-believe. As with *The Importance of Being Earnest*, a distinction needs to be drawn between discovering dramatic elements that we can understand as occasional or isolated references to a homosexual subculture and seeing in them the dramatic motor of the play. For if we do try to understand Chiltern's past as that of the compromised homosexual then the dynamic behind the relationships of the other characters becomes dramatically and structurally incomprehensible. In particular it becomes difficult to understand Chiltern's relationship with Lady Chiltern and the ways in which the tensions between the two are used to explore the nature of love—more specifically, the difference between a love based on realism (that is, on a knowledge of and ability to forgive the loved one's imperfections and mistakes), and a love centred on idealism, on placing the loved object on a pedestal (a theme that had also been explored in *Lady Windermere's Fan*).

Act II of the play closes with Chiltern's eloquent plea to his wife that the truest test of love is that it endures despite "weaknesses ... follies ... [and] imperfections." As Chiltern puts it—in quasi-Christian terms that in turn anticipate the language of the later parts of *De Profundis*: "It is not the perfect, but the imperfect, who have need of love. It is when we are wounded by our own hands, or by the hands of others, that love should come to cure us—else what use is love at all? All sins, except a sin against itself, Love should forgive. All lives, save loveless lives, true Love should pardon" (Ross, ed., *An Ideal Husband*, 132). Of course it is very tempting to read these lines biographically and to substitute Wilde and his wife Constance for Sir Robert and Lady Chiltern. As Neil McKenna has argued:

> There are many parallels between [their] situations.... Like Oscar, Sir Robert had committed a terrible sin and hides a terrible secret from his wife and the world. That Oscar's sins are plural and sexual, as opposed to Sir Robert's single, financial sin, makes little difference. Sir Robert speaks of his single sin as if it were, in fact, plural and sexual. He describes his sin as "my secret and my shame," evoking the Uranian meaning of shame as love and sex between men. (McKenna, 244)

If we are disposed to see Chiltern's past as involving a homosexual scandal, we must also give full attention (as McKenna fails to do) to the way in which the play develops and so treats such a misdemeanour. And this requires us to read Chiltern's speech in Act II in its entirety and to recognize that his aim is not only to ask for his wife's understanding of and forgiveness for a compromising relationship with another man, but also to regain her love for the future. As he confesses to Goring in Act III: "I love her more than anything else in the world.... Love is the great thing in the world. There is nothing but love, and I love her" (Ross, ed., *An Ideal Husband*, 161). We might now find these lines overly melodramatic or even overly sentimental, but structurally they stand as Chiltern's attempt to find a form of closure for his earlier wrongdoing—to present it as an isolated aberration, now firmly in his past, one never to be repeated. In other words, even if we see Chiltern's friendship with Arnheim as possessing a sexual element, then we also have to acknowledge what a very Victorian—indeed conservatively Victorian—conclusion the end of Act II represents dramatically.

In this reading homosexuality would have to be seen as an aberration of youth, a younger man led astray by an older (exactly what Edward Carson accused Wilde of doing to Douglas); the mature, and fundamentally heterosexual man bitterly repents of his earlier "weakness" or "folly," a sentiment which is reiterated several times in the remainder of the play. Of course one might wish to attribute that view of homosexuality to Chiltern's hypocrisy—to see his speech as mere cant, an attempt to cover his back, as it were, and to preserve his marriage in order to maintain his grasp on political power. The difficulty with this interpretation, though, is that Chiltern's view of his past is explicitly endorsed by Goring. As Goring later explains to Mrs. Cheveley, "It was an act of folly done in his youth, dishonourable, I admit, shameful, I admit, unworthy of him, I admit, and therefore ... *not his true character*" (Ross, ed., *An Ideal Husband*, 177; Wilde's ellipsis, our emphasis); and then, later still, to Lady Chiltern: "Why should you scourge him with rods for a sin done in his youth, before he knew you, *before he knew himself?*" (Ross, ed., *An Ideal Husband*, 228; our emphasis). It is interesting to note that it was in precisely these terms that the older Alfred Douglas accounted for the homosexual promiscuity of his own youth. It was not unusual, he claimed, for boys in public schools, or young men in universities, to be "led astray" in such a way. Of course we do not have to see the play in biographical terms, but if we do feel tempted to pursue the personal allusions, then we should acknowledge that they appear to make the play more, not less, conservative, for they present homosexuality in a conventional and ultimately unthreatening way. Such an account of course bears no relation to the realities of Wilde's own sexual life.

The themes of financial and moral corruption in *A Woman of No Importance* can also lend themselves to that kind of homoerotic reading that has been found in parts of *An Ideal Husband*. On its surface *A Woman of No Importance* concerns the rivalry between Lord Illingworth and Mrs. Arbuthnot for the attention and the care of their illegitimate son, Gerald Arbuthnot. Here, as we hinted earlier, the relationship between Illingworth and Gerald is, on the surface, not easy to understand. It is one where the older man seems to treat the younger as a kind of possession: despite his illegitimacy he will gain his inheritance, but only under certain conditions, ultimately that of spending (like the Persephone of Greek mythology) half of his life with Illingworth. The comparison with Persephone is not as far-fetched as it first sounds, because Illingworth's offer has sinister overtones to it, and his relationship with Gerald has often been seen as one which makes most sense when understood in sexual rather than parental terms (even though we are told explicitly that Illingworth and Gerald *are* father and son). This interpretation was expressed most provocatively by the iconoclastic modernist Lytton Strachey, who in a letter informed Duncan Grant of his reactions to Herbert Beerbohm Tree's 1907 revival of the play:

> "It was rather amusing," he told Duncan Grant (2 June 1907), "as it was a complete mass of epigrams, with occasional whiffs of grotesque melodrama and drivelling sentiment. The queerest mixture! Mr Tree [who played Lord Illingworth] is a wicked Lord, staying in a country house, who has made up his mind to bugger one of the other guests—a handsome young man of twenty. The handsome young man is delighted; when his mother enters, sees his Lordship and recognizes him as having copulated with her twenty years before, the result of which was—the handsome young man. She appeals to Lord Tree not to bugger his own son. He replies that that's an additional reason for doing it (oh! he's a *very* wicked Lord!). She then appeals to the handsome young man, who says, 'Dear me! What an abominable thing to do—to go and copulate without marrying! Oh no, I shall certainly pay no attention to anyone capable of doing *that*, and—' when suddenly enter (from the garden) a young American millionairess, shrieking for help, and in considerable disorder. The wicked Lord Tree, not content with buggering his own son, has attempted to rape the millionairess, with whom (very properly) the young handsome man is in love. Enter his Lordship. Handsome Y. M.: 'You devil! You have insulted the purest creature on God's earth! I shall kill you!' But of course he doesn't, but contents himself with marrying the millionairess, while his mother takes up a pair of gloves and slashes the Lord across the face. It seems an odd plot, doesn't it? But it required all my penetration to find out that this *was* the plot, as you may imagine…. The audience was of course charmed."[5]

As Alan Sinfield helpfully reminds us, had the plot of *A Woman of No Importance* "been read generally in this way, it could not have been performed on the West End stage in 1907 or initially in 1893" (Sinfield, 34). The fact that Strachey might have been alone, or in a tiny minority, in his deliberately provocative understanding of the play does not, however, necessarily invalidate it. As we have argued, the relative visibility of biographical allusions (which will obviously change with the passage of time and the differing degrees of knowledge held by the plays' audiences) is important, though it remains a literary-historical issue. By contrast the principal literary-critical question is how those allusions affect our interpretation and evaluation of the play. As we put matters earlier, how do the private and public domains fit together, and how do they allow us to glimpse the play's politics? In order to examine this topic, it will be useful to revisit briefly those details of Wilde's personal life which most forcefully underwrite a biographical reading like Strachey's.

In January and February 1893, while the play was in preparation and about to be put into rehearsal, Wilde was staying at Babbacombe Cliff, near Torquay in Devon, in the house of Lady Mount-Temple, a distant relative of Constance, his wife. The trip began as a family holiday, but in due course Constance left with the children (a circumstance which might have some bearing on the series of jokes in the play made at the expense of Mr. Kettle, whose wife and children are also apart from him during the action of the first two acts). In the absence of his family, Wilde set up what he called a mock "academy," writing in a letter of "Babbacombe School," with himself as headmaster, with Lord Alfred Douglas, who represented the "Boys," and with Campbell Dodgson, Douglas's private classics tutor at Oxford, acting as "second master." The mock rules Wilde invented included "tea for headmaster and second master, brandy and soda (not to exceed seven) for boys" (*Complete Letters*, 555–56). Here life—at least Wilde's life—seems to have been perilously close to art. Further details about that life came to light a couple of years later during Queensberry's trial. The relationship between Wilde and Walter Grainger, Douglas's Oxford servant, who was employed by Wilde as a member of the household staff at Babbacombe Cliff (and then again as an under-butler when he rented a cottage for himself and Douglas in the summer of 1893 in Goring), became the subject of a heated exchange, in which Carson attempted to demonstrate that Wilde's interest in Grainger was chiefly sexual.

If Wilde's admission in *De Profundis* that he found completing *A Woman of No Importance* difficult is to be believed, it was because of the demands made upon his time by Alfred Douglas and Douglas's constant need to be entertained. So if we wish to construe Wilde's writing as autobiographical, then it is tempting to see how once again he might have used *A Woman of No Importance* to articulate some of the tensions between his public (and familial) and private (and gay) selves which he was experiencing at this time. In such an interpretation the overt and explicitly heterosexual concerns of the play (aristocrats and their mistresses, Victorian sexual double standards, the concern with legitimacy and inheritance, and what male writers in the 1890s labelled the Woman Question) are read so that they code homosexual desire, where the older man must compete with both older and younger women for the affection and loyalty of young men, a theme also to be found in the extant scenario of *The Cardinal of Avignon*, a project about which Wilde was thinking at around the same time as he was writing *A Woman of No Importance*, and which we discuss in more detail below.

In contrast to the rather forced interpretation of one speech in *An Ideal Husband*, a biographical reading of *A Woman of No Importance* can be developed with some consistency and plausibility and may appear to resolve what otherwise might seem structural or thematic weaknesses in the play, particularly (as Strachey noticed) the imbalance of its main dramatic tension, ostensibly a conflict between a selfless maternal and a selfish paternal love. These imbalances are quite far reaching: so, for example, in the course of the play we and the characters learn with Illingworth that he is Gerald's father but we never really find out the reasons why he wishes so strongly to "own" his son by having his exclusive company for six months of the year. Moreover, we never see Gerald in a situation that explains any of the qualities that make him such a good prospect for Illingworth both as secretary and as a companion—which particular qualities, that is, that would make him "of considerable use" (Ross, ed., *A Woman of No Importance*, 17), apart from his boyishness and looks.

Another imbalance is the length of the scenes given to the play's dowagers, such as Lady Hunstanton, Lady Stutfield, and Mrs. Allonby, who contribute nothing to the play's action, but who in Act II discuss quite openly the attractions of the male body. This scene is there, of course, principally for comic effect, but collectively the openness of the dowagers contrasts with the milk-and-water, and sexually unthreatening, younger woman—Hester. She is a rich but tedious American heiress, much more of a one-dimensional character than the witty Mabel Chiltern. Why she comes to Britain, why she is so attractive to Gerald (and why he is so attractive to her) are, once again, questions which the play studiedly ignores. Moreover the young heterosexual lovers, Gerald and Hester, are the most stereotyped and for that reason dramatically the least interesting characters in the whole play. Then there is the slightly ambivalent presentation of Mrs. Arbuthnot. As the seduced and deserted single mother she ought to invite at least some of our sympathy, even if we take account of the fact that Victorian attitudes to premarital sex and illegitimacy were quite different from modern ones. In contrast, as the play progresses she is given long, over-melodramatic, and self-pitying speeches, and sometimes seems to be on the side of the priggish, coldhearted puritanism that Wilde consistently mocks in all his work, and here specifically in the character of Hester.

A reading of the play that stresses its gay subtexts may seem to make sense of these imbalances in that it gives reasons for the shortcomings in the representation of heterosexual love—in Sir John and Lady Pontefract, in Mrs. Arbuthnot and Illingworth, in Kelvil and his offstage wife, as well as in Hester and Gerald. At the same time, however, it makes the discussion of love in the play much more cynical and certainly less comic and romantic. What is professed to be love invariably turns out to be simple desire or possessiveness, and therefore the play's ostensible theme of love as selflessness, articulated by Mrs. Arbuthnot, becomes marginal. If we pursue Strachey's homoerotic reading, this "darkening" of the play's themes manifests itself again in the way we now have to understand the role of Gerald, that obscure object of Illingworth's desire, who is at the same time his own son. A biographical reading adds to gay desire the altogether more difficult (and far less comic) topic of incest. So some imbalances are resolved, but at the cost of producing new ones. The problem—as Strachey hints—now becomes that of reconciling incestuous desires (if that is what they are) with Illingworth's witty nonchalance: like Lord Henry Wotton in *The Picture of Dorian Gray*, he is an attractive villain and is given the best comic lines in the play. Even in *The Picture of Dorian Gray*, it is hard to see the dandy as such a straightforwardly sinister figure as incestuous desire threatens to make Illingworth here: his ability to make outrageous comments about hypocrisy and double standards derives from, and is reinforced by, his relative remoteness from the world of real emotions and from real desires which can disturb or damage. The dandy's ability to embarrass others is a direct function of his imperturbability.

We ought to remind ourselves that the plays, taken as a sequence, develop the role of the dandy with considerable sophistication. In *Lady Windermere's Fan*, Darlington is either an amoral but purely verbal cynic or a compromised would-be adulterer: he is never both. The play keeps these different aspects of Darlington quite separate; moreover Wilde showed little interest in developing the dandy's role as an adulterer. It was a difficult subject to broach in the drama of the late nineteenth century, and it only figures as a topic of gossip in the other plays. In *A Woman of No Importance* the dandy is given a more prominent role than in *Lady Windermere's Fan*, for unlike Darlington, Illingworth is very much at the centre of the power structures and social world that the play alludes to. However, as we noted, a cynical detachment remains central to his characterization and is the source of most of the comedy: the audience can appreciate Illingworth's wit while simultaneously deprecating his immorality. Such a delicate dramatic balance would be overturned by the theme of incest. Illingworth would soon reveal himself as a monster, and the society of which he is the centre would by extension become monstrous too. Pursuing the homoerotic subtexts in *A Woman of No Importance* may give it a particular kind of darkness, one in tune with modern sensibilities, but it exacts a huge price in doing so because it makes it incomprehensible as a comedy of manners. It also has the unfortunate consequence of presenting male-male desire as something so unnatural that incest is no longer a taboo; and in this way (as with *An Ideal Husband*) it can be seen as reinforcing contemporary conservative prejudices about the pathology of homosexuality.

The logic of our discussion of the society comedies is that it is difficult to develop the occasional hints about homoerotic or homosocial lives in a way which makes sense of the plays' overall themes or of what we know of Wilde's attitudes to his own sexuality. Moreover—and surprisingly—it is perfectly possible to pursue the biographical allusions in *An Ideal Husband* and *A Woman of No Importance* to produce a homophobic interpretation of those plays, one in which homosexuality is depicted either as a one-off lapse excusable in a basically heterosexual young man or as monstrous behaviour in his more mature homosexual counterpart. These views are hardly compatible with anything we know of Wilde's intentions or of the plays' first reception. We should not, however, take all this to imply that Wilde had no interest in exploring in his dramas the complexities of male-male relations. In fact that theme does figure much more centrally in some of his lesser-known works, in particular in *Salome*, *A Florentine Tragedy*, *La Sainte Courtisane*, and the scenario of *The Cardinal of Avignon*. Significantly, the settings of this group of plays—they are all placed in distant Renaissance or biblical times—are far removed from the social topicality of the society comedies, from that domain of "public" knowledge which, we have argued, seems to conflict with the occasional glimpses into the "private" world which was the arena for Wilde's own sexual life. It is as if this very remoteness from late-nineteenth-century social mores gave Wilde the freedom to explore the concerns closest to his own life. In other words, it is paradoxically those plays that seem to be the least about the world in which Wilde lived which may repay best a biographically motivated reading.

The Private World of the Unfinished & Unperformed Plays

Complaining, as usual, about the demands that Douglas made on his time, Wilde wrote in *De Profundis* of an exceptionally productive period in his life that followed his lover's departure to Egypt. He described how he had "collected again the torn and ravelled web of my imagination, got my life back into my own hands, and not merely finished the three remaining acts of *An Ideal Husband* but conceived and had almost completed two other plays of a completely different type, the *Florentine Tragedy* and *La Sainte Courtisane*" (*Complete Works*, II: 40). Readers and scholars of Wilde have been so habituated to thinking of *Salome* as the exception in his dramatic *oeuvre*—"his most experimental play isolated as an apparent aberration among the complete works," as one theatre historian has put it—that they have been apt to forget that it was two other pieces which in *De Profundis* Wilde himself singled out for their "difference."[6]

Categorizing Wilde's dramatic output is not a straightforward task. That body of writing could be divided into the early and the late works: a period of nearly a decade separates Wilde's first theatrical experiments—*Vera; Or, the Nihilists*, written in 1880, and *The Duchess of Padua*, written in 1883—from the run of successful West End comedies that began with *Lady Windermere's Fan* (completed and first performed in 1892) and ended with *The Importance of Being Earnest* (in 1895). Or one might choose the finished and the unfinished. For most of the plays that were completed and either performed or published in Wilde's lifetime—that is, *Vera*, the four society comedies, *Salome*, and *The Duchess of Padua* (published in an edition of twenty copies, at Wilde's expense and probably in 1891); for those there is another group of dramatic works that exist only as scenario or as unfinished draft. This latter group includes *La Sainte Courtisane*, written sometime after 1893 but (as Karl Beckson notes) incomplete in mid-1895; *A Florentine Tragedy*, an incomplete one-act drama again written in the years after 1893; *The Cardinal of Avignon* (a lengthy scenario of which was sketched out by Wilde in 1894, although the first idea for the play came to him as early as 1882); *A Wife's Tragedy* (probably written in the late 1880s, and surviving only in a manuscript fragment which was published by Rodney Shewan in 1982); and *Mr. and Mrs. Daventry*, a scenario which Wilde wrote in the summer of 1894 and which he eventually sold to Frank Harris, who completed the play in 1900.[7] Finally, one might be tempted to divide the plays by genre or theme, separating *Vera* and the society comedies with their contemporary settings from those more melodramatic or tragic works concerned with historical or biblical subjects.

The very least we can agree upon is that Wilde's interest in the theatre was more wide-ranging than an exclusive concern with the society comedies might lead us to believe. On the other hand, it does seem significant that the works Wilde found most difficult to complete were, overwhelmingly, those with little or no topical reference. There is, of course, a straightforwardly pragmatic explanation for this state of affairs. Wilde worked hardest on those genres that offered the best prospect of commercial success; and it was the fashionable contemporaneity of the society comedies, rather than the stylized and perhaps archaic Renaissance tragedies, which brought the much-needed commissions and cash advances. Yet the failure of his attempt to have *Salome* staged, and the contrasting success of *Lady Windermere's Fan*, did not blunt Wilde's interest in those plays "of a completely different type": *La Sainte Courtisane*, *A Florentine Tragedy*, and *The Cardinal of Avignon*. They all postdate *Salome*, and provide evidence of Wilde's continuing (even compulsive) interest in dramatizing those fierce emotions and desires that had no place in the politely ordered, normative, and strictly gendered world of the drawing rooms of London society. It seems from his scattered references to these projected works that they possessed a powerful hold over his imagination, even while he was preoccupied with the more popular and conventional society comedies. That Wilde was unable to sell the scenarios for any of these works probably explains why they were never finished. However, what must have been failures or disappointments for him do present the modern reader with a number of opportunities. The very fact that *La Sainte Courtisane*, *A Florentine Tragedy*, and *The Cardinal of Avignon* were never placed before the public when Wilde was alive means that other hands, whether they belonged to actors, managers, or publishers, did not—so far as we know—intervene in or interfere with Wilde's creative process by forcing or persuading him to modify his first ideas.[8] As a consequence, it may be that it is in these incomplete and fragmentary works that we see Wilde at his most raw and personal, using drama or theatre (however inexpertly) to explore emotions that were closest to his own life.

Before continuing with our argument it may be helpful to offer a brief word of explanation about how we will develop our discussion in the remainder of this chapter. The plots and situations of the society comedies are so well known and have—as we noted earlier—been the subject of so much critical explication that we have assumed that the reader will be able to place those particular or local episodes we have discussed in relation to the plays as a whole. However, the same is not true of the unfinished plays; these works are not widely available and the fundamental precondition of a critical debate about them—the establishing of reliable and authoritative texts—has yet to be put in place. And it is because they are relatively unexamined in comparison with the rest of Wilde's *oeuvre* that we think it worthwhile to provide the reader with accounts of their themes and—when necessary—their plot structures. (They are reprinted, with full bibliographical information, in the Appendix.) In this way and for these reasons we offer much more of a close reading or explication of these works than with any of the better-known pieces in Wilde's *oeuvre*.

The fact that the potential of *La Sainte Courtisane*, *A Florentine Tragedy*, and *The Cardinal of Avignon* has been so little explored by modern critics can be explained, as we said, by the fact that the texts themselves are only infrequently reprinted. Moreover, those that have been published are not always consistent with each other, as editors make different decisions about how to piece together the various surviving manuscript fragments. Merlin Holland reproduced *A Florentine Tragedy* (along with *La Sainte Courtisane*) in his revised *Complete Works of Oscar Wilde* (1994), although Terence Brown, who wrote the introduction to the section on the plays in Holland's edition, does not mention either of them. The only other easily available printing of *A Florentine Tragedy* is to be found in Richard Allen Cave's Penguin edition of *The Importance of Being Earnest and Other Plays* (2000), the introduction to which, unlike Brown's, does discuss some of the work's themes as well as its theatrical novelty and dramatic power. Readers might also go to Robert Ross's 1909 edition, although they would notice that Ross's text is significantly different from that of Holland or Cave, for it includes a first scene of some 200 lines composed by the writer Thomas Sturge Moore after Wilde's death. To complicate matters further, manuscript fragments of what appears to be the missing opening which Moore's lines had been composed to replace came to light after Ross's edition had gone to press, and were reprinted in part in Stuart Mason's *A Bibliography of Oscar Wilde*. None of the Mason fragments appears in the few modern editions of the work. By contrast the scenario of *The Cardinal of Avignon* is virtually unknown to all except a handful of experts: it has been printed only in bibliographical works directed towards the specialist reader. The few surviving lines of dialogue of the play (probably an opening for Act II) contained in a notebook (currently held in the Taylor Collection at Princeton) have never been reprinted.

The Cardinal of Avignon

The 1894 scenario of *The Cardinal of Avignon* is quite detailed, giving both an outline of the play's plot as well as some indication of the principal dramatic exchanges. It centres on a Cardinal who is about to be elected Pope. In the opening scene he is soliciting votes by promising to fulfil the "personal aims and desires" of various "Nobles and Princes" whose "vices and pleasures" he knows well. He also has the guardianship of what the scenario describes as "a beautiful young girl." In a later scene she reveals to him that she is in love with "a handsome young man" who has "been made much of by the prelate" (and who, we soon learn, is in fact the Cardinal's illegitimate son). Full of "rage and sorrow" the Cardinal, who is also secretly in love with the girl, makes her promise not to relate their conversation to her lover. Later, on finding out that the two lovers have indeed met, the Cardinal, determined not to "lose the only thing he loves," lies to the girl's lover by telling him that she is in fact his sister and he must therefore "pluck this impossible love from his heart and also kill it in the heart of the girl." The young man carries out this demand. In the final act, the Cardinal is struggling with his conscience, anxious that the "sin in his soul"— his illicit love for his ward and his lie to his son—will prevent him from being elected Pope. But he is elected, and in his elation reveals to the young man that the lie was merely a "test" and that he can now marry his ward and "ride away from Rome." But the girl has already killed herself in despair. The scenario ends with a violent argument, conducted over the corpse of the girl, between the Cardinal (now Pope) and his son; in the course of that confrontation the son threatens to kill his father. In order to save his life, the Pope first appeals to the sanctity of his office; then, on revealing his identity as a father, draws attention to the "hideousness of the crime of patricide." Finally, he reveals his love for his ward—"I too loved her"—at which point the young man throws himself on the corpse and stabs himself. In the final tableau, reminiscent of a Jacobean revenge tragedy, the Pope is seen blessing the dead bodies, an action witnessed by the "soldiers, Nobles, etc." who have burst into the palace.

This potent mix of parental power, sexual rivalry between an older and a younger man, and the hint of incest (as both quasi-parental and fraternal feelings are translated into sexual ones) we have of course seen before, though with a much less explicit treatment. Wilde was composing the scenario for *The Car-*

dinal of Avignon less than a year after he had completed *A Woman of No Importance*, in which similar themes have been detected. In both plays a young woman (an entirely blameless, and thus a dramatically uninteresting victim) is a device by which Wilde can dramatize a conflict between two men, one in which good looks and youthfulness are set against age, knowledge, and power. It is clear from the scenario that the scenes that interested Wilde most—and that are afforded the most extensive treatment by way of his marking out potential lines of dialogue—are the exchanges between the Cardinal and his son. By contrast, the conventional love scenes between the son and the ward are given only a perfunctory mention. As Wilde curtly puts it: "The girl now re-enters, and the Cardinal explains that her lover finds he has made a serious mistake and does not love her sufficiently to wed her. The portion of the play winds up with a powerful scene between the two lovers, the young man rigidly carrying out the promise exacted from him by the Cardinal." Wilde gives no indication of the kinds of exchanges that might be exhibited in this "powerful scene." We might also notice the lack of women characters in the scenario: the Cardinal/Pope (as one would expect) operates within an entirely male world of nobles, princes, and soldiers. The dowager-duchesses and the wronged middle-aged women who populate the society comedies and whose influence is exercised only in a domestic environment are significantly absent; and so too, therefore, are the male-female power struggles which help to ground the society comedies in the conventional sexual ethics and traditions of the well-made play. As a result Wilde's interest in the complexities of male-male relationships is very much at the forefront of *The Cardinal of Avignon*. In that work, as in the periodical version of *The Picture of Dorian Gray*, Wilde's personal concerns seem right on the surface. Richard Ellmann, who sees the scenario as an "emulation" of Shelley's *The Cenci*, is certainly right when he comments that Wilde is "not interested in the subject of incest" and that "the tragedy is one of thwarted love [where] family relationships of lovers and rivals do not seem to matter" (Ellmann, 386). Oddly, though, Ellmann does not tease out the nature of that nonfamilial love.

A Florentine Tragedy

As we noted earlier, in order to understand some of the problems involved in interpreting *A Florentine Tragedy*, modern readers need some information about its textual status. They can choose between two different texts: that printed by both Holland and Cave, or that given by Ross in his 1909 edition. In fact, the only (though substantial) difference between the Ross and the Holland and Cave texts concerns the latter editors' omission of those opening 200 lines which had been commissioned from Sturge Moore. Ross himself, according to an introduction he wrote for the American edition of that work, had based his text on a typescript of the play (now presumed lost) which had been given to him by the actor Edward Smith Willard (Willard in turn claimed that the typescript had been sent to him by Wilde). Significantly, that typescript, according to Ross, began at the same place as some loose manuscript fragments of the play which he had in his own possession, having retrieved them from Wilde's Tite Street home in 1895 following Wilde's bankruptcy proceedings. Ross's fragments in turn were almost certainly the same incomplete manuscript draft that is now held in the collection of the Clark Library in the University of California; the first page of that draft—numbered as it is in Wilde's hand—begins (as we must presume the Willard typescript did) with the stage direction "*Enter the Husband*" followed by Simone's first speech. Simone enters a stage already peopled with two other characters—Guido and Bianca—whose presence has not been explained to the audience. This detail, in combination with the absence of a description of the scene or of the *dramatis personae*, led Ross to conclude that Wilde had failed, for whatever reason, to write an opening scene for the play. Later in *De Profundis* Wilde acknowledged that the play was indeed incomplete at the time of his conviction, though he did not explain precisely what work remained to be done.

However, as we hinted earlier, other surviving manuscript fragments, which were not in Ross's possession when he put together the 1909 edition of *A Florentine Tragedy*, show that Wilde had indeed worked on a beginning for his play, although whether these lines had been composed before or after the typescript made for Willard is not clear. That these fragments are on unnumbered pages may seem to suggest that they came from a very early draft, as Wilde tended to number manuscript pages only when he was making a fair copy for a typist. On the other hand, we know from Wilde's other works that he habitually had drafts typed up, and that these would subsequently be heavily corrected, and new manuscript pages interleaved with them. The typescript he sent to Willard, then, did not necessarily represent finished work, and the unnumbered pages where he is apparently drafting out a possible opening do not necessarily represent discarded ideas.

These details about the composition of *A Florentine Tragedy* may seem unnecessarily complex, an example of exactly the sort of arcane scholarship or dry-as-dust facts that we have deprecated as being of interest only to scholars. However, as we will show, they turn out to be important for an interpretation of the play, and particularly for how we understand its main themes.

A Florentine Tragedy is written in blank verse; it represents an achievement in striking contrast to some of the dully artificial language of *Poems* (1881), the pseudo-Elizabethan diction of *A Duchess of Padua*, and the occasionally overwrought Decadent verse of *The Sphinx*. In many ways *A Florentine Tragedy* can lay claim to be Wilde's most accomplished and mature verse in the sense that it is completely of a piece with the play's themes and action. Its plot is simpler than that indicated in the scenario of *The Cardinal of Avignon*, though it has many thematic similarities, in that it is concerned with power, sexual attraction, and male-male rivalry. The entire action takes place in a single scene, one which (as we have noted) seems to possess no proper opening, or none that Wilde completed. The scene provided by Sturge Moore was thus an attempt to frame and to explain the abrupt beginning and spare action of Wilde's typescript. (The play, using Moore's opening, was first performed privately in the King's Hall in London by the Literary Theatre Society in 1906.) However, these additional lines produce a different effect than the one we would expect from a simple scene-setting addition: they act as a controlling or preemptive paratext for it. In Moore's opening, we learn that Guido Bardi, the son of the Duke of Florence, has attempted to buy the favours of Bianca, the wife of a Florentine trader, Simone Dario, for 40,000 crowns, a sum Bianca returns to Guido. All of this information is related in a conversation between Bianca and her "tire-woman" Maria (a character invented by Moore), who has been acting—as female servants typically do in Renaissance dramas—as a kind of go-between for her mistress and that mistress's putative lover. Indeed, in this version most of our information about Guido, prior to his entrance, comes to us via Maria, who is explicitly weighing him as a potential suitor (and, for her, a potential employer). Thus she emphasizes his "blue" aristocratic blood and his conventional manly virtues: that he is rich and "handsome," with his "doublet," "chains" and "hose," and his "revered legs."

Guido's entrance in Moore's opening then initiates a familiar Renaissance theatrical courtship ritual, in which he celebrates Bianca's grace and beauty and

---

Wilde & Renaissance Drama   For those readers, almost certainly the majority, who associate Wilde's dramatic energies with his four society comedies, it may come as something of a surprise to learn that he had such a sustained interest in historical and particularly Renaissance drama. One of his favourite works was Shelley's *The Cenci*—in a letter to the editor of the *Daily Telegraph*, dated 19 February 1892, he described it as one of only "two great plays" to have been produced "in this century, in England" (*Complete Letters*, 519). In the mid-1880s he reviewed several Shakespearean productions for the *Dramatic Review*, including those of *Hamlet*, *As You Like It*, *Henry IV*, and *Twelfth Night*, and he also wrote more generally on contemporary methods of staging Shakespeare, engaging with what was then a lively debate about archaeological accuracy in costume and scenery. There is also evidence of a more widespread public interest in seventeenth-century drama. In 1887 Henry Havelock Ellis (who would later find fame as a sexologist) established the Mermaid Series of Old Dramatists, published by Vizetelly. It was designed to make available to a wider audience texts of Renaissance and Jacobean dramas. Early editors included John Addington Symonds, Edmund Gosse, Algernon Charles Swinburne, Arthur Symons, Ernest Rhys, and Roden Noel. Wilde's sustained commitment to the subgenre, then, was far from being unusual.

then asks what he could purchase from Simone for 100,000 crowns, finally telling Bianca that it is her whom he wishes to buy. At the close of the scene Bianca directs Guido to "bargain" for her with Simone. It is important to stress that
all of these exchanges are an invention by Moore (even though they pick up
certain details in Wilde's text, such as the amounts of money mentioned when
Simone is trying to sell Guido a "robe of state"). Their cumulative effect is to
establish Bianca, and the exchange value of female beauty, as the pivot of the
play's action; and they also suggest an overt connection between money, sex, and
power in a way which is once again familiar from the sexual politics of Eliza-
bethan and Jacobean drama. Moore seems to be transforming Wilde's play into
a conventional period piece.

Wilde's own incomplete draft openings to the play (printed in the Appendix) could not be more different. They give no hint that Guido has attempted
to "buy" Bianca, nor, more importantly, that either or both parties understand
their relationship principally in economic terms. Bianca, in particular, is presented (as her name suggests) as virtue personified. So what we call Fragment
B (published by Mason) centres on a conventional lover's language of longing
and anxiety; Bianca stands alone near an open window lamenting the prob-
lems of an involvement in an illicit love affair—the "loveless days | Wearily
passed and patiently endured"—and calling on the "Holy Mother" to witness
her patience and her pain. In what we call Fragment C (first published in full
by Small in 1993), her piety is given yet greater weight, as we meet her "kneeling before an image of the Madonna ... simply but beautifully dressed." Moreover, when Guido enters by the window, it is her own unworthiness which
preoccupies Bianca—that, as a "common burgher's unloved wife," it would be
enough for her (using a Dante-like phrase) just to have "looked on" her "terrible Lord," on his "fair" face, with his "throat like milk," "mouth a scarlet flow-
er," and eyes where "wild woodland wells" and "dark violets see | Their purple
shadows drown." Here, in Wilde's opening, we should notice that it is the beauty of Guido (rather than of Bianca) that is dwelt upon. In neither of Wilde's
manuscript fragments is Guido given any lines celebrating Bianca's appearance.
Moreover, Bianca's dreamily sensuous appreciation of the male body, so reminiscent of the Decadent language in works such as *The Picture of Dorian Gray*, is
completely at odds with Maria's description of Guido (as imagined by Moore),
which emphasizes his possessions and his public standing. In Wilde's draft opening, it is the male (rather than the female) body that is established as a "price-
less" object of desire—a detail to which we shall return.

As we noted, the text of Willard's typescript (and those of Holland and Cave)
opens suddenly with Simone returning to his own house to discover his wife
Bianca in the company of Guido. Simone begins with a series of apparently
innocent questions about the identity and purpose of the visit of his wife's guest

which make immediate sense in terms of the themes of manners and courtesy, as one would expect from a play whose setting is Renaissance Italy. However, the specificity of that setting is largely irrelevant to the play's plot. It is important only insofar as it permits Wilde to rehearse his themes of desire and jealousy. For Simone, Guido's presence must be explained by the fact that he is "some friend" or "kinsman"; no other man could properly be entertained by Bianca with "such courtly grace" in a house "lacking a host"—that is, without an adult male, and presumably the husband—present. Simone then makes explicit the sexual impropriety of such an encounter when, in imagery ironically anticipating how he will describe the duel he is later to fight with Guido, he describes his house as "a scabbard without steel to keep it straight." When Guido's identity is explained—he is the "son | Of that great Lord of Florence"—Simone then chooses to understand his presence, his acceptance of "hospitalities," in terms of trade, and in a series of long exchanges attempts, via flattery, to sell Guido some rich and luxurious clothing. That flattery, however, centres explicitly on paying tribute to Guido's sexual attractiveness and sexual prowess— that "highborn dames" of the court "throng like flies" around him; and that in his presence "husbands ... wear horns, and wear them bravely, | A fashion most fantastical." When Guido refuses to barter with him (by offering a sum so extravagant that Simone will be "richer far | Than all other merchants"), Simone then tries to engage his attention with other subjects, speaking first of politics (the tensions between the Pope and King of France) and then of music, requesting Guido to "draw melodies from [his] lute | To charm my moody and o'er-troubled soul." The implication, of course, is that Guido could only have brought his lute to entertain Bianca; Simone's challenge, however, is to demand that Guido pay court to him, a man, and not to his wife. Finally he invites Guido to drink with him at a table already set, once more explicitly inviting Guido to transfer his romantic attention from Bianca to him (Simone).

These exchanges, which dominate the action of the play, are briefly and periodically interrupted by asides between Bianca and Guido, in which the former confesses her revulsion at her husband's vulgarity—that he speaks like "a common chapman" and has a "soul [that] stands ever in the market-place." Matters come to a climax when Guido makes a move to leave, despite Simone's pressuring him to "stay awhile." Simone duly fetches Guido's cloak and sword; but before his guest can depart he reminds him that he has "drunk of my wine, and broken bread, and made | Yourself a sweet familiar." He then confronts Guido in language whose metaphors lay bare the source of the tension between the two men:

> Why, what a sword is this!
> Ferrara's temper, pliant as a snake,
> And deadlier, I doubt not. With such steel

One need fear nothing in the moil of life.
I never touched so delicate a blade.

Simone then challenges Guido to test "Whether the Prince's or the merchant's steel | Is better tempered"; and in a long monologue observes that although his own sword "is somewhat rusted now," he too is an accomplished swordsman and has killed a thief "on the road to Padua." A duel ensues in which Guido wounds Simone. Undaunted Simone fights on, and disarms Guido, noting that "My gentle lord, you see that I was right. | My sword is better tempered, finer steel." Simone finally kills Guido and "looks at Bianca." At this point the reader or the audience expect Simone to kill Bianca as well—such a conclusion would clearly fit the Renaissance setting and context. But instead *"she comes towards him as one dazed with wonder and with outstretched arms."* Thereafter the play concludes quickly and enigmatically with a reconciliation of husband and wife over the corpse and blood of the wife's dead lover, one that makes overt the relationship between male physical power and attraction:

> Bianca: Why
> Did you not tell me you were so strong?
> Simone: Why
> Did you not tell me you were so beautiful?

How are we to make sense of the play and in particular its surprising and sudden denouement? Karl Beckson helpfully suggests that it was modelled upon the example of Alfred de Musset's *proverbes dramatiques,* "brief dialogues with a dramatic reversal at the end to illustrate a moral point" (Beckson, 103). But what is that moral exactly? Does it amount to anything more than a crude display of sexual power and prowess, a suggestion that the potency of the "sword" is mightier than any amount of "red gold"? Some critics, following up the hints in Moore's opening scene, have attempted to elaborate that connection linking desire, money, and value in terms more relevant to Wilde's own society. Thus Regenia Gagnier, probably the best-known of those critics, has glossed those themes by finding analogues to them in the discourses of late-nineteenth-century classical economics, particularly in the ways in which the market was held by some contemporary theorists to underwrite all forms of human behaviour. In other words, primed, it would seem, by the example of the society comedies, Gagnier looks for some form of social or topical reference—that domain of "public" knowledge that we mentioned earlier—to explain Wilde's interest in a Renaissance setting:

> And where is the "priceless love" Bianca longed for? It is inspired by the merchant's strength, finally revealed when activated by competition. In classic terms, as Guido's language of seduction makes clear, Bianca is the Beautiful: the small, the smooth, the soft, curvaceous, and bright; while Simone is the Sublime: the rugged, the rigid, the dark, the timeless. By the end of the play, one is to be embraced, the other to be saluted.

Inevitably, they are the pair that audiences are hard-wired, according to Hume, to find most productive of pleasure. In economic terms, it's the oldest trope in market society: Beauty loves not so much the man with money (the idle aristocrat) as the man who *makes* money, in historical chronology, the merchant, the capitalist, the entrepreneur, the financier, the arbitrageur. Love is not only on the market, it is driven by market forces. (Gagnier, 80)

There are some obvious problems with this reading (though it is useful in helping point out the strengths and weaknesses of the play). First it blurs the distinction between Wilde's text and the lines added by Moore. The foregrounding of love as an economic exchange, and the consequent understanding of the play's "moral" as centring on a choice (made by Bianca) between two different kinds of moneymaking, is directed by Moore's interpretative paratext. Read without his 200-line introduction, Bianca, as we have argued, is a much less prominent and attractive figure; certainly she has much less dramatic agency. Her name, which translates as "the white woman" or "the white female," and her status are reflected in the fact that she is given only a handful of lines in the play (about one-twelfth of the total). Moreover, this impression is reinforced by Wilde's fragmentary openings which have survived. There, as we noted, Bianca is conventionally pious and submissive: she is in no sense (as Moore portrays her) an agent in her own selling, and neither is she—as Gagnier suggests—a modern consumer or a prototypical "new woman," choosing the man who is (economically speaking) the more productive.

Second, and more important, the principal or dominating "language of seduction," to borrow Gagnier's phrase, belongs not to Guido but to Simone. In Wilde's text, it is *he* (not Bianca) who most explicitly "courts" Guido, who flatters him with increasingly voluptuous and sexually explicit language. He claims, for example, to have "a curious fancy" to see Guido "in this wonder of the loom | Amidst the noble ladies of the court, | A flower among flowers"; later he again refers to Guido as "the flower in a garden full of weeds." Moreover, at the very beginning of the play Simone had also used botanical imagery (that self-same language of horticulture innocently given to Miss Prism and Dr. Chasuble in *The Importance of Being Earnest*) to describe himself, explaining that a house without a host was "A flowerless garden widowed of the sun." (Here we might usefully also recall that Wilde habitually, but less innocently, referred to Douglas in flower-imagery as his "jonquil," or his "narcissus," or his "fleur-de-lys.") Simone's Decadent language—of "pearls | As thick as moths in summer streets at night | And whiter than the moons that madmen see"—is, ironically, very far from that of the "common chapman" which Bianca and Guido insist on calling Simone. The following lines, for example, where Simone, in Keatsean fashion, exalts the lasting beauty of art over the transience of nature—of the attraction of roses made of "Lucca damask" over real blossoms—would not be amiss in Wilde's own lyrics:

I think the hillsides that best love the rose
At Bellosguardo or at Fiesole
Throw no such blossoms on the lap of spring
Or if they do their blossoms droop and die.
Such is the fate of all the dainty things
That dance in wind and water. Nature herself
Makes war on her one loveliness and slays
Her children like Medea.

Such images explicitly echo the language of desire in which (in a fragment we have already referred to) Bianca herself had described her lover. In other words, the play's language of love—that familiar Wildean lexicon of "curious" fancies, of "silver and roses," of "blossoms," of "pomegranates," of "pearls," and of "rubies"—is used principally by Simone to engage Guido's attention: it seems, that is, to refer to male, rather than female, beauty.

Throughout this attempted verbal seduction of Guido—he beseeches him at one point to "ravish my ears with some sweet melody"—Simone repeatedly insists on his wife's plainness: she is "uncomely," and her virtues are those of the traditional wife. She should "kneel down upon the floor"; upon such a surface she is "better so," and she should be merely "made to keep the house and spin." In a startlingly misogynistic line Simone implicitly compares her to "the meanest trencher-plate | From which I feed mine appetite." Such sentiments are hard to account for simply in economic terms: attributing to Simone a mercantile sensibility, as Bianca does—he is a man whose "soul stands ever in the market-place"—may explain why he sees his relationship with his wife as one of ownership, but not why he professes to Guido that that particular possession has such little worth. (If we follow Gagnier's economic analogies, we should remember that in market economics rarity carries the highest price; yet Simone insists on his wife's *ordinariness*, that she has "virtues as most women have, | But beauty is a gem she may not wear.") Nowhere in Wilde's text is Bianca, as Gagnier proposes, "soft, curvaceous, and bright"; she is, like Sybil Vane and a host of Wildean women before her, much more of a cipher.

But there is, of course, another way to make sense of the dynamic of the play's dialogue: that the affair between Bianca and Guido is a framing device that allows Wilde to stage a much more compelling contest, one in which Bianca and Simone are competing with each other for Guido's attention, and where women's "foolish chatterings," as Simone calls them, are displaced by a male language of desire which, in places, is Shakespearean in its eloquence:

There are times when the great universe,
Like cloth in some unskilled dyer's vat,
Shrivels to a handsbreadth, and perchance
That time is now! Well! Let that time be now.
Let this room be as that mighty stage

Whereon kings die, and our ignoble lives
Become the stakes God plays for.

We might recall that, as we commented in chapter two, Wilde had used similar phrases to describe the tragedy of his own life in *De Profundis:* "[For] me the
world is shrivelled to a handsbreadth, and everywhere I turn my name is written on the rocks in lead." By far the greatest proportion of the lines, and all of
the long speeches, are given to Simone and directed to Guido. Simone domi-
nates the action; the other two characters, by contrast, are barely realized. It is
thus hard to resist concluding that Wilde's failure to complete the opening scene
of *A Florentine Tragedy*—the scene preceding Simone's entrance—was due (like
the underwritten elements of the scenario to the *Cardinal of Avignon*) to a lack
of interest in dramatizing heterosexual desire. We might also note that, for some
critics, the weakest elements in the society comedies are those exchanges—for
example between Lord Darlington and Lady Windermere in Act II of *Lady Windermere's Fan*—in which men profess their love for women and vice versa.

This representation of male-male rivalry as a process in which men exhibit
themselves to each other (rather than to a woman) can be found elsewhere in
Wilde's *oeuvre*: it is hinted at in the competition between Lord Henry Wotton
and Basil Hallward for Dorian Gray's attention (in *The Picture of Dorian Gray*),
in the competition between Darlington and Lord Windermere (in *Lady Windermere's Fan*), and in the threatened physical encounter between Lord Illingworth
and Gerald Arbuthnot (in *A Woman of No Importance*). Wilde's text of *A Florentine Tragedy* clearly shows more interest in the power relationship between Guido and Simone than in any sexual relationship between Guido and Bianca, or
between Simone and Bianca. And that male-male relationship has some obvious similarities to the personal situation of its author in the mid-1890s. Simone is given little social distinction; he is a kind of outsider who has to make
his way in the market-place, which reminds us of how Wilde felt himself con-
strained to write for money—"How poor a bargain is this life of man, | And
in how mean a market are we sold!" Simone exclaims. More importantly Guido, the younger and more attractive man, is the son of a prince; he, like Wilde's lover Douglas (the son of an aristocrat) assumes he has the money to buy
any sexual object he desires. Here we should recall that the year when Wilde
was writing the play, 1893, was also the time when his relations with Douglas
were at their most fraught, and when Douglas had been dispatched to Egypt
to avoid engulfing them both in scandal following Douglas's and Wilde's relationship with a sixteen-year-old youth. The lesson that Guido learns in the play,
that sexual power depends more on possessing a "better tempered steel" than
on youth and money, seems very personal—wishful thinking, perhaps. If we
are tempted to read Wilde's fictions and plays as disguised dramatizations of the
sexual and psychological tensions he was experiencing in his own life, then *A*

Florentine Tragedy is a far richer seam to mine than the society comedies, in the sense that it positively invites such a reading. The themes of money and power, the excitement of male–male rather than male–female relationships, and a focus on class, require little scholarly excavation once we understand what comprises Wilde's text: those themes are, to revert to Henry James's phrase, all on the surface of the piece.

La Sainte Courtisane

La Sainte Courtisane survives in a much more fragmentary form than *A Florentine Tragedy*; moreover the version of it published by Ross in his 1908 *Collected Edition* (and subsequently reprinted in the Collins *Complete Works*) was considerably "tidied up" by its first editor. Wilde's manuscript has no names of characters or stage directions; there are just heavily corrected blocks of speech. To make dramatic sense of this material, Ross had both to rearrange and edit the speeches, and then to attribute them to characters. In so doing he imposes a dramatic structure on Wilde's text, inventing *dramatis personae* such as "first man" and "second man," and making decisions about which lines belong to which character. As with his editing of *A Florentine Tragedy*, these interventions have had some interesting implications for how the play has been understood.

Few critics have drawn attention to the title of *La Sainte Courtisane*, which draws upon French religious language used to describe Mary—"la Sainte Vierge," "the Blessed Virgin." Wilde's title translates as "the blessed harlot" or "prostitute," which should immediately alert us to its similarity to *Salome*. Like that play it centres on the desire of a lascivious and beautiful heroine for a celibate holy man who "will not look on the face of woman." Also like *Salome*, it combines biblical and erotic language as, for example, in the heroine Myrrhina's enticing promise to Honorius: "I will smear your body with myrrh and pour spikenard on your hair. I will clothe you in hyacinth and put honey in your mouth."

The fragment, as rearranged by Ross, begins with two unnamed men discussing the beauty of Myrrhina, who has in turn come to consult them about the "beautiful young hermit," Honorius. By far the longest speech is given to Myrrhina as she tries to coax Honorius from his hermit's cave. She tempts him by recounting the number and beauty of her young male lovers: there is "the minion of Caesar" who is "pale as a narcissus" with a "body ... like honey"; there is the "son of the Praefect" who "slew himself in my honour"; there is the "Tetrarch of Cilicia" who "scourged himself for my pleasure"; and there are the "young men wrestling" who have "bodies ... bright with oil and ... brows [which] are wreathed with willow sprays and with myrtle." The strange courtship of a man (Honorius) with images of male beauty and of male masochistic violence is worlds away from the genteel language of wooing that we find in the society comedies. As with *A Florentine Tragedy* and *The Cardinal of Avignon*, the scenario of *La Sainte Courtisane* appears to have provided Wilde with an opportunity to rehearse the themes of male eroticism, sinfulness, and a Decadent theatre of cruelty. That these passages seem, in Wilde's text, to have been composed as autonomous units—as freestanding pieces of prose—lends further weight to such conjecture. It is as if Wilde wrote the speeches first and then tried to find a dramatic structure to contain them, one in which they could be made to make sense.

The draft ends with a double role reversal: the chaste Honorius wishes to "taste of the seven sins" while the courtesan Myrrhina longs for "a cavern in the desert" so that her "soul may become worthy to see God." Myrrhina invokes in her final speech a sense of "Sin" and "Shame" that is explicitly to do with sexual transgression. The homoerotic language of *La Sainte Courtisane* places that sin and shame much closer to Wilde's own life than the more elusive hints in the society comedies. Indeed, the speed with which desire is transformed into its opposite (both here and in *A Florentine Tragedy*) is reminiscent of the way Wilde interrogates sin in *De Profundis*: there the moral life and tasting the fruit of the trees on the "other side of the garden" are two equal and equally necessary modes of experience. This relativization of desire was simply not a theme that could be explored in those plays which, like the society comedies, are set in such a contemporary and precisely realized social world, where transgression—especially sexual transgression—has real consequences. Such themes are sustainable only within the stylized world and highly stylized language of Decadence. They have no place in comedy and exist only fleetingly in *An Ideal Husband*—as we noted, to be dismissed immediately by Goring.

Conclusion

We began this chapter by noting that academics have tended to find three layers of reference or allusion in Wilde's plays: the literary, the biographical, and the social or topical. We have also tried to show that the different kinds of knowledge that these references call upon—particularly the distinction between what we termed "private" biographical knowledge as opposed to "public" topical information—do not always interact with each other in coherent or consistent ways, a circumstance which in turn can make it difficult for the general reader to make sense of the vast body of scholarly material produced on these works. One way around this dilemma is to acknowledge that not all lines of scholarly enquiry are equally useful in enhancing our enjoyment of Wilde's dramas. We have argued quite forcefully that, despite their apparent closeness to Wilde's own life, pursuing the occasional and isolated personal allusion in the society comedies is a fairly fruitless task, producing surprisingly conservative (even homophobic) interpretations of the plays. By contrast, those lesser-known, unfinished plays—the *Cardinal of Avignon*, *A Florentine Tragedy*, and *La Sainte Courtisane*—provide rich pickings for critics disposed to see some of Wilde's writings as autobiographical; the conflicts dramatized in this group of works make most sense in terms of Wilde playing out the anxieties that were produced by his own relationship with Douglas. It is therefore something of an irony that they have been all but ignored by Wilde's biographers, and particularly by Neil McKenna, who is so insistent in his biographical treatment of Wilde's writings. In our final chapter we will examine another group of works which are habitually ignored by scholars (though not, interestingly, by general readers): Wilde's short fiction.

Notes

1.   This is not the only way of understanding Wilde's place within a theatrical tradition. Rather than seeing Wilde as a dramatist constrained by the conventions of his time, there have been a number of attempts to locate Wilde's comedic style within particular modern—that is, twentieth-century—dramatic traditions. Here Wilde is typically seen as the starting point of a modern comedy of manners, which is developed through the works of Noel Coward and, more recently, Joe Orton. In this tradition of modern farce, Wilde becomes a truly original and originating voice, not an echo of Arthur Wing Pinero or of W. S. Gilbert. Far from manipulating fundamentally conservative late-nineteenth-century dramatic devices, he becomes a dramatist developing patterns and forms that later generations exploit.

2.   See, for example, the argument that underwrites Sos Eltis's account of Wilde's revisions to the society comedies in her *Revising Wilde* (Oxford: Clarendon Press, 1996).

3.   The same exchange is to be found in *The Trials of Oscar Wilde*, H. Montgomery Hyde, ed. (London: Hodge, 1948), but in a version that—as we noted in chapter two—makes Wilde's comments seem considerably wittier.

4.   Suttons was and is a large British horticultural firm.

5.   Quoted in Michael Holroyd, *Lytton Strachey: Vol. I. The Unknown Years (1880–1919)* (London: Heinemann, 1967), 319–20fn.

6.   William Tydeman and Steven Price, *Wilde: Salome* (Cambridge: Cambridge University Press, 1996), 1; Tydeman and Price go on to counter this assumption by pointing out how some of the themes and theatrical devices of *Salome* are anticipated in two earlier works, *Vera* and *The Duchess of Padua*.

7.   There may also be fragments of another play, a blank verse tragedy called *Beatrice and Astone Manfredi*; see Beckson, 23–24.

8.   There were of course other hands involved in both the writing and the translation of *Salomé*. More still were involved in its publication, in both Britain and France.

Works Cited & Consulted

Bateson, F. W. "The Function of Criticism at the Present Time," *Essays in Criticism*, 3 (1953), 1–27.

Beckson, Karl. *The Oscar Wilde Encyclopedia*. New York: AMS Press, 1998.

Behrendt, Patricia. *Oscar Wilde: Eros and Aesthetics*. London: Macmillan, 1991.

The Complete Letters of Oscar Wilde, Merlin Holland and Rupert Hart-Davis, eds. London: Fourth Estate, 2000.

The Complete Works of Oscar Wilde, Merlin Holland, ed. London: Collins, 2000.

Craft, Christopher. "Alias Bunbury: Desire and Termination in *The Importance of Being Earnest*," *Representations*, 31 (Summer 1990), 19–46.

Dickson, Sarah Augusta, ed., *The Importance of Being Earnest: A Trivial Comedy for Serious People in Four Acts as Originally Written by Oscar Wilde*. 2 vols. New York: New York Public Library, 1956.

Ellmann, Richard. *Oscar Wilde*. London: Hamish Hamilton, 1987.

Eltis, Sos. *Revising Wilde*. Oxford: Clarendon Press, 1996.

Gagnier, Regenia. "*A Florentine Tragedy*," *Modern Drama*, 37 (1994), 71–83.

Holland, Merlin. *Irish Peacock and Scarlet Marquess: The Real Trial of Oscar Wilde*. London: Fourth Estate, 2003.

Kaplan, Joel. "Staging Wilde's Society Plays: A Conversation with Philip Prowse (Glasgow Citizens Theatre)," *Modern Drama*, 37 (1994), 192–205.

_____. "A Puppet's Power: George Alexander, Clement Scott, and the Re-plotting of *Lady Windermere's Fan*," *Theatre Notebook*, 46 (1992), 59–73.

F. R. Leavis, ed. *A Selection from Scrutiny*. 2 vols. Cambridge: Cambridge University Press, 1968.

Mackie, W. Craven. "Bunbury Pure and Simple," *Modern Drama*, 41 (1998), 327–30.

McKenna, Neil. *The Secret Life of Oscar Wilde*. London: Century, 2003.

Oscar Wilde's The Importance of Being Earnest: The First Production, Joseph Donohue, with Ruth Berggren, eds. Gerrards Cross, Bucks.: Colin Smythe, 1995.

Raby, Peter. "'The Persons of the Play': Some Reflections on Wilde's Choice of Names in *The Importance of Being Earnest*," *Nineteenth Century Theatre*, 23 (1995), 67–75.

Sinfield, Alan. "'Effeminacy' and 'Femininity': Sexual Politics in Wilde's Comedies," *Modern Drama*, 37 (1994), 34–52.

Stowell, Sheila and Joel Kaplan. *Theatre and Fashion: Oscar Wilde to the Suffragettes*. Cambridge: Cambridge University Press, 1994.

Small, Ian. *Oscar Wilde Revalued*. Greensboro: ELT Press, 1993.

Sutton and Sons, *The Culture of Vegetables and Flowers*. London: Hamilton, Adams & Co., 1884.

Tydeman, William and Steven Price, *Wilde: Salome*. Cambridge: Cambridge University Press, 1996.

Wilde, Oscar. *An Ideal Husband*, Robert Ross, ed. London: Methuen, 1908.

_____. *An Ideal Husband*, Russell Jackson, ed. Second and revised ed. London: A. and C. Black, 1993.

_____. *A Woman of No Importance*, Robert Ross, ed. London: Methuen, 1908.

_____. *The Importance of Being Earnest*, Robert Ross, ed. London: Methuen, 1908.

_____. *The Importance of Being Earnest and Other Plays*, Peter Raby, ed. Oxford: Oxford University Press, 1995.

_____. *The Importance of Being Earnest and Other Plays*, Richard Allen Cave, ed. London: Penguin, 2000.

____. *Intentions and The Soul of Man*, Robert Ross, ed. London: Methuen, 1908.

____. *Lord Arthur Savile's Crime and Other Prose Pieces*, Robert Ross, ed. London: Methuen, 1908.

____. *Salome. A Florentine Tragedy. Vera*, Robert Ross, ed. London: Methuen, 1908.

Zatlin, Linda Gertner. *Aubrey Beardsley and Victorian Sexual Politics*. Oxford: Oxford University Press, 1990.

| VI | *Dorian Gray* and the Short Fiction:
Choosing Between "Sinburnianism" and Pleasing the British Public

IN THE PREVIOUS CHAPTER we discussed the ways in which the society comedies have been central in shaping our modern conception of what is a typically Wildean play. In this chapter we will make a similar case about the centrality of *The Picture of Dorian Gray* in shaping our views of Wilde as a writer of fiction. That work tells us emphatically—should we need to be told—that Wilde was quite unlike the great Victorian novelists who preceded him. From the point of view of form and structure, he was one of the first writers to exploit the possibilities afforded by the new, short, one-volume novel. He was also happy to engage creatively with the enormous changes taking place in the late-nineteenth-century periodical trade and publish a complete novel in a single issue of a magazine (rather than the more usual practice of serializing it). Wilde was not interested in realism, nor in depth or "roundness" of characterization, nor in representing what earlier writers had called the "great web" of contemporary social life. For Wilde the outcome of all the assiduous moralizing which had underwritten the popularity of the three-decker novel was simply that "the good end happily and the bad unhappily" (as Miss Prism defines fiction in Act II of *The Importance of Being Earnest*).

The themes of *Dorian Gray*, particularly its anticipation of twentieth-century concerns like conspicuous consumption and the pleasures of city life, seem to align it with a nascent modernity. We see Dorian wining and dining, going to the theatre and to art galleries, visiting opium dens, being a member of a shooting party in the country but, in contrast to his worthy mid-Victorian fictional predecessors, never working, and never talking about work. The anxieties which animate his life could not be further from those tensions between duty and personal gratification, between money and morality, and between work and leisure, which had formed the subject matter of so many earlier novels. In fact what makes *Dorian Gray* seem so quintessentially Wildean—exactly that sort of

novel one might expect Wilde to write—is its opposition to what we habitually take to be traditional Victorian values.

This sense of *Dorian Gray*'s "difference" is also to be found in its interpretative
openness or plurality: the novel's resistance to any single or simple reading has
allowed it to be seen as a precursor to the full-blown modernist fiction of, say,
Joyce, Woolf, or Ford. That resistance is also what permits us to glimpse Wilde's
apparent interest in male-male desire, a subject which is constantly suggested in
the novel, but only via nuance and innuendo (as we noted in chapter two it is
perfectly possible to read *Dorian Gray* as a straightforward morality tale, at the
centre of which is the doomed romance between Dorian and Sybil Vane). As
numbers of critics have noted, *Dorian Gray* succeeds in combining a variety of
what might on the surface seem to be incompatible themes and styles. It debates
complex ideas about art and its relation to life, liberally paraphrasing or directly
quoting parts of Pater's *Renaissance*. It simultaneously exploits subgenres, such as
detective fiction and magic picture stories, whose popularity depended on their
accessibility to a wide audience and their ability to entertain. In a similar vein,
those long set-piece rehearsals of connoisseurship and taste, reminiscent of the
dialogues in *Intentions*, which take up so much of the early section of the novel, are paced quite differently from the dramatic events which occupy its other
chapters, such as Dorian's macabre and sinister arrangements for the disposal of
Basil's body and his terrified flight from the avenging James Vane. The contrast
between moments such as these, designed to thrill, and the studied intertextuality found in other parts of the novel—where, for example, Wilde "borrows"
verbatim long passages from contemporary accounts of ancient Rome, or of fine
stones and jewels, or of tapestries—is unique in late-nineteenth-century British or Irish fiction. Moreover, all of these elements have proved to be meat and
drink to scholars and literary historians, who have identified a wide range of

---

Wilde's "Sources" for *Dorian Gray*   The works upon which Wilde drew when he was writing *Dorian Gray* may be divided into four categories. First, there are those which may have
inspired the basic conception of his story—his use of the *doppelgänger* motif and the idea
of the changing picture. Here numerous possible influences have been suggested, including Charles Maturin's *Melmoth the Wanderer* (1820), Edgar Allan Poe's "The Oval Portrait"
(1842), Wilhelm Meinhold's *Sidonia the Sorceress* (1847–1848), Edmond de Goncourt's *La
Faustin* (1882), Robert Louis Stevenson's *Dr. Jeykll and Mr. Hyde* (1886), and Edward Heron-
Allen's *Ashes of the Future (A Study of Mere Human Nature): The Suicide of Sylvester Gray*
(1888). Second, there are *Dorian Gray*'s debts to other "aesthetic" works or novels, notably Walter Pater's *Studies in the History of the Renaissance* (1873) and *Marius the Epicurean*
(1885), as well as Joris-Karl Huysmans's *A Rebours* (1884); this last work is assumed by most
critics to be the model for the "yellow book" given to Dorian by Lord Henry—that "novel
without a plot, and with only one character"—which so absorbs his attention.

analogues and sources from French, German, and English literature for many of the descriptive details in the novel.

Alongside its strong melodramatic storyline—murder, suicide, and failed love—*Dorian Gray* also has passages of broad and witty social satire (similar, and occasionally identical, to that found in the society comedies), and these work to undermine the reader's ability to locate the story's moral. The dull self-righteousness of the working-class "hero" (James Vane) is as much a target of Wilde's wit as the carelessness of the aristocracy; similarly, the sinister, Svengali-like aspect of Lord Henry's character is constantly undermined by his sharp verbal repartee, his habit (as Dorian puts it) of cutting "life to pieces with his epigrams" (*Complete Works*, III: 251).[1] Here again scholars have found much to discuss in Wilde's representation of the customs and manners of the upper and working classes: so the etiquette of gentlemen's clubs, of smoking, of dressing for dinner, of social ostracism, as well as the deference expected of working-class subjects for their "betters," and the social geography of London can all be usefully elucidated for the modern reader. So too can the details and myths surrounding opium dens and the troping of the novel's latent Orientalism.[2] And then there are the famous passages of purple prose typically used in moments of heightened emotional tension: they include those occasions when Basil is trying to articulate his feelings to Lord Henry, or Dorian is contemplating his own imminent social ruin. As some scholars have argued, it is possible to see in these passages a stylistic self-consciousness which once again anticipates modernism. Certainly in these passages it is difficult for a reader to know how seriously the emotions which they register are to be taken.

---

continued   Third, there are a number of specialist studies upon which Wilde drew for certain descriptive details of the novel, volumes such as A. H. Church's *Precious Stones Considered in their Scientific and Artistic Relations* (1886), William Jones's *History and Mystery of Precious Stones* (1880), and Alan S. Cole's translation of Ernest Lefébure's *Embroidery and Lace* (1888) (which Wilde had reviewed for the *Woman's World*). Fourth, for many of the historical elements of the novels—the accounts of classical Rome or Renaissance Italy—Wilde made use of such well-known works as Suetonius's *Life of the Caesars* and some parts of John Addington Symonds's seven-volume study *The Renaissance in Italy* (1875–1898). In addition to all these materials, the novel also contains numerous allusions to, and quotations from, contemporary French Decadent writing, particularly by Théophile Gautier and Charles Baudelaire.

In its witticisms, its brevity, its interpretative openness, its themes, as well as the controversy which surrounded its first publication, *Dorian Gray* seems to embody everything we associate with the name of Wilde. It even has a cast of characters with whom we can readily identify the author and his social milieu. There are dandies and artists; there is the cultured older man who educates a younger *ingenu*; there has, though, been much debate about who, if any, from Wilde's young male acquaintances inspired the character of Dorian—as far as we know he had not yet begun his relationship with Alfred Douglas when he wrote the novel. There are also those powerful dowager-duchesses who police the activities of attractive young men, as well as the dowdy dull daughters they are trying to marry off, and those pushy nobodies who are attempting to enter London society. (Moreover, the names of some of them, such as "Mrs. Erlynne" and "Lady Gwendolen," Lord Henry's sister, reappear in the society comedies.) There is even a beleaguered member of the professional classes, Alan Campbell, whose skills as a chemist Dorian ruthlessly exploits to dispose of the body of Basil Hallward.

For all these reasons, the publication of *Dorian Gray* is often seen to mark the beginning of that exceptionally productive four-year period in which Wilde wrote all the works for which he is best remembered today—*Dorian Gray*, *Intentions*, the four society comedies, and *Salome*—and which culminated in 1895 in *An Ideal Husband* and *The Importance of Being Earnest* running simultaneously and to huge popular and critical acclaim in the West End. That moment of success has in turn typically been understood as one following a long period of journeyman work, and the point of transition (in the early 1890s) has been described

---

A Book for "Perverted Telegraph Boys"   A month before "The Picture of Dorian Gray" was published in *Lippincott's Monthly Magazine* (1890) Wilde had written to another publisher claiming that his work would "make a sensation" (*Complete Letters*, 425). This judgment proved prophetic, though not perhaps in quite the sense that Wilde had been anticipating. Some publications, like *Punch*, merely mocked his efforts. But others—particularly the *Scots Observer*, *St James Gazette*, and *Daily Chronicle*—were openly condemning, complaining about the novel's "ordure," and its offensiveness to all "decent persons." Such comments in turn led W. H. Smith, the largest (and also perhaps most conservative) bookseller in the country, to remove all copies of the British edition of *Lippincott's* from its shelves, on the grounds that the story had been "characterised by the press as a filthy one" (Holland, 310). So vituperative and personal were these hostile reviews that Wilde felt obliged to respond, vigorously defending his story in letters to those newspapers which had so offended him. This negative publicity proved less than helpful when Wilde tried to find a publisher for a book version of his story; the prestigious house of Macmillan, for example, noted sourly in their rejection letter that there was something "rather repelling" about it (Guy and Small, 70).

as coinciding with Wilde becoming aware of the real nature of his own sexuality. As we mentioned in chapter two, Richard Ellmann most forcefully articulated this argument by asserting that homosexuality "fired" Wilde's creativity. This narrative, combining sexual awakening with a new artistic sophistication, has, however, a number of rarely acknowledged consequences.

The first is that *Dorian Gray* is seen principally as a starting point, the beginning of what is seen as Wilde's mature style. This in turn has meant that the novel is usually linked—at least in terms of themes, wit, satire, and so forth—with the works which followed it, particularly the society comedies, and not those which preceded it. As we noted in chapter five, reinforcement for this view can be found in the reappearance in *Lady Windermere's Fan* of some of the jokes and epigrams in *Dorian Gray*. Second, as we mentioned in chapter two, if we see the early 1890s marking a change in Wilde's attitudes to his own sexuality, then biographical readings of *Dorian Gray*—in which the novel is seen as rehearsing both the pleasures and the anxieties of the more promiscuous gay life he was leading—become almost impossible to resist. As a consequence critics have looked for equally rich personal references and subtexts in the works which succeeded the novel: the idea of Wilde's "mature style" thus comes to be defined (at least in part) by its self-disclosure. This concept of his mature style, as we argued in the previous chapter, has tended to obscure the nature of the success enjoyed by the society comedies, as well as the significance of some of the late unfinished plays, which are much more personal in the themes they explore.

A final and for us more telling consequence of this narrative is that Wilde's novel is rarely seen in the context of his other works of fiction. If we view

---

continued   When the book version was eventually brought out in 1891, with six new chapters and numerous other stylistic changes, by Ward, Lock & Co. (the British publisher of *Lippincott's*), it sold slowly and relatively poorly. The first and only reprint in Wilde's lifetime, issued in 1895, was a commercial disaster, and was remaindered within a year. Yet it is hard to know whether such failure was due to the story's notoriety—that "decent" readers had indeed been put off—or whether the earlier and much cheaper periodical version had simply exhausted the market (in the winter of 1890 three specially bound numbers of *Lippincott's* had been issued with material from the earlier six months' issues: all three had "The Picture of Dorian Gray" as the lead item). Furthermore modern critics remain divided over the reasons for, and the significance of, the revisions Wilde made for the book version of his story. For some, they were an act of self-censorship, an attempt to tone down the controversial homoeroticism of the periodical text by working up the melodramatic, and more conventional, elements of the tale (the figure of James Vane, for example, does not appear in the *Lippincott's* version). Others, however, have pointed to a pragmatic need to expand that shortish periodical text to justify republication in book form, noting that some of the new material, such as the witty account of Lady Narborough's dinner and the shooting party, merely replaces one form of social provocation with another.

Dorian Gray as developing out of Wilde's career as a writer of short stories, rather than the beginning of his period of success as a dramatist, we have a much more rounded sense of Wilde's accomplishments as a writer of prose fiction as well as a firmer understanding of why the novel works as well as it does. We suggested that the unfinished plays allow us to understand that the popularity of the society comedies exists in part in their use of familiar genres and in their resistance to programmatic biographical interpretation. In a similar way, Wilde's earlier short stories help us to appreciate those powers of synthesis which define the singular achievement of *Dorian Gray*. In that novel, Wilde developed a style, unique in his *oeuvre*, in which revelation and concealment, transgression and conformity, self-conscious intellectualism and simple entertainment, are held in a perfect balance. *Dorian Gary* is simultaneously both "high" and "low" art: a popular story which entertains without any academic mediation, but one which has also provided opportunities for richly detailed scholarly commentaries.

Intertextuality and Allusion in Wilde's Fiction

It is easy to overlook the fact that, in addition to his short novel, Wilde produced three other volumes of fiction: *The Happy Prince and Other Tales* (1888), *Lord Arthur Savile's Crime and Other Stories* (1891), and *A House of Pomegranates* (1891). Although the last two books appeared after *Dorian Gray*, nearly all the stories in them had been written some years earlier—probably in the late 1880s, when most were published in magazines such as the *Court and Society Review* and the *Lady's Pictorial*. The three volumes amount to some thirteen stories; the total reaches fourteen if we include "The Portrait of Mr. W.H.," a piece which was published separately and which is also sometimes classified as criticism.

"The Portrait of Mr. W.H.": Criticism or Fiction?   Like *Dorian Gray*, "The Portrait of Mr. W.H." exists in two quite different versions. The first takes the form of a short "story" (to borrow the term which Wilde asked to be used in an advertisement for the piece) published in the July 1889 issue of *Blackwood's Monthly Magazine*. The second is a manuscript reworking of that story (currently held in the Rosenbach Foundation in Philadelphia) which consists of the marked-up periodical text with much additional material on interleaved folios. This longer version expands and complicates the story's critical elements, so it becomes less a work of prose fiction and more like the kind of writing we find in *Intentions*. However, this version was never published in Wilde's lifetime, and we cannot therefore be certain whether it represents finished work. Nonetheless, this is the text of "Mr. W.H." which most modern readers encounter, for since it was first published in 1921 by Mitchell Kennerley, it has provided the basis of several popular editions (including the text published in the Collins *Complete Works*).

Of these, however, there are probably only three or four which can lay claim to a genuine and long-lasting popularity like that of *Dorian Gray* and the society comedies. They are: the often reprinted and much anthologized "The Happy Prince" and "The Selfish Giant," now considered classics of children's fiction; "The Canterville Ghost," which has been turned into an animated film; and also (perhaps) "Lord Arthur Savile's Crime." The first two stories are probably the only works in Wilde's entire *oeuvre* which have had a life completely independent of their author, in the sense that the majority of readers (children) will have first encountered them without any knowledge of Wilde's controversial private life. In this respect, they stand as polar opposites to *Dorian Gray*, a work which, as we suggested in chapter two, is virtually impossible to read without Wilde's presence looming over every page. "The Happy Prince" and "The Selfish Giant" may also seem the least relevant to the overall argument of the present book, for an appreciation of them hardly seems to require any form of academic mediation or specialized knowledge. In particular, the spare, straightforward language of "The Selfish Giant" resists any kind of intertextual or contextual framing, although an observant reader might notice how the central motif— the solitary weeping child trapped in the wintry corner of the garden—seems to be recapitulated in *De Profundis*, when Wilde observes that "wherever there was sorrow, though but of a child in some garden weeping over a fault that it had or had not committed, the whole face of creation was completely marred" (*Complete Works*, II: 107).

To say that some of Wilde's short stories do not need academic mediation or specialist knowledge does not mean that scholars have had nothing to say about them. A modern editor of "The Happy Prince," for example, might wish to draw the (adult) reader's attention to a number of topical and literary allusions which it contains, as well as to the ways in which it rehearses images, phrases, and themes to be found in several of Wilde's later works. In other words, in this early story we can see the multiplicity of interests and styles which characterize *Dorian Gray*, but worked through in a much less sophisticated manner. So that same editor might want to comment on how the comic elements of "The Hap-

---

continued Because those same readers usually come to "Mr. W.H." after reading Wilde's better-known works, especially *Dorian Gray*, they are also inclined to understand what Wilde called his "Willie Hughes theory" as rehearsing a similarly dangerous homoeroticism. Yet in distinction to his novel, there is little evidence to suggest that Wilde's short story aroused any such suspicions in the minds of its original reviewers. It was in fact quite favourably received, and only a few reviews discussed the piece from the point of view of morality; most preferred to focus on the vexed question as to whether Wilde's story was just whimsy.

py Prince," such as the swallow's courtship of the reed—an attachment viewed
as "ridiculous" by his avian companions because the reed "has no money and
far too many relations"—echo in a rather laboured way Wilde's later satire in
both *Dorian Gray* and the society comedies on contemporary marriage customs.
She might also draw attention to the fact that the journey eastward made by the
swallow's friends makes use of imagery in Théophile Gautier's poem "Ce que
disent les hirondelles" in *Emaux et camées* (a volume Wilde knew well and to
which he also alluded several times in *Intentions*, and again in chapter fourteen of
the book version of *Dorian Gray*). Scholarly exegesis can also illuminate the significance of the reference to the "great granite throne" where "the God Memnon ... watches the stars, and when the morning star shines he utters one cry of
joy, and then is silent," a sentence which anticipates the following lines in Wilde's
poem *The Sphinx*: "Still from his chair of porphyry gaunt Memnon strains his
lidless eyes | Across the empty land, and cries each yellow morning unto Thee"
(*Complete Works*, I: 192). Moreover the Prince's description of the "young man
in a garret" with his "lips red as pomegranate" and his "large and dreamy eyes"
anticipates Wilde's later (and often more obviously homoerotic) descriptions of
male beauty which also concentrate on those facial features. Then there is the
"Art Professor's" comment on the statue of the Prince—"As he is no longer
beautiful he is no longer useful"—the surface meaning of which is enriched
by a knowledge of its contemporary reference within a complex late-Victorian debate about beauty and utility, and more particularly its connection to the
writings of William Morris, a critic of Aestheticism who argued forcefully for
a necessary connection between utility and beauty. Again these ideas are picked
up in later works, most famously in the final aphorism in the Preface to *Dorian
Gray*—that "All art is quite useless"—but also, of course, in *Intentions*.

So although "The Happy Prince" seems straightforward—it is designed, after
all, to appeal to children—academic commentary of the kind we have outlined
can help us to see traces of an ambition which exceeds the simple moralizing
of the genre which was familiar to Victorian readers of children's fiction. At the
same time, though, it also needs to be acknowledged that when we attempt to
deepen our understanding of that ambition and, say, tease out the significance of
the allusions we mentioned above, we come to a curious dead end, in the sense
that an appreciation of the story's intertextual references does little to help us
understand its main themes. "The Happy Prince" may contain the same mixture
of styles as *Dorian Gray*, combining witty social satire with conventional Christian moralizing and those elaborately sensuous descriptions which we associate
with Wilde's "purple prose," but these styles are not synthesized with anywhere
near the same subtlety, sophistication, and elegance. We can better appreciate this
distinction by comparing the uses Wilde makes of the same source—Gautier's
Emaux et camées—in both works.

In "The Happy Prince," the swallow is talking to the Prince about his impatience to migrate south and east, and the terms which he uses to describe the attractions of Egypt are familiar elements in what readers have come to recognize in Wilde's later works as a Decadent lexicon: that is, a concentration on rare and precious jewels, on unfamiliar flora and fauna, on strange peoples, and on mysterious buildings and artifacts:

> "I am waited for in Egypt," answered the Swallow. "To-morrow my friends will fly up to the Second Cataract. The river-horse couches there among the bulrushes, and on a great granite throne sits the God Memnon. All night long he watches the stars, and when the morning star shines he utters one cry of joy, and then he is silent. At noon the yellow lions come down to the water's edge to drink. They have eyes like green beryls, and their roar is louder than the roar of the cataract." (Ross, ed., *A House of Pomegranates*, 175)

And a little later:

> "In Egypt the sun is warm on the green palm-trees, and the crocodiles lie in the mud and look lazily about them. My companions are building a nest in the Temple of Baalbec, and the pink and white doves are watching them, and cooing to each other. Dear Prince, I must leave you, but I will never forget you, and next spring I will bring you back two beautiful jewels in place of those you have given away. The ruby shall be redder than a red rose, and the sapphires shall be as blue as the great sea." (Ross, ed., *A House of Pomegranates*, 177–78)

And finally:

> He told him of the red ibises, who stand in long rows on the banks of the Nile, and catch gold fish in their beaks; of the Sphinx, who is as old as the world itself, and lives in the desert, and knows everything; of the merchants, who walk slowly by the side of their camels, and carry amber beads in their hand; of the King of the Mountains of the Moon, who is as black as ebony, and worships a large crystal; of the great green snake that sleeps in a palm-tree, and has twenty priests to feed it with honey-cakes; and of the pygmies who sail over a big lake on large flat leaves, and are always at war with the butterflies. (Ross, ed., *A House of Pomegranates*, 179)

At one level, these images are being used in the service of a typical, and typically unspecific, Victorian Orientalism, whose function has nothing to do with the actuality of Egypt, but merely represents a familiar Victorian "other." In the story it stands as a colourful, sensual, and exotic alternative to the grim "ugliness" and "misery"—as the narrator puts it—of the Prince's recognizably late-Victorian English city. But we might pertinently ask what difference it makes if we are alert to the fact that parts of that description—for example, the reference to the "Second Cataract" and "Temple of Baalbec"—originated in a poem by Gautier. What particular "point" does the allusion give to that generalized or unspecific Orientalism?

Most obviously a recognition of the allusion serves to remind the (adult) reader that the exoticism of the East also involved what the philistine "Town Councillors" in "The Happy Prince" would have considered sexual "otherness"—that is, those forms of desire that were forbidden in Victorian Britain. In French Decadent authors like Gautier the sensual appreciation of beautiful and rare objects, such as precious gems or statuary, is usually eroticized. In turn that appreciation is identified with an interest in uncommon forms of sexuality, such as hermaphroditism. That Wilde was fully aware of this quality of Gautier's writing, that he knew it was part of Gautier's attraction for him, and that he expected most adult readers to share that reading experience, can be seen in a somewhat supercilious letter, written a couple of years later to the *Daily Chronicle* in defence of *Dorian Gray*, in which he paired *Emaux et camées* with the "*Satyricon* of Petronius Arbiter," explaining that both were "literary books ... that any fairly educated reader may be supposed to be acquainted with" (*Complete Letters*, 436).

The allusion to Gautier in "The Happy Prince" might thus lead the informed (and again adult) reader to recall the role which the "foreignness" of Egypt could have played in the lives of middle-class and aristocratic Victorian homosexuals. The modern reader might also recollect the role Egypt played in the sexual life of Douglas, and how it was to provide him with a temporary escape from the constricting censure of Victorian morality. However, if we are predisposed to think of the allure of the East in these terms, then we must also acknowledge that the story (like Wilde's society comedies) leaves little space for such hints to be developed. For the attractions of the East (whatever they are) are invoked only to be systematically dismissed. In the conclusion of the story Egypt is displaced by what is presented as an altogether more noble and permanent alternative to the hard-heartedness of Victorian London, that Christian transfiguration to be found in "the garden of Paradise." Moreover, the Prince is only able to enter that garden when (with the swallow's help) he has given away all his exotic worldly goods, his jewelled features, and the gold leaf that covers his body.

What Wilde appears to be doing with his French source is appropriating its Decadent images, but in so doing removing those values which gave French Decadence its suggestive power—its ability to subvert and provoke. In this respect Wilde's use of Gautier in "The Happy Prince" has a recognizably "British" quality, familiar from contemporary British dramatists' use of the French well-made play, or from contemporary British novelists' use of French naturalism. Despite its criticism of Victorian materialism, Wilde's tale—like all fairy tales—is at heart conservative; its moral is that self-denial on earth is rewarded in heaven. In contrast to what we see in *Dorian Gray*, Wilde seems not yet to have been able to integrate Decadent themes into a conventional morality while simultaneously leaving the values of both intact. This of course explains why "The Happy Prince" has a straightforward and uncomplicated appeal to the child reader; it also explains why academics can "do" relatively little with it. Teasing out the literary allusions and explaining Wilde's use of French Decadent imagery does not alter our sense of the story's moral, because that imagery does not disrupt the tale's hierarchy of discourse. To put this another way: a knowledge that the images are imported from Gautier does not change the way we view their narrative function.

This limitation—if that is the right word—becomes clear if we compare Wilde's later use of exactly the same source in chapter fourteen of the book version of *Dorian Gray* (chapter twelve of the *Lippincott's* text).[3]

> He sighed, and took up the volume again, and tried to forget. He read of the swallows that fly in and out of the little café at Smyrna where the Hadjis sit counting their amber beads and the turbaned merchants smoke their long tasselled pipes and talk gravely to each other; he read of the Obelisk in the Place de la Concorde that weeps tears of granite in its lonely sunless exile, and longs to be back by the hot lotus-covered Nile, where there are Sphinxes, and rose-red ibises, and white vultures with gilded claws, and crocodiles, with small beryl eyes, that crawl over the green steaming mud; he began to brood over those verses which, drawing music from kiss-stained marble, tell of that curious statue that Gautier compares to a contralto voice, the "*monstre charmant*" that couches in the porphyry-room of the Louvre. But after a time the book fell from his hand. He grew nervous, and a horrible fit of terror came over him. (*Complete Works*, III: 305)

Wilde's Ideal Reader   When Wilde felt obliged to defend works which had been labelled immoral—that is, principally *Dorian Gray* and his second volume of fairy tales, *A House of Pomegranates*—his tactic was typically to question the intelligence of the reviewer by claiming that any "fairly educated reader" or "fairly educated person" would have no difficulty at all in understanding his work. This may seem an odd tactic, given that it was precisely the allusiveness of his writing—its intertextual quality—which gave it its suggestive power: we gain more insight into Dorian's character from what he reads than from what he does. But Wilde's concept of "education" meant more than simply catholic reading, ploughing through what he termed in *Intentions* "the monstrous multitudinous books that the world has produced." Much more important was the attitude with which one read, particularly when it came to "literary" books. As Gilbert explains: "We, in our educational system, have burdened the memory with a load of unconnected facts, and laboriously striven to impart our laboriously acquired knowledge. We teach people how to remember, we never teach them how to grow. It has never occurred to us to try and develop in the mind a more subtle quality of apprehension and discernment" (Ross, ed., *Intentions*, 216). From this perspective, being "fairly educated" meant reading with an attitude appropriately receptive to the works to which Wilde alludes. In the case of literary art, this meant (as Wilde explained in a pithy but unpublished epigram) that "in the presence of a work of art the public should applaud and the journalist be silent" (*Oscar Wilde Revalued*, 131).

The passage occurs shortly after Dorian has killed Basil Hallward. While he is waiting for Alan Campbell to arrive to help him dispose of the corpse, he takes up a book as a distraction, to forget that "the dead man was still sitting there." The nature of that reading has in turn already been indicated very precisely. In the preceding paragraphs we have been told that the particular book which Dorian has in front of him, given to him by a young male friend, Adrian Singleton, is *Emaux et camées* in "Charpentier's Japanese-paper edition, with the Jacquemart etching." Wilde is thus not only explicitly signposting his allusion, but he is also placing it in a very obvious context: Dorian's reading habits are being defined in recognizably Decadent terms, as a form of connoisseurship. Decadent too is his manner of reading, a dreamy self-immersion and forgetting—he pauses, from time to time, to reflect upon certain lines with "half-closed eyes"—and this blurs the distinction between the world he is inhabiting (where he is a murderer) and the world he is imagining. The suggestive power of that reading can be seen in the fact that the selfsame edition of *Emaux et camées*, with its "eau-forte par Jacquemart," was still available for Ezra Pound to use in his 1920 poem *Hugh Selwyn Mauberley* as an evocation of a decadent life.

Just before trying to lose himself in the exoticism of Gautier's East, Dorian has read aloud—and Wilde has quoted—some verses from another poem in *Emaux et camées*, "Variations sur le Carnaval de Venise." The first stanza that Dorian reads plays upon images of water and upon the juxtaposition of red and white: "*Sur une gamme chromatique, | Le sein de perles ruisselant, | Le Vénus de l'Adriatique | Sort de l'eau son corps rose et blanc*" ("As though upon a chromatic scale, her pearly breast streaming, the Venus of the Adriatic emerges from the waters, her body red and white"; *Complete Works*, III: 304). The red and white images of these lines in turn call to mind Basil's final conversation with Dorian (in the preceding chapter) before he was stabbed. Horrified by what had happened to Dorian, Basil had suggested that they should "pray" together, quoting from Isaiah 1:18: "Though your sins be scarlet, yet I will make them white as snow." Basil's injunction of course fails, and it is difficult not to see this failure partly as a function of rhetoric: Basil can unfortunately remember only fragments from the Bible. Alongside the verse from Isaiah, he mentions a line or two from the Lord's Prayer—"Lead us not into temptation. Forgive us our sins"—and a phrase from the *Lavabo* prayer of the Mass—"Wash away our iniquities" (*Complete Works*, III: 299).

These spare phrases of Christian forgiveness have thus to compete for attention with the rich sensuality of Gautier's verse which Dorian will go on to quote and paraphrase at length. In contrast to "The Happy Prince," then, here the relationship between the values of Decadent art (Gautier) and of Victorian morality (the Bible) seems much more finely poised. And it is in this context that the reader encounters the Orientalism in the passage we quoted above from chapter fourteen; it is part of a discourse which has been opposed to, but not superseded by, conventional Christian piety. Its attraction thus remains intact, at least until Dorian's musings are rudely interrupted by the "horrible fit of terror" which forcefully reminds him, and the reader, of "the dead thing" upstairs.

A further difference between the use of *Emaux et camées* in "The Happy Prince" and *Dorian Gray* is that Dorian's paraphrase of Gautier's poems explicitly foregrounds the oscillation between an imagined Egypt and the source of that imagining—a contemporary, if Decadent, Paris ("the Obelisk in the Place de la Concorde" and the "porphyry-room of the Louvre").[4] In this way, the "otherness" of the East is made more tangible and less foreign, and also, therefore, more dangerous—a movement opposite to that which takes place in "The Happy Prince." (There is, of course, a long tradition in Victorian literature of using France and French culture to represent various freedoms—artistic, political, and sexual—that were unavailable to British subjects.) As the swallow grows weaker, the possibility of his reaching Egypt recedes and in the process the power of those pleasures which it represents is diminished. However, Dorian's self-absorbed reading brings Eastern exoticism progressively closer, locating it (in the culmination of the passage) in a statue which some of Wilde's readers, and certainly Wilde himself, would have seen.

The "*monstre charmant*" in the Louvre which Gautier describes in his poem "Contralto" (also in *Emaux et camées*) was popularly known as the "Sleeping Hermaphrodite." The phrase Wilde quotes occurs in the following lines which make explicit the transgressive eroticism of the Decadent imagery: "Monstre charmant, comme je t'aime | Avec ta multiple beauté!" ("Charming monster, how I love you with your multiple beauty!").[5] We can get a useful sense of the symbolic value of that statue in late-nineteenth-century British culture from the poet Algernon Charles Swinburne. Another admirer of *Emaux et camées*, Swinburne had written his own poem in celebration of the statue, entitled "Hermaphroditus" and published in his 1866 collection *Poems and Ballads*. That volume had in turn been the subject of a series of vitriolic and highly personal attacks, with "Hermaphroditus" singled out for condemnation. In a vigorous defence of his work, published in the same year in a pamphlet entitled *Notes on Poems and Reviews*, Swinburne attempted, in a manner similar to Wilde's later defence of *Dorian Gray*, to turn the language of his detractors against them, provocatively accusing them of harbouring a "rottenness" beneath their prudery:

> There is nothing lovelier, as there is nothing more famous, in later Hellenic art, than the statue of Hermaphroditus.... [T]he delicate divinity of this work has always drawn towards it the eyes of artists and poets. A creature at once foul and dull enough to extract from a sight so lovely, from a thing so noble, the faintest, the most fleeting idea of impurity, must be, and must remain, below comprehension and below remark. It is incredible that the meanest of men should derive from it any other than the sense of high and grateful pleasure.... I am not the first who has translated into written verse this

sculptured poem: another before me, as he says, has more than once "caressed it with a sculptor's love." ... I cannot see why this statue should not be the text for yet another poem. Treated in the grave and chaste manner as a serious "thing of beauty," to be for ever applauded and enjoyed, it can give no offence but to the purblind and the prurient.... [U]nclean and inhuman the animal which could suck from this mystical rose of ancient loveliness the foul and rancid juices of an obscene fancy. It were a scavenger's office to descend with torch or spade into such depths of mental sewerage, to plunge or peer into subterranean sloughs of mind impossible alike to enlighten or to cleanse.[6]

At this point we might note that Wilde uses exactly the same allusion to Gautier's poem in "Pen, Pencil, and Poison" when he describes the personality of another murderer, Thomas Griffiths Wainewright: "like Gautier, he [Wainewright] was fascinated by that 'sweet marble monster' of both sexes that we can still see at Florence and in the Louvre" (Ross, ed., *Intentions*, 68).[7]

In both "Pen, Pencil, and Poison" and *Dorian Gray* a character's tastes in art are presented as identical with a fascination with crime; yet they are simultaneously also a justification, or mitigation, for that criminality. It is precisely Dorian's and Wainewright's "superior" aesthetic sensibility which prevents them from being seen just as murderers (as simple stage villains from a melodrama), and this in turn maintains our interest in them as characters. Moreover, the reader needs to know something about the sort of writer Gautier was, and his reputation among late-nineteenth-century British readers, in order to understand the nature of the connection between the values which his writing celebrated and the characters of Dorian and Wainewright. (After all, Dorian could hardly have escaped the horrors of his situation in the same way by reading a three-decker novel.) At the same time, however, this does not mean that the reader who knows nothing about Gautier, or who is insensitive to (or repelled by) the verses which Dorian quotes, necessarily misunderstands this particular episode in the novel: that sort of reader will simply come to a different and more melodramatic conclusion about Dorian's actions. Probably he or she will be appalled that he can even think of reading poetry—any poetry—with a dead man upstairs. The skill of Wilde's writing is that it allows for both sorts of readings, and both sorts of responses to Decadent art, to be simultaneously available to readers.

In comparing "The Happy Prince" to *Dorian Gray* we can see how in the later work Wilde is able to exploit the subversive potential of Decadence through a more sophisticated manipulation of its allusive and intertextual nature. This in turn helps to explain why such a popular and entertaining novel can also repay the dense scholarly commentary that it has attracted: the deeper one investigates the literary allusions, the more morally ambiguous, and thus more "modern," the work becomes. By contrast, teasing out the allusions in "The Happy Prince" only reinforces its conservatism. The full nature of Wilde's achievement can be better appreciated by a comparison with another of Wilde's short stories, "The Fisherman and His Soul," in which he seems to be striving for the same effect he was to achieve in *Dorian Gray*—that is, for a similar kind of moral ambiguity in which the distinction between sinfulness and goodness is collapsed into a concept of beauty. This story, however, has proved to be much less popular than "The Happy Prince."

Experimenting with Decadence

"The Fisherman and His Soul" is Wilde's longest, most complex, and most ambitious short story. It was first published in 1891 in his second volume of fairy tales, *A House of Pomegranates*, a book which sold poorly, and which received lukewarm reviews. The tale had had its origins some years earlier: significantly, it seems to have begun life as a possible contribution to the Philadelphia-based journal, *Lippincott's Monthly Magazine*. Wilde had been commissioned around August 1889 to write a story for that publication by the managing editor, James Stoddart, who was in Britain attempting to find material by promising young British and Irish authors. At the end of September, Stoddart wrote to Wilde to chase up his commission. Wilde, complaining of illness, equivocated; he later wrote that he was "unable to finish" the story he had begun and was "not satisfied with it as far as it goes." A letter dated 17 December reveals the identity of this first piece: Wilde now claimed that he had "invented a new story, which is better than 'The Fisherman and his Soul'" (*Complete Letters*, 414, 416). That new story was, of course, "The Picture of Dorian Gray," which Stoddart went on to publish in the summer of 1890. The problematic unfinished story, "The Fisherman and His Soul," was almost certainly set aside for some months, and unlike most of Wilde's other short stories, it was not published in a periodical form.

That *Dorian Gray* developed out of Wilde's work on "The Fisherman and His Soul" goes some way to explaining the thematic and stylistic similarities between the two works, particularly that interest in presenting sinfulness and goodness as just two sides of the same coin—or, as Wilde would later call them, different modes of life to be realized. (We have already seen the same pattern emerging in the unfinished *The Cardinal of Avignon* and *La Sainte Courtisane*.) In both novel and story the narrative invites us to identify and sympathize with the feelings of the main protagonists, both of whom are beautiful young men (the fisherman, like Dorian, is described as a "pretty boy"); in addition both are tempted to part with their souls in order that they might follow desires which their society judges to be transgressive. For Dorian this means pursuing the "new Hedonism" proselytized by Lord Henry, and for the fisherman it means pursuing his love for one of the "Sea-folk." Dorian's liberation comes about via the magical properties of Basil's portrait of him. The fisherman, in a reversal of the Hans Christian Andersen tale it draws upon, is able to cut away his soul from his body with a magic knife given to him by a witch. Both young men find that in some senses they have made a pact with the Devil, and both are haunted by the consciences they have tried to leave behind. Dorian has the changing picture in his attic, which he is unable to ignore; the fisherman is three times confronted by his soul, which finally succeeds in returning (unwanted) to the fisherman's body. Both characters also find that the self which continues to haunt them is frighteningly cruel: the picture, for Dorian, becomes increasingly "loathsome" (*Complete Works*, III: 356); the fisherman's soul, without a heart, is transformed into "an evil Soul" (Ross, ed., *A House of Pomegranates*, 118). At the end of both stories body and soul are reunited, although on both occasions the price of that union is the death of the main character. When attempting to free himself from the picture's influence, Dorian unwittingly stabs and kills himself; the fisherman, in a final show of defiance towards his soul, refuses to flee from the encroaching waves and is drowned while kissing "with mad lips the cold lips of the mermaid" (Ross, ed., *A House of Pomegranates*, 126).

In both stories the richly enticing sensual world "of the body" (as it is termed in "The Fisherman and His Soul") is opposed by a judgmental Christianity represented, respectively, by Basil and the priest. In both fables the young male protagonists consistently ignore the advice and remonstrations of that older male authority, and although they both die for their transgressions, neither fully regrets the choice they have made. The moral agency of those figures of authority is thus significantly diminished: Basil dies virtually inarticulate and unnoticed by society; the priest finds himself "troubled" by the spectres of the dead fisherman and his mermaid lover, and is not able afterwards to preach "of the wrath of God," but only "of the God whose name is Love" (Ross, ed., *A House of Pomegranates*, 128). In this sense, then, the death of the transgressive figure does not represent a straightforward triumph of good over evil. Rather—and in a manner which anticipates Wilde's account of Christ's attitude to sin in *De Profundis*—the values of a transgressive life remain intact, even in disgrace or death.

A further similarity between the novel and story lies in the way in which Wilde registers the realm of the body, for desire takes two distinct forms in both works. There is the all-consuming and self-annihilating yearning for an unattainable other—or simply "Love," as it is termed in both novel and story. Examples of this kind of devotion are to be found in Sybil's idolization of Dorian and in the fisherman's adoration of the mermaid. We can also note here that, despite the thematic importance of this idealized and idealizing form of (hetero)sexual love, Wilde—as in the unfinished plays which we discussed in chapter five—seems relatively uninterested in exploring its specificity. In *Dorian Gray* most of the narrative, particularly in the *Lippincott's* version, focuses on Dorian's relationships with Lord Henry and Basil (rather than with Sybil). In the same way, in "The Fisherman and His Soul," the fisherman's transactions with the priest and his soul are recounted in considerable detail, but his emotional relationship with the mermaid is a complete blank—when he plunges into the waves to join the "Sea-folk" he simply disappears from the reader's view. It is thus the drama of a young man's confrontation with forms of male authority that (again as in the unfinished plays) provides the dynamic of both novel and story.

Alongside "Love," novel and story also describe a more generalized kind of desire, a longing for sensual gratification which typically takes the form of a covetousness, whether of art objects, of "curiosities" (a favourite Wildean term which appears in both works), or of increasingly rarefied experiences. Moreover, this form of desire is also explicitly empowering, an aspiration to dominate others which stands in obvious opposition to the sense of "wonder" and unworthiness that accompanies "Love." As Sybil explains to her mother: "why does he [Dorian] love me so much?... [W]hat does he see in me? I am not worthy of him" (*Complete Works*, III: 222); and as the fisherman says to the mermaid: "I will be thy bridegroom ... and all that thou desirest I shall do" (Ross, ed., *A House of Pomegranates*, 72). We see this second kind of desire in Dorian's frenetic pursuit of "sensations that would be at once new and delightful, and possess the element of strangeness that is essential to romance" (*Complete Works*, III: 280), as well as in the exotic "marvels" with which the soul tries to tempt the fisherman. In both story and novel Wilde seems interested in setting these two forms of desire—one static and selfless, and the other dynamic and selfish—against each other, but the effect achieved is different in each case, and it is this difference which in turn helps us to understand both why *Dorian Gray* is the more successful work, and why Wilde may have been unsatisfied with "The Fisherman and His Soul."

In the novel the language of "Love" is also the language of melodrama; this language brings with it melodrama's fixed concepts of good and evil. However, melodrama, as we noted earlier, is not a particularly sophisticated subgenre, and for this reason the values it embodies, though conventionally "worthy," are not necessarily to be taken too seriously. So Sybil's death may be tragic, but the reader's ability to respond to her as a victim is consistently undermined by the novel's social satire, and more particularly by the flippant way in which Lord Henry treats Dorian's emotional entanglement. He comments to Dorian at one point: "I was afraid I would find you plunged in remorse, and tearing that nice curly hair of yours" (*Complete Works*, III: 251). In a similar manner, Dorian's impassioned description of his romance with Sybil, of her "little flower-like face ... small Greek head with plaited coils of dark-brown hair, eyes that were violet wells of passion, lips that were like the petal of a rose," is met by Lord Henry's withering (and Wilde's famous) paradox: "When one is in love, one always begins by deceiving one's self, and one always ends by deceiving others. That is what the world calls romance" (*Complete Works*, III: 213–14). By contrast, the language of personal gratification is conspicuously Decadent: sophisticated and allusive, as well as verbally extravagant, it is in itself a form of seduction, both sensual and intellectual. And this in turn is why it is difficult to dismiss the various temptations to which Dorian falls prey, even as we recognize their devastating effects on his character. So, for example, the *tour de force* that is chapter eleven (chapter nine in the *Lippincott's* version) of *Dorian Gray*, in which Dorian's pursuit of the "new Hedonism" is so richly laid out for the reader, is much more eloquently suggestive than the few words that Sybil can muster to describe her self-denying love, even though we recognize the moral rightness of her assertion that "love is more than money" (*Complete Works*, III: 221). Another way of putting this is to say that much of the richness of reading *Dorian Gray*, that plurality to which we referred earlier, derives from the way in which Wilde's use of different styles, with their different rhetorical effects, disturbs our ability to make judgments about the various kinds of desire he is portraying.

"The Fisherman and His Soul," by contrast, does not have this stylistic complexity or, indeed, any stylistic variation: all the ways of describing desire—the fisherman's love for the mermaid as well as the soul's search for a rival to that love—employ the same Decadent language. Moreover, as in "The Happy Prince," that language is straightforwardly aligned with the narrative voice: it is the descriptive technique which is employed throughout the whole story. Furthermore, none of the images is mediated via clearly signposted allusions. So even though it is clear (from the comparisons with *Dorian Gray*) that Wilde's descriptions of the soul's exotic journeys to the East were influenced by his reading of Gautier and of works such as J.-K. Huysmans's *A Rebours*, these are not debts which he wished to acknowledge. We are not, in other words, explicitly invited to understand the exotic worlds and experiences which the story invokes as possessing the ambiguous values of Decadence, even though they are described in recognizably Decadent terms. And this results in a moral confusion, one quite different from the moral pluralism of *Dorian Gray*. For example, the fisherman falls in love with the mermaid chiefly because of her great beauty; and the manner in which that beauty is described, in the cadence of the phrasing, its repetitions, and the choice of modifiers, would not be out of place in *Salome*:

> Her hair was as a wet fleece of gold, and each separate hair as a thread of fine gold in a cup of glass. Her body was as white as ivory, and her tail was of silver and pearl. Silver and pearl was her tail, and the green weeds of the sea coiled round it; and like sea-shells were her ears, and her lips were like sea-coral. The cold waves dashed over her cold breasts, and the salt glistened upon her eyelids. (Ross, ed., *A House of Pomegranates*, 68)

Similarly the underwater world which the mermaid inhabits, and of which she sings to the fisherman, is described in terms of familiar Decadent exotica—that is, of rare stones, of remote and precious flora and fauna:

> [S]he sang of ... the palace of the King which is all of amber, with a roof of clear emerald, and a pavement of bright pearl; and of the gardens of the sea where the great filigrane fans of coral wave all day long, and the fish dart about like silver birds, and the

anemones cling to the rocks, and the pinks burgeon in the ribbed yellow sand. (Ross, ed., *A House of Pomegranates*, 70–71)

Confusingly, however, the various other "worlds" which the story invokes are described using exactly the same type of language. So the description of the Devil who appears at the witches' Sabbath is not very different from that of the mysterious "Sea-folk" whom the priest must learn to bless (and not different either from the descriptions of male beauty that we find elsewhere in Wilde's *oeuvre*):

> His [the Devil's] face was strangely pale, but his lips were like a proud red flower.... On the grass beside him lay a plumed hat, and a pair of riding-gloves gauntleted with gilt lace, and sewn with seed-pearls wrought into a curious device. A short cloak lined with sables hung from his shoulder, and his delicate white hands were gemmed with rings. (Ross, ed., *A House of Pomegranates*, 83–84)

Similar again are the sensual delights of those faraway places with which the soul tempts the fisherman to win him back from the mermaid. For example, when the soul travels to the East he comes across a garden where

> The priests in their yellow robes moved silently through the green trees, and on a pavement of black marble stood the rose-red house in which the god had his dwelling. Its doors were of powdered lacquer, and bulls and peacocks were wrought on them in raised and polished gold. The tiled roof was of sea green porcelain, and the jutting eaves were festooned with little bells. When the white doves flew past, they struck the bells with their wings and made them tinkle. (Ross, ed., *A House of Pomegranates*, 95)

Inside this house he is shown an "idol standing on a lotus of jade hung with great emeralds. It was carved out of ivory.... On its forehead was a chrysolite, and its breasts were smeared with myrrh and cinnamon. In one hand it held a crooked sceptre of jade, and in the other a round crystal. It ware buskins of brass, and its thick neck was circled with a circle of selenites" (Ross, ed., *A House of Pomegranates*, 97). The long descriptions of the soul's three journeys, where Wilde heaps up image upon exotic image, can seem self-indulgent, diversions from the main narrative.

One senses that Wilde enjoyed writing virtuoso passages of this sort; they have an element of exhibitionism in them and (like the draft of *La Sainte Courtisane*) a freestanding quality, which would enable them to be easily transferred to other works. One can, for example, see obvious similarities between the descriptions of the soul's journeys and the list of "treasures" which Dorian collects in chapter eleven of *Dorian Gray*—that is, those "jewels" and "stories about jewels," embroideries, and tapestries. The problem, however, with such stylized writing in "The Fisherman and His Soul" is that the soul's accounts of its travels do not provide a sufficient contrast with what has gone before: it is indistinguishable in style from the descriptions of the world inhabited by the mermaid and fisherman, and this makes it difficult for the reader to appreciate the nobility of the fisherman's love. Although we understand that such love is "better than wisdom, and more precious than riches, and fairer than the feet of the daughters of men," how can the reader not be struck by the fact that in wanting to be constant to his mermaid, with her enticing "mauve-amethyst eyes" and her enchanting undersea life, the fisherman has chosen a "valley of pleasure" which is little different from the temptations offered him by his soul. In the story's terms, the world of selfless love and the world of sensual gratification are too similar: both seem equally exotic, equally foreign to that everyday world where, as the priest puts it, "love of the body is vile." Or, to adapt again Wilde's biblical language from *De Profundis*, the fruits of the trees in all parts of the garden seem to taste alarmingly the same.

This blurring of categories is further reinforced when, at the end of the story, the priest is so overcome by the "strange" and "curious" beauty of the white flowers that have come from the unhallowed ground where the mermaid and fisherman are buried, that he feels compelled to bless "the sea, and all the wild things that are in it" (Ross, ed., *A House of Pomegranates*, 127, 129). "Strange" and "curious," we should remember, are also terms used to describe the Devil. The reader is thus left unsure about what sort of wildness exactly—what sort of bodily desire—the priest's blessing is actually endorsing, diabolic or romantic. ("Wild" things also remind us of the author's own name, and his own kind of Wilde-ness.) It needs to be reiterated that this uncertainty is different from the moral relativism of *Dorian Gray*. In the novel we see clearly that there is a difference between Sybil's "Love" and Dorian's self-gratification; our difficulty (and our reading pleasure) resides in trying to decipher which form, if any, of desire the novel is actually endorsing. And this is why it has proved possible to make sense of *Dorian Gray* both as a conventional morality tale and as its opposite, a celebration of an amoral hedonism.

The problem in "The Fisherman and His Soul" is knowing what exactly is meant by the kind of love which fills "the people with joy and wonder": we are not so much choosing between alternative moral codes (the priest, we should remember, has been converted from his rigid Christianity), as trying to work out what constitutes this "strange" morality of "the heart" (Ross, ed., *A House of Pomegranates*, 129). The story appears to suggest that it is the *quality* of an individual's love—that it can be defined by constancy and fidelity—which is paramount, and that the experience of loving is thus much more important than the worth of the loved object. Such a conclusion can of course be affiliated to a humane Christianity, one which emphasizes (as the priest learns to do, and Wilde later did in *De Profundis*) the inclusive forgiveness and suffering of Christ: "*All* the things in God's world he blessed" (including "wild(e) things"). But, as the Decadent imagery so insistently reminds those readers who recognize its origins, that same view of love can also be used to legitimate same-sex

desire, or indeed any form of desire that is maintained with intensity and loyalty—or, in terms with which the 1890s would have been familiar, maintained
with that Paterian "hard gem-like flame." In this way what is conventionally
considered sinful can quickly become its "other," something beautiful and good.
Thus sinfulness and goodness, as in *La Sainte Courtisane*, become interchangeable
terms. Here we might recall how this same idea is briefly rehearsed in the closing chapter of *Dorian Gray* when Dorian nostalgically remembers Lord Henry's
description of the "unstained purity of his boyhood" as "rose-white" (*Complete
Works*, III: 354). That oxymoronic image recalls the Decadent "rose et blanc"
body of Venus in Gautier's poem. But just as insistently it also reminds us of
the Christian imagery which runs through the novel, in which white and red
exist as opposites—of how "scarlet sins" can be made "white as snow," but only
through a transfiguring act of repentance and through God's grace.

   Although we can understand why Wilde might have been interested in
exploring such an idea—this combining of sin with its opposite—it is possible
that he realized that the way in which the idea is presented in his story was just
too "strong" (to use Macmillan's term) for nineteenth-century readers' tastes,
particularly for a family magazine like *Lippincott's*. We do not know how much
of his story he had completed when he wrote to Stoddart claiming that he was
"not satisfied with it as far as it goes." Nor do we know exactly what about it
displeased him. But it is tempting to speculate that he was beginning to realize
the artistic limitations of Decadence, certainly for commercial writing addressed
to ordinary readers, or to what Wilde disparagingly termed at about this time
"public opinion." When used as the sole mode of narrative description, it was
too suggestive. A contemporary reviewer glimpsed this when he knowingly
complained that the "pretty poetic and imaginative flights" of the stories in *A
House of Pomegranates* "wandered off too often into something between a 'Sinburnian' ecstasy and the catalogue of a high art furniture dealer."[8]

   To make his exploration of sin and beauty acceptable to a wider reading public—a public which either did not know, or if it did know did not approve of,
the "Sinburnian" quality of Decadent writing—Wilde needed to find a narrative foil for it. Here it may be worth recalling the difficulties he experienced over
his other "fully" Decadent works: *Salome* was never performed on the English
stage in his lifetime, *La Sainte Courtisane* and *The Cardinal of Avignon* were never
finished, and *The Sphinx* took years to complete, and when published sold only
in very small numbers. Of course Wilde found that foil in *Dorian Gray*; his method there was to combine Decadence with social satire and the more straightforward moralizing of melodrama: taken together, these last two styles, as we have
shown, allowed for a conservative and morally "safe" reading of the novel. Yet
they did so without wholly obliterating the subversive implications of its Decadent origins. Interestingly we seem to see Wilde "rehearsing" or experiment-

ing with such a stylistic synthesis in the other stories in *A House of Pomegranates*, particularly in "The Young King" and "The Birthday of the Infanta." It is worth examining them in detail, as they shed further light on the full nature of Wilde's achievement in *Dorian Gray*.

The Development of Wilde's Mature Style

Both "The Young King" and "The Birthday of the Infanta" had their first publication in magazines, in the *Lady's Pictorial* in 1888 and *Paris Illustré* in 1889, and were thus almost certainly written before "The Fisherman and his Soul," and probably just a little after "The Happy Prince." These details serve to remind us just how compelling Wilde was beginning to find Decadent imagery and themes, and how often he attempted to find an appropriate place for them in his own writing.

"The Young King" has elements familiar from both *Dorian Gray* and "The Happy Prince." So we learn that "curious" stories are told about the protagonist; he is in turn described in ways that suggest a prototype for Dorian Gray. He is discovered "gazing, as one in a trance, at a Greek gem carved with the figure of Adonis," and on another occasion "pressing his lips to the marble brow of an antique statue ... inscribed with the name of the Bithynian slave of Hadrian" (Ross, ed., *A House of Pomegranates*, 7). That slave, as any of the story's classically educated adult readers would have recognized, is Antinoüs, the beautiful page boy of the Roman emperor Hadrian, who, according to legend, drowned in the Nile in order to save Hadrian's life. (Wilde, or his publishers, wavered between the forms "Antinoüs" and "Antinous": both are correct.) The page was a favourite subject of sculptors and appeared—as a select few of Wilde's adult readers would also have known—in a number of works by late-nineteenth-century gay writers, for example, in John Addington Symonds's "The Lotus-Garland of Antinoüs" in *Many Moods: A Volume of Verses* (1878). Wilde himself had earlier described Antinoüs's beauty in much more obviously homoerotic terms in his poem "The Burden of Itys": "And through the vale with sad voluptuous smile | Antinous had wandered, the red lotus of the Nile | Down leaning from his black and clustering hair, | To shade those slumberous eyes' caverned bliss" (*Complete Works*, I: 65). Reading these lines might prompt us to recall that the Orientalism imagined by Dorian also involved a longing to be back by the "hot lotus-covered Nile." Later in *The Sphinx* Wilde would write of how the Sphinx "heard from Adrian's gilded barge the laughter of Antinous ... and watched with hot and hungry stare | The ivory mouth of that rare young slave with his pomegranate mouth!" (*Complete Works*, I: 183). And Antinoüs represents one of Basil Hallward's artistic ideals when he comments that "what the invention of oil-painting was to the Venetians, the face of Antinoüs was to late Greek sculpture" (*Complete Works*, III: 176).

The Young King's Decadent credentials are strengthened by the fact that he is also intensely preoccupied with "all rare and costly materials," particularly his coronation robe "of tissued gold, and the ruby-studded crown, and sceptre with its rows and rings of pearls." As in so many of Wilde's descriptions of young male beauty, the King has a feral quality; he has "boyish lips" and "dark woodland eyes," and he is surrounded by the familiar array of beautiful and striking objects, including "a large press, inlaid with agate and lapis-lazuli," "a curiously wrought cabinet with lacquer panels of powdered and mosaiced gold, on which were placed some delicate goblets of Venetian glass, and a cup of dark-veined onyx," a "laughing Narcissus in green bronze," and "a flat bowl of amethyst" (Ross, ed., *A House of Pomegranates*, 9). Narcissus, too, was one of Wilde's favourite classical images of male beauty; he often called Alfred Douglas Narcissus, and—as we might by now expect—in *Dorian Gray* Lord Henry describes Dorian to Basil as "a Narcissus." Then, in a manner similar to "The Happy Prince," this conspicuous and "strange" luxury is juxtaposed with a series of images (presented to the King in three dreams) of the poverty and degradation of those who produce the goods he so carelessly enjoys. These images, some conveyed in quasi-biblical language, lead the King to renounce his riches and to clothe himself—Christlike, and (as we might again anticipate) against the advice of his bishop, that familiar older figure of male authority—in the garments of a humble goatherd. This humility is rewarded by a Christian apotheosis: the final image of him is of a man with "the face of an angel" upon whom no one dares look.

"Sinburnianism" In calling Wilde's writing "Sinburnian" reviewers were punning on the reputation of an earlier and equally controversial writer, Algernon Charles Swinburne, once called "the libidinous laureate" by John Morley, himself an eminent, if radical, Victorian. The label "Sinburnian" had been applied to Swinburne's *Poems and Ballads* (1866), a volume whose publication had met with unusually hostile reviews, with its author being accused of paganism, blasphemy, sensuality, and immorality. Swinburne's second volume of poetry, *Songs before Sunrise* (which appeared in 1871), met with similar condemnation, and was one of the targets of a vituperative attack on what its author, Robert Buchanan, famously termed the "fleshly school of poetry." Swinburne (or "Swine-born," as *Punch* preferred to call him) reacted to these criticisms with spirited defiance, publishing two pamphlets in defence of poems which had been described as "loathsome and abominable" and full of "unspeakable foulness." These pamphlets were *Notes on Poems and Reviews* (1866) and *Under the Microscope* (1872). Ironically, at the time when Wilde was being accused of writing in a similarly immoral and scurrilous vein, Swinburne himself had become a more conservative and much less controversial figure, and his quarrels with his critics were by then nearly two decades in the past. Nevertheless, his earlier reputation lived on and his name continued to resonate as a byword for Decadent dissipation.

For the child reader, the moral of this story needs little explication—it seems to be as straightforward as that of "The Happy Prince." Yet for the adult reader who recognizes the allusions, it is oddly disconcerting. The structure seems designed not so much to exemplify an overt Christian message, but to provide Wilde with opportunities to exercise his taste for exotic description, for that "Sinburnianism" identified by contemporary reviewers. So although, as in "The Happy Prince," the plot ostensibly works to displace Decadent themes by a conventionally moralizing ending, those themes somehow refuse to disappear. Most strikingly they seem to be reasserted in the final image of the King at a point where Wilde describes his divinity using his favourite oppositions of red and white and of jewels and flowers. We might remember here that in order for the Happy Prince to enter the "garden of Paradise" it was necessary for him to divest himself of his jewels—the "great ruby" in his sword hilt, the "rare sapphires" of his eyes, and the "leaf" after "leaf" of "fine gold" that covered his body. By contrast the last image of the Young King seems to marry the Decadent to the Christian:

> The dead staff blossomed, and bare lilies that were whiter than pearls. The dry thorn blossomed, and bare roses that were redder than rubies. Whiter than fine pearls were the lilies, and their stems were of bright silver. Redder than male rubies were the roses, and their leaves were of beaten gold. (Ross, ed., *A House of Pomegranates*, 95)

Does that marriage work, however? Academic explication might put the general reader in a better position to make such a judgment. The first sentence contains an allusion to the *Tannhäuser* legend, which had become popular in late-nineteenth-century Britain, in large measure because of Wagner's opera, first performed there in 1876. Its libretto was based on a sixteenth-century German ballad which tells how a poet becomes enamoured of a beautiful woman who beckons him into the grotto of Venus where he spends the next seven years in a life of sensual pleasure. He subsequently meets Elizabeth, daughter of a local count, and wishing to marry her, travels to Rome to ask for absolution from the Pope; but he is told that it is as impossible as it is for the Pope's dry staff to blossom. Three days after (that Christian symbol again) the staff does indeed break into flower and the Pope calls for the poet's return. However, it is too late—on returning to the grotto of Venus the poet has discovered (like the Cardinal of Avignon) that Elizabeth has died and Tannhaüser subsequently falls dead on her funeral bier.

Scholarship Again

Contemporary literary treatments of the *Tannhäuser* legend, about which Wilde and many of his adult readers would have known, had included Swinburne's controversial "Laus Veneris" (another one of those pieces in *Poems and Ballads* deemed to be "Sinburnian" by reviewers), William Morris's "The Hill of Venus"

(1870), as well as Pater's retelling of the tale in "Two Early French Stories" in *The Renaissance*. The *Tannhäuser* motif could therefore be enlisted into the service of both Decadent and conventionally Christian interpretations. Pater, for example, had typically blurred the distinction between such readings when he compared the fate of the "erring knight" to that of the Christian Abelard. In Pater's account both knight and monk (as Abelard later became) are seen as a prefiguring of "the character of the Renaissance, that movement in which, in various ways, the human mind wins for itself a new kingdom of feeling and sensation and thought, not opposed to but only beyond and independent of the spiritual system then actually realised."[9] Interestingly in *Dorian Gray* Wilde was also to use *Tannhäuser*, but as an explicitly Decadent motif, attributing Dorian's continued fascination with the opera, when he had "wearied" of so many other art forms, to the fact that he saw "in the prelude to that great work of art a presentation of the tragedy of his own soul" (*Complete Works*, III: 282). What exactly, then, does the loaded reference symbolize in the context of "The Young King"?

For some readers, certainly for children, the allusion will go unnoticed, just like the origins of the Orientalism in "The Happy Prince." For them it will work as a straightforwardly moral tale. For those who recognize only the Christian elements in the allusion, and who fail to grasp the significance of the Decadent troping of the Prince's taste, the tale will also be straightforward. But for others aware of the literary tradition in which Wilde was working, the *Tannhäuser* allusion is almost certainly more subversive; it might have been seen as slyly endorsing those "curious" (that is, homoerotic) elements of the Young King's character which the story's denouement so conspicuously fails to banish. And at this point knowledge of another scholarly detail may be helpful: the erotic potential of the tale was exploited a few years later by Aubrey Beardsley, who provided the illustrations for the English edition of *Salome* of 1893. Beardsley's *The Story of Venus and Tannhäuser* concentrated on the knight's sexual adventures with Venus, rehearsed in a manner which parodied contemporary pornography. The piece was first published in 1896 in a heavily expurgated version, entitled "Under the Hill," in the *Savoy* magazine.

Teasing out the implications of the *Tannhäuser* motif in order to gain a sense of what the allusion could imply requires quite a detailed knowledge of late-nineteenth-century literary culture, and this, as we argued earlier, is exactly the sort of information which an academic can supply for the modern reader. The example of Wilde's use of the *Tannhäuser* motif also reminds us that Decadence seems to work best for Wilde when he is able to exploit elements of its intertextuality, to use allusion to gesture toward the more subversive implications of its exotic language. So at this point we can see in "The Young King" some evidence of Wilde developing those techniques he would later use in *Dorian Gray*. In the story, as in the novel, it is as if he is searching for a way to preserve the values of Decadence, even though the function of the plot (like that of "The Happy Prince") is ostensibly to dismiss them.

The Limitations of the Decadent Trope

"The Birthday of the Infanta" represents a rather different use of Decadence, although it is one which also resonates with *Dorian Gray*. We encounter Wilde's familiar lists of Decadent objects in his descriptions of the Infanta's birthday entertainments, most of which, we might note in passing, involve beautiful young men—a toned-down version, as it were, of Myrrhina's parade of male entertainers in *La Sainte Courtisane*. There are the "noble boys" who play at being toreadors, the African juggler and the "charming" "dancing boys" from the Church of Nuestra Senora Del Pilar, as well as the "troop of handsome Egyptians" with their dancing bear and monkeys. Familiar, too, are the lengthy descriptions of the luxuriously fitted-out royal apartments: the throne room with its black velvet canopy "studded with silver tulips and elaborately fringed with silver and pearls." The walls of the apartment are covered in "pink-flowered Lucca damask"—that selfsame damask, perhaps, with its "roses | So cunningly wrought that they lack perfume merely" with which Simone tempts Guido in *A Florentine Tragedy*. In the royal rooms there are "screens broidered with parrots and peacocks" and a floor of "sea-green onyx" (Ross, ed., *A House of Pomegranates*, 41–42, 59–60). In this tale the contrast to such conspicuous consumption is, predictably enough, simply "love," as it is exemplified in the Dwarf's devotion to the Infanta. Yet his dedication to pleasing her, far from transfiguring him—as it does to characters like the swallow in "The Happy Prince" or the fisherman in "The Fisherman and His Soul"—merely forces him to confront his own ugliness, that he is "misshapen and hunchbacked, foul to look at and grotesque" (Ross, ed., *A House of Pomegranates*, 62). In this instance the integrity of the lover's feelings is no compensation for their inappropriateness, and so the Dwarf remains at best an object of pathos. Moreover in the resolution of the story the final word is given to the Infanta, who dismissively comments, "for the future let those who come to play with me have no hearts" (Ross, ed., *A House of Pomegranates*, 64).

If we are looking for parallels with *Dorian Gray*, it is hard not to be struck by the similarity between the fates of the Dwarf and Sybil Vane: the devotion of both is bought at the cost of self-delusion, and although both die for their love, their self-sacrifices arouse relatively little sympathy in the reader. Neither of them is able to inhabit (or appreciate) the Decadent world to which the objects of their desires belong. Sybil never meets Dorian in his elaborately decorated rooms in which Lord Henry is so at ease, and the Dwarf is uncomfortable in the Infanta's palace, caring "nothing" for its "magnificence." That Sybil is female and the Dwarf a male but ugly "monster" might lead us to conclude that the Decadent world which seems to fascinate Wilde, and on which his narratives dwell so insistently, is one in which only beautiful young men—be they princes, kings, or mere fishermen—can live. Here too it is worth recalling the marginal roles given to Bianca and the Cardinal's ward in *A Florentine Tragedy* and the scenario for *The Cardinal of Avignon*. By contrast, Salome and Myrrhina can be fully part of a Decadent world because they are participants in, rather than banished from, the homoeroticism of *Salome* and *La Sainte Courtisane* respectively—that is, Salome's desire for Iokannan can be seen as inflaming that of Herod, just as Myrrhina courts the hermit with images of male, not female, beauty.

Second and more importantly, the values of the non-Decadent worlds where Sybil and the Dwarf do feel at home are constantly the targets of Wilde's satire. In *Dorian Gray*, as we have noted, the melodramatic aspects of working-class life to which Sybil belongs are the butt of Lord Henry's withering wit; in "The Birthday of the Infanta" Lord Henry's counterparts are the garden flowers. Their comments are an anticipation of the snobbery of the dowager duchesses we later encounter in the society comedies. The flowers' observations undercut the simple bucolic attraction of forest life: they note of the birds, the creatures with which the Dwarf has most affinity: "what a vulgarising effect this incessant rushing and flying about has. Well-bred people always stay in exactly the same place.... [B]irds have no sense of repose, and indeed birds do not even have a permanent address" (Ross, ed., *A House of Pomegranates*, 51). (The chatter of the water-rat, duck, and linnet in "The Devoted Friend," another of Wilde's tales which takes self-denial as its theme, performs the same sort of role, and in the process the moralizing function of the fairy-tale subgenre is ironized.) What distinguishes "The Birthday of the Infanta" from *Dorian Gray* is of course the absence of any plot mechanism by which the dangerous—and in this story explicitly cruel—values of Decadence can be safely banished for the reader: there is no nemesis for the Infanta or her courtiers for their spitefulness. And this is probably why those reviewers who were looking for a Victorian moral found only "Sinburnianism," and why, too, *A House of Pomegranates* succeeded in appealing only to a small group of readers.[10]

Decadent Traces

In terms of their themes and styles, the pieces which Wilde collected in another volume of short stories, *Lord Arthur Savile's Crime and Other Stories*, seem to have few links with *Dorian Gray*. With the possible exception of "The Sphinx without a Secret," none has a Decadent setting, and none explores Decadent themes. This effect may be explained in part by Wilde's need to appeal to the interests of the readers of the magazines in which the stories were first published. All of them appeared in the late spring and early summer of 1887; three were in various issues of *The Court and Society Review* and one in the *World*. The light-hearted plots all centre on contemporary domestic events, on life in the drawing rooms, country houses, and gentlemen's clubs that later figure so strongly in the society comedies, the works to which they are nearest in tone and sub-ject matter. The stories gently mock a variety of topical upper-middle-class enthusiasms—chieromancy, psychic phenomena, and philanthropy. In addition they rehearse many of what will soon become a veritable litany of jokes about marriage and courtship rituals, American vulgarity, and German dullness. Even some of the names are familiar: those of Lady Windermere and Gerald both reappear in later works. For the alert reader, though, amid this witty social sat-ire there are also occasional (and surprising) suggestions of those "other" sorts of lives and experiences that were more provocatively hinted at in *Dorian Gray* and the other two volumes of short fiction.

For example, the framing device of "The Sphinx without a Secret" is a con-versation between two men which takes place in a restaurant located in Par-is near the "Bois"—that is, the Bois de Boulogne, a wooded park which at the time had a reputation as a haunt of prostitutes, renters, and their clients. Then there is the "wonderfully good-looking" Hughie Erskine in "The Model Mil-lionaire," with his "crisp brown hair." Dorian Gray also has "crisp" hair, but this time "golden" (*Complete Works*, III: 181). Interestingly Hughie is "as popu-lar with men as he was with women." We know this popularity can have noth-ing to do with conventional manly virtues, for we have also been informed that Hughie (like, we suspect, the later character Gerald Arbuthnot in *A Wom-an of No Importance*) is neither intelligent nor good at making money: his high-est recommendation is simply that he is "a delightful, ineffectual young man with a perfect profile and no profession" (Ross, ed., *Lord Arthur Savile's Crime*, 136). Lord Arthur Savile, too, is hardly the usual sort of Victorian hero: young and handsome with "finely-chiselled lips," he, like so many of Wilde's boyishly beautiful young men, has "lived a delicate and luxurious life, … a life exquisite in its freedom from sordid care, its boyish insouciance" (Ross, ed., *Lord Arthur Savile's Crime*, 16, 18). Arthur also possesses a "very finely-wrought" nature via which he can be "dominated" by the "exquisite physical conditions of the moment" (Ross, ed., *Lord Arthur Savile's Crime*, 26). And it is this heightened sen-suality which seems to explain his rhapsodic reaction, not to his wife-to-be (to whom he is only conventionally attracted) but rather to some "white-smocked carters, with their pleasant sunburnt faces and coarse curly hair" and a "chub-by boy" with a "bunch of primroses in his battered hat" whom he encounters at dawn on their way to Covent Garden market. That reaction in turn betrays a nascent yet discernible Decadent sensibility:

> [T]he great piles of vegetables looked like masses of jade against the morning sky, the masses of green jade against the pink petals of some marvellous rose. Lord Arthur felt curiously affected, he could not tell why. There was something in the dawn's delicate loveliness that seemed to him inexpressibly pathetic, and he thought of all the days that break in beauty, and that set in storm. The rustics, too, with their rough, good-humoured voices, and their nonchalant ways, what a strange London they saw…. He

wondered what they thought of it, and whether they knew anything of its splendour and its shame, of its fierce, fiery-coloured joys, and its horrible hunger, or all it makes and mars from morn to eve.... It gave him pleasure to watch them as they went by. Rude as they were, with their heavy, hob-nailed shoes, and their awkward gait, they brought a little of Arcady with them. (Ross, ed., *Lord Arthur Savile's Crime*, 23–24)

By now we should recognize the all-too-familiar list of Decadent objects: beautiful flowers, precious stones, things both "curious" and "strange." "Fiery-coloured" was yet another of Wilde's favourite epithets. He used it in many of his reviews as well as in a number of his poems where it typically describes a moment of sensual or spiritual ecstasy—as in, for example, the "One fiery-coloured moment: one great love" in "Panthea" or the "One fiery-coloured moment of great life!" in "Sen Artysty" (*Complete Works*, I: 113, 147). In chapter two of *Dorian Gray*, Lord Henry's transforming influence over Dorian is also described in these terms: "Yes; there had been things in his boyhood that he had not understood. He understood them now. Life suddenly became fiery-coloured to him. It seemed to him that he had been walking on fire. Why had he not known it?" (*Complete Works*, III: 184). The implications of Arthur's reverie in "Lord Arthur Savile's Crime" are perhaps better appreciated by comparing its description with a passage from *Dorian Gray*:

As the dawn was just breaking he [Dorian] found himself close to Covent Garden. The darkness lifted, and, flushed with faint fires, the sky hollowed itself into a perfect pearl. Huge carts filled with nodding lilies rumbled slowly down the polished empty street. The air was heavy with the perfume of the flowers, and their beauty seemed to bring him an anodyne for his pain. He followed into the market, and watched the men unloading their wagons. A white-smocked carter offered him some cherries. He thanked him, wondered why he refused to accept any money for them, and began to eat them listlessly. They had been plucked at midnight, and the coldness of the moon had entered them. A long line of boys carrying crates of striped tulips, and of yellow and red roses, defiled in front him, threading their way through the huge jade-green piles of vegetables. (*Complete Works*, III: 244)

Here we have a much more explicitly homoerotic description of what is basically the same encounter. Similar too are the tantalizing questions which the passages provoke: why is Arthur so "curiously affected" by the carters he gazes at? Why does the carter whom Dorian encounters refuse to accept money for the cherries he offers? In neither case does the "knowing" reader have to think very hard to supply the answer. The perfumed air and jade-coloured vegetables give all the clues that are needed: the market in Covent Garden promises to become a garden of (forbidden) sensual fruits. Of course nothing much is made of these hints in "Lord Arthur Savile's Crime": the plot (like that of "The Model Millionaire") is resolved by a conventional, and conventionally happy, marriage. That such hints are there at all, though, is interesting: a style of writing that would become so complex, so assured, and so winning in *Dorian Gray*—that

synthesis of satire and purple prose—is here, in these early stories, in an embry-
onic and incomplete way, being simultaneously formed and tested.

Conclusion

Reviewing Wilde's entire body of fictional work, particularly comparing the
short stories with *Dorian Gray*, helps us to appreciate just how a novel that
some have argued was "'designed,' 'intended' and 'understood' by its readers to
be a book about sodomy and those men who practised sodomy" could nevertheless—as Wilde's counsel Charles Clark reminds us—remain for "five years
... upon the bookstalls and at bookshops and in libraries" without provoking
any form of official complaint. Today we have become so habituated to reading *Dorian Gray* biographically through the lens of the trials that we can easily overlook the complexity and subtlety of Wilde's achievement—that is, the
nature of those stylistic clues which take us back to the biography in the first
instance. *Dorian Gray*, like some parts of the short stories, derives its suggestive power not from any simple expressive transparency, but rather its opposite—a highly contrived and self-consciously "literary" style which alternately
suggests and insinuates by allusion. Moreover, that style requires of its readers a
fairly sophisticated literary education in order that they recognize and follow
the chains of association which the allusions simultaneously set in motion and
allow to be understood. The subversive values of Decadence only become fully
visible once we are alert to the literary tradition with which Wilde was aligning
himself. It follows that the most fruitful way of unlocking the novel's subversive
secrets for the modern reader is not by means of that relentless pursuit (made
by McKenna and others) of the supposed parallels with Wilde's own life—the
search, that is, for the "real" analogues to Dorian and Lord Henry. Rather, traditional forms of academic scholarship may be more useful: by patiently explaining Wilde's allusions, and spelling out the values which they encode, modern
critics and editors of Wilde's fiction can enable modern readers to understand
why the novel can still be "dangerous" without any knowledge of Wilde's personal life. And, equally pertinently, why a knowledge of who Wilde was does
not debar one from reading *The Picture of Dorian Gray* as a straightforward and
entertaining morality tale.

Notes

1.   Unless specified to the contrary, all quotations from *Dorian Gray* are from the 1891 version,
as it appears in the text established by Joseph Bristow in *Complete Works*, III.

2.   One might be tempted to think that an attention to social details, such as an East-End
opium den, indicates some interest in realism. However Wilde seemed very concerned to dispel
any such literalism, by leaking to the contemporary trade journal *The Bookman* that "the opium
den scene (which occurs only in the revised-volume form) is, for all its fidelity of detail, a purely

imaginary description, as Mr Wilde recently said that he had never set foot in an opium den in his life." *The Bookman*, I (1892), 88.

3.   There are relatively few differences between these passages in the periodical and book versions of *Dorian Gray*, and this suggests that Dorian's reading of Gautier was crucial to Wilde's conception of his character (see also note 5 below).

4.   Dorian's description of Egypt borrows images from two poems in *Emaux et camées*. From "Ce que disent les hirondelles" ("J'ai ma petite chambre | A Smyrne, au plafond d'un café. | Les Hadjis comptent leur grains d'ambre | Sur le seuil, d'un rayon chauffé"); and from "Nostalgies d'obélisques" ("Sur cette place je m'ennuie, | Obélisque dépareillé: | Neige, givre brunie et pluie | Glacent mon flanc déjà rouillé").

5.   In the text of the periodical version of *Dorian Gray* Wilde had been slightly more circumspect, so there is no mention of Dorian brooding, nor of the marble statue being "kiss-stained": he just "reads … of that curious statue that Gautier compares to a contralto voice, the '*monstre charmant*' that couches in the porphyry-room of the Louvre" (*Complete Works*, III: 144). The more overt homoeroticism of the book version is a useful reminder that not all of Wilde's revisions to his story can be seen as an attempt to tone it down.

6.   Algernon Charles Swinburne, *Notes on Poems and Reviews* (1866); reprinted in Josephine M. Guy, ed., *The Victorian Age: An Anthology of Sources and Documents* (London: Routledge, 1998, 2002), 378–79.

7.   There is a further allusion in this quotation: the "sweet marble monster" appears in Shelley's "Studies for Epipsychidion": "And others swear you're a Hermaphrodite; | Like that sweet marble monster of both sexes, | Which looks so sweet and gentle that it vexes | The very soul that the soul is gone | Which lifted from her limits the veil of stone" (57–61).

8.   Karl Beckson, ed. *Oscar Wilde, The Critical Heritage* (1970; London: Routledge, 1997), 113–14.

9.   Walter Pater, *Studies in the History of the Renaissance*, ed. Donald Hill (London: University of California Press, 1980), 5.

10.   The reasons for the critical and commercial failure of *A House of Pomegranates* are in fact complex. The volume was also very expensive, and it may have been the price, as much as the contents, which deterred contemporary readers.

Works Cited & Consulted

Baker, Houston J., Jr. "A Tragedy of the Artist: *The Picture of Dorian Gray*," *Nineteenth Century Fiction*, 24 (1969), 349–55.

Brown, R. D. "Suetonius, Symonds and Gibbon in *The Picture of Dorian Gray*," *Modern Language Notes*, 71 (1956), 264.

The Complete Letters of Oscar Wilde, Merlin Holland and Rupert Hart–Davis, eds. London: Fourth Estate, 2000.

The Complete Works of Oscar Wilde. I. Poems and Poems in Prose, Bobby Fong and Karl Beckson, eds. Oxford: Oxford University Press, 2000.

The Complete Works of Oscar Wilde. Volume II. De Profundis. "Epistola: In Carcere et Vinculis." Ian Small, ed. Oxford: Oxford University Press, 2005.

The Complete Works of Oscar Wilde. III. The Picture of Dorian Gray, Joseph Bristow, ed. Oxford: Oxford University Press, 2005.

Cook, Lucius H. "French Sources of Wilde's *Picture of Dorian Gray*," *Romantic Review*, 19 (1928), 25–34.

Gillespie, Michael Patrick. "Picturing Dorian Gray: Resistant Readings in Wilde's Novel," *English Literature in Transition*, 35 (1992), 7–25.

Guy, Josephine M. and Ian Small. *Oscar Wilde's Profession: Writing and the Culture Industry*. Oxford: Oxford University Press, 2000.

Holland, Merlin. *Irish Peacock and Scarlet Marquess*. London: Fourth Estate, 2003.

Marez, Curtiz. "The Other Addict: Reflections on Colonialism and Oscar Wilde's Smoke Screen," *English Literary History*, 64 (1977), 257–87.

Maurer, Oscar, Jr. "A Philistine Source for *Dorian Gray*?" *Philological Quarterly*, 26 (1947), 84–86.

Murray, Isobel. "*Children of Tomorrow*: A Sharp Inspiration for *Dorian Gray*," *Durham University Journal*, 80 (1987), 69–76.

_____. "Oscar Wilde in his Literary Element: Yet Another Source for *Dorian Gray*?" in *Rediscovering Oscar Wilde*, C. George Sandulescu, ed. Gerrards Cross: Colin Smythe, 1994, 283–96.

_____. "Strange Case of Dr Jekyll and Oscar Wilde," *Durham University Journal*, 79 (1987), 311–19.

Murray, Isobel, and Louis J. Poteet, "*Dorian Gray* and the Gothic Novel," *Modern Fiction Studies*, 17 (1971), 239–48.

Pater, Walter. *The Renaissance*, Donald Hill, ed. London: University of California Press, 1980.

Powell, Kerry. "Tom, Dick, and Dorian Gray: Magic Picture Mania in late Victorian Fiction," *Philological Quarterly*, 62 (1983), 147–70.

_____. "Who was Basil Hallward?" *English Language Notes*, 24 (1986), 84–91.

Schroeder, Horst. *The Portrait of Mr. W.H.: Its Composition, Publication and Reception*. Braunschweig: Braunschweiger Anglistische Arbeiten, 1984.

Small, Ian. *Oscar Wilde Revalued*. Greensboro: ELT Press, 1993.

Wilde, Oscar. *A House of Pomegranates, The Happy Prince and Other Tales*, Robert Ross, ed. London: Methuen, 1908.

_____. *Intentions and The Soul of Man*, Robert Ross, ed. London: Methuen, 1908.

_____. *Lord Arthur Savile's Crime and Other Prose Pieces*, Robert Ross, ed. London: Methuen, 1908.

_____. *The Picture of Dorian Gray*, Donald Lawler, ed. London: W. W. Norton, Ltd., 1988.

Appendix:
Wilde's Unfinished Plays and Scenarios

The Cardinal of Avignon

The text is taken from the appendix to Stuart Mason, *Bibliography of Oscar Wilde* (London: T. Werner Laurie Ltd., 1914), 583–85. The Clark Library has a manuscript copy of the same scenario in the hand of Wilde's friend, More Adey; it is reprinted in Small, *Oscar Wilde Revalued* (Greensboro: ELT Press, 1993), 120–23.

Sketch of the Scenario of an unpublished play by Oscar Wilde, written in April 1894:—

The play opens in the palace of the Cardinal at Avignon. The Cardinal is alone and somewhat excited for he has received news that the Pope is sick and about to die. "What if they were to elect me Pope?" he says, thus giving the keynote of his inordinate ambition. Nobles and Princes enter; and the Cardinal, who knows the vices and pleasures of each one, solicits and obtains promises of their votes by promising each of them the fulfilment of their personal aims and desires. *Exeunt*, and the Cardinal says: "Will God place me on such a pinnacle?" and he has a fine speech with regard to the Papacy. A servant enters and says that a lady wishes to see the Cardinal. He refuses; but the lady, a beautiful young girl, a ward of the Cardinal, enters. She upbraids him for refusing to see her, and a very pretty and affectionate scene occurs between them. In the course of the conversation the girl says: "You have spoken to me of many things, but there is one thing you never told me about, and that is Love." "And do you know what Love is?" "Yes, for I love." Then she explains to the Cardinal that she has plighted her troth to a handsome young man who some time since came to the Cardinal's Court and has been made much of by the prelate. The prelate is much upset and makes her promise not to mention this conversation to her lover. When his ward has left him, the Cardinal is filled with rage and sorrow. "And so my sin of twenty years ago has risen up against me and come to rob me of the only thing I love!" The young man is his son.

The scene now changes to some gardens at the rear of the Palace. The Cardinal's ward and her betrothed are together. They have a passionate love scene. The young man, mindful of what they both owe to the Cardinal, asks his betrothed whether she has told the Cardinal of their betrothal. She, also mindful of her promise, says "No." He urges her to do so as soon as possible.

At this point there enters a pageant, and suddenly a Masque of Death appears. This alarms the girl who sees in it a presage of some coming woe. Her lover scouts the idea, saying: "What have you and I, with our new-born love, to do with Death? Death is not for such as you and me." The pageant comes to an end, and the lovers part. The girl, in leaving, drops her glove.

The Cardinal comes out of the Palace, picks up the glove, and at the same time sees the young man. He is furious. "So they have met!" He is determined that he will not lose the only thing he loves, and so in the course of conversation he tells the young man, who desires to be told about his father, that, years ago, a mighty prince, on his death-bed, entrusted his two children to the Cardinal's care. "Am I one of those children?" "You are." "Then I have a brother?" "No; but a sister." "A sister! Where is she? Why do I not know her?" "You do know her. She is the girl to whom you have betrothed yourself." The young man is horror- and grief-stricken. The Cardinal, without, however, betraying his own relationship, urges him to pluck this impossible love from his heart and also to kill it in the heart of the girl. The girl now re-enters, and the Cardinal explains that her lover finds that he has made a serious mistake and does not love her sufficiently to wed her. This portion of the play winds up with a powerful scene between the two lovers, the young man rigidly carrying out the promise exacted from him by the Cardinal.

The scene now changes back to the interior of the Palace, as in the opening of the play. The Cardinal is alone and already repenting of the deed of yesterday. He is miserable. A struggle is going on within him between his ambition and his love. He is desperately in love with his ward; and at the same time he doubts whether, with such a sin on his soul, God will raise him to the Papacy. Trumpets are heard. Nobles and Princes enter. The Pope is dead, and the Cardinal has been elected Pope in his place. He is now the Pope. The Nobles and others, after making obeisance, *exeunt*. The Cardinal is radiant. "I who was but now in the mire am now placed so high, Christ's Vicar on earth!" and so on. A fine speech. Now his ambition conquers. He sends for the young man. "What I told you yesterday was done simply to test you. You and your betrothed are no relations. Go, find her, and I will marry you to her to-night before I ride away to Rome." At this moment the huge doors at the end of the hall are thrown open and there enter friars bearing a bier covered with a pall which they proceed to set down in the centre of the hall, and then *exeunt* without speaking a word. Both men intuitively feel who is the occupant of the bier. The young girl has killed herself in despair at the loss of her lover. The Cardinal opens the doors and says to the soldiers outside: "Do not enter here, whatever you may hear, until I walk forth again." He then re-enters the room and draws a heavy bolt across the doors. The young man then says: "Now I am going to kill you." The Pope answers: "I shall not defend myself, but I will plead with you." He then urges upon the young man the sanctity of the papal office etc., etc. and represents the horrible sacrilege of such a murder. "No, you cannot kill the Pope." "Such a crime has no horror for me: I shall kill you." The Pope then reveals to him that he is the young man's father, and places before him the hideousness of the crime of patricide. "You cannot kill your father!" "Nothing in me responds to your appeal. I have no filial feelings: I shall kill you." The Pope now goes to the bier and, drawing back the pall, says: "I too loved her." At this the young man runs and flings open the doors and says to the soldiers: "His Holiness will ride hence to-night on his way to Rome." The Pope is standing, blessing the corpse, and as he does so, the young man throws himself on the bier between the Pope and stabs himself. The soldiers, Nobles, etc. enter. The Pope still stands blessing.

[Curtain.]

A Florentine Tragedy

There is no proper edition of *A Florentine Tragedy*. The text which Ross published in his 1908 *Collected Edition* is usually taken as copy-text. Ross's 1909 *Second Collected Edition*, and his 1910 *Collected Edition*, issued for America, also prints Thomas Sturge Moore's additional opening scene. We do not reproduce that scene; rather we print the additional manuscript material given by Stuart Mason in his *A Bibliography of Oscar Wilde* (1914), supplemented by that printed by Ian Small in *Oscar Wilde Revalued*. Mason reprints a "reduced facsimile" of the "original manuscript" of the piece's "Scene" and "Characters" (463), which is given below as Fragment A. He also prints a transcription of "a manuscript of *A Florentine Tragedy*" which "contains the following unpublished fragments" (464–65). This is given below as Fragment B. In addition Mason prints the first part of yet another fragment of an alternative opening for the play (465); the whole of this fragment (the manuscript of which is in the Clark Library) is also reprinted by Small (132–33). The only difference between the readings of the part of the text printed by Mason and by Small is as follows. In the third line of Guido's first speech, Mason prints "visit" as a variant of "follow," rather than part of the line. This is given below as Fragment C.

Fragment A

Scene

The scene represents a room in a burgher's house at Florence. A large window at the back opens on a moonlit sky. The city towers are faintly seen. There is a door L.C. A large tapestried bed with close drawn curtains L.U. The time is XVIth century. There is a table set with supper for one. A lamp. Stools. A chest, etc.

Characters

Simone Dario (a merchant)

Bianca (his wife)

Guido Bardi (a young Florentine of high birth)

Time. XVI. century.

Place

Florence

Fragment B

The scene represents a room in the house of a Florentine Burgher. The time is night, and through the open window at the back of the stage one can see the moon and the tall towers of the ... and the roofs of many houses and many bright stars.

BIANCA:

Oh! I had thought Love came with winged feet

And not with feet of lead! [*'Tis past the hour.*]

                Why does he tarry?

These foolish lights were better quenched.

'Tis past the hour, and the [*dull*] slow-ticking clock

Like an unskilful player on the lute,

Makes harsh divisions of each point of Time

And sickens expectation. Mary Mother!

Thou knowest all my love and loveless days

Wearily passed and patiently endured,

Days without light or laughter, or such joys

As are [*a*] the common heritage of those

Who lack both food and raiment.

                      Holy Mother,

Thou knowest them all? And if it be thy will,

. . . . .

Oh! he has come! He has come

Guido's voice outside

. . . . .

BIANCA:

Sing! Sing again! The thorn-pierced nightingale

[*That all night long makes music for the moon*]

[*Is not so sweet. She does but sing of pain*]

That every eve calls to the listening moon

Is not so sweet, for all her ecstasies,

She does but sing of pain, and bleeding loves,

[Of bleeding loves and pain she does but sing]

[*And*] fierce misery her melody.

Therefore she hides herself in forest leaves

And to the deepest darkness makes her moan,

And with false echoes fills that hollow shell,

Guido's voice

BIANCA

SIMONE DARIO:

My good wife you come slowly. Were it not seemlier

                                [*better*]

To run to meet your lord? Here take my cloak.

[*And*] First store this pack. 'Tis heavy. I have sold nothing

Fragment C

Bianca, a beautiful woman, is kneeling before an image of the Madonna. She is simply but beautifully dressed.

Enter by Window, GUIDO

GUIDO:
Last night it snowed in Florence, but tonight
It rained red roses. Nay, my gentle dove,
Why do you lure the hawk to follow you, visit
And then grow timorous? Do you know my name?

BIANCA:
Too well. Too well.
You are that terrible Lord, who men call love,
                                        homely

And I a common burgher's unloved wife.
It is enough that I have looked on you.

GUIDO:
No, by St James, but it is not enough.

BIANCA:
Tell me your name. Nay do not tell me your name.
Love having many names has yet but one.
I am content, so I may touch your cheek,
Or smooth these tangled blossoms.
                        How fair you are!
Fair as that young St. Michael on the wall
Of Santa Croce where we go and pray.
Your throat like milk, your mouth a scarlet flower
Whose petals prison music, and your eyes
Wild woodland wells in which dark violets see
Their purple shadows drown.

Our Florence lilies
Are white and red, but you have lily and rose
Yet in one garden.

[The text of Ross's 1908 edition begins here]

[*Enter* THE HUSBAND]

SIMONE.

My good wife, you come slowly, were it not better
To run to meet your lord? Here, take my cloak.
Take this pack first. 'Tis heavy. I have sold nothing:
Save a furred robe unto the Cardinal's son,
Who hopes to wear it when his father dies,
And hopes that will be soon.
                              But who is this?
Why you have here some friend. Some kinsman doubtless,
Newly returned from foreign lands and fallen
Upon a house without a host to greet him?
I crave your pardon, kinsman. For a house
Lacking a host is but an empty thing
And void of honour; a cup without its wine,
A scabbard without steel to keep it straight,
A flowerless garden widowed of the sun.
Again I crave your pardon, my sweet cousin.

BIANCA.

This is no kinsman and no cousin neither.

SIMONE.

No kinsman, and no cousin! You amaze me.
Who is it then who with such courtly grace
Deigns to accept our hospitalities?

GUIDO.

My name is Guido Bardi.

SIMONE.

                    What! The son
Of that great Lord of Florence whose dim towers
Like shadows silvered by the wandering moon

I see from out my casement every night!
Sir Guido Bardi, you are welcome here,
Twice welcome. For I trust my honest wife,
Most honest if uncomely to the eye,
Hath not with foolish chatterings wearied you,
As is the wont of women.

GUIDO.

                  Your gracious lady,
Whose beauty is a lamp that pales the stars
And robs Diana's quiver of her beams
Has welcomed me with such sweet courtesies
That if it be her pleasure, and your own,
I will come often to your simple house.
And when your business bids you walk abroad
I will sit here and charm her loneliness
Lest she might sorrow for you overmuch.
What say you, good Simone?

SIMONE.

                  My noble Lord,
You bring me such high honour that my tongue
Like a slave's tongue is tied, and cannot say
The word it would. Yet not to give you thanks
Were to be too unmannerly. So, I thank you,
From my heart's core.

                  It is such things as these
That knit a state together, when a Prince
So nobly born and of such fair address,
Forgetting unjust Fortune's differences,
Comes to an honest burgher's honest home
As a most honest friend.

                  And yet, my Lord,
I fear I am too bold. Some other night
We trust that you will come here as a friend,
To-night you come to buy my merchandise.
Is it not so? Silks, velvets, what you will,
I doubt not but I have some dainty wares
Will woo your fancy. True, the hour is late,
But we poor merchants toil both night and day

To make our scanty gains. The tolls are high,
And every city levies its own toll,
And prentices are unskilful, and wives even
Lack sense and cunning, though Bianca here
Has brought me a rich customer to-night.
Is it not so, Bianca? But I waste time.
Where is my pack? Where is my pack, I say?
Open it, my good wife. Unloose the cords.
Kneel down upon the floor. You are better so.
Nay not that one, the other. Despatch, despatch!
Buyers will grow impatient oftentimes.
We dare not keep them waiting. Ay! 'tis that,
Give it to me; with care. It is most costly.
Touch it with care. And now, my noble Lord—
Nay, pardon, I have here a Lucca damask,
The very web of silver and the roses
So cunningly wrought that they lack perfume merely
To cheat the wanton sense. Touch it, my Lord.
Is it not soft as water, strong as steel?
And then the roses! Are they not finely woven?
I think the hillsides that best love the rose,
As Bellosguardo or at Fiesole,
Throw no such blossoms on the lap of spring,
Or if they do their blossoms droop and die.
Such is the fate of all the dainty things
That dance in wind and water. Nature herself
Makes war on her own loveliness and slays
Her children like Medea. Nay but, my Lord,
Look closer still. Why in this damask here
It is summer always, and no winter's tooth
Will ever blight these blossoms. For every ell
I paid a piece of gold. Red gold, and good,
The fruit of careful thrift.

GUIDO.

                              Honest Simone,
Enough, I pray you. I am well content,
To-morrow I will send my servant to you,
Who will pay twice your price.

SIMONE.

My generous Prince!

I kiss your hands. And now I do remember
Another treasure hidden in my house
Which you must see. It is a robe of state:
Woven by a Venetian: the stuff, cut-velvet:
The pattern, pomegranates: each separate seed
Wrought of a pearl: the collar all of pearls,
As thick as moths in summer streets at night,
And whiter than the moons that madmen see
Through prison bars at morning. A male ruby
Burns like a lighted coal within the clasp.
The Holy Father has not such a stone,
Nor could the Indies show a brother to it.
The brooch itself is of most curious art,
Cellini never made a fairer thing
To please the great Lorenzo. You must wear it.
There is none worthier in our city here,
And it will suit you well. Upon one side
A slim and horned satyr leaps in gold
To catch some nymph of silver. Upon the other
Stands Silence with a crystal in her hand,
No bigger than the smallest ear of corn,
That wavers at the passing of a bird,
Yet so cunningly wrought that one would say
It breathed, or held its breath.

Worthy Bianca,
Would not this noble and most costly robe
Suit young Lord Guido well?

Nay, but entreat him;
He will refuse you nothing, though the price
Be as a prince's ransom. And your profit
Shall not be less than mine.

BIANCA.

Am I your prentice?
Why should I chaffer for your velvet robe?

GUIDO.
Nay, fair Bianca, I will buy the robe,

And all things that the honest merchant has
I will buy also. Princes must be ransomed,
And fortunate are all high lords who fall
Into the white hands of so fair a foe.

SIMONE.

I stand rebuked. But you will buy my wares?
Will you not buy them? Fifty thousand crowns
Would scarce repay me. But you, my Lord, shall have them
For forty thousand. Is that price too high?
Name your own price. I have a curious fancy
To see you in this wonder of the loom
Amidst the noble ladies of the court,
A flower among the flowers.

                        They say, my lord,
These highborn dames do so affect your Grace
That where you go they throng like flies around you,
Each seeking for your favour.

                        I have heard also
Of husbands that wear horns, and wear them bravely,
A fashion most fantastical.

GUIDO.

                    Simone,
Your reckless tongue needs curbing; and besides,
You do forget this gracious lady here
Whose delicate ears are surely not attuned
To such coarse music.

SIMONE.

                    True: I had forgotten,
Nor will offend again. Yet, my sweet Lord,
You'll buy the robe of state. Will you not buy it?
But forty thousand crowns. 'Tis but a trifle,
To one who is Giovanni Bardi's heir.

GUIDO.

Settle this thing tomorrow with my steward
Antonio Costa. He will come to you.
And you will have a hundred thousand crowns

If that will serve your purpose.

SIMONE.

A hundred thousand!
Said you a hundred thousand? Oh! be sure
That will for all time, and in everything
Make me your debtor. Ay! from this time forth
My house, with everything my house contains,
Is yours, and only yours.

A hundred thousand!
My brain is dazed. I will be richer far
Than all the other merchants. I will buy
Vineyards, and lands, and gardens. Every loom
From Milan down to Sicily shall be mine,
And mine the pearls that the Arabian seas
Store in their silent caverns.

Generous Prince,
This night shall prove the herald of my love,
Which is so great that whatsoe'er you ask
It will not be denied you.

GUIDO.

What if I asked
For white Bianca here?

SIMONE.

You jest, my Lord,
She is not worthy of so great a Prince.
She is but made to keep the house and spin.
Is it not so, good wife? It is so. Look!
Your distaff waits for you. Sit down and spin.
Women should not be idle in their homes.
For idle fingers make a thoughtless heart.
Sit down, I say.

BIANCA.

What shall I spin?

SIMONE.

Oh! spin

Some robe which, dyed in purple, sorrow might wear
For her own comforting: or some long-fringed cloth
In which a new-born and unwelcome babe
Might wail unheeded; or a dainty sheet
Which, delicately perfumed with sweet herbs,
Might serve to wrap a dead man. Spin what you will;
I care not, I.

BIANCA.

               The brittle thread is broken,
The dull wheel wearies of its ceaseless round,
The duller distaff sickens of its load;
I will not spin to-night.

SIMONE.

                    It matters not.
Tomorrow you shall spin, and every day
Shall find you at your distaff. So, Lucretia
Was found by Tarquin. So, perchance, Lucretia
Waited for Tarquin. Who knows? I have heard
Strange things about men's wives. And now, my lord,
What news abroad? I heard today at Pisa
That certain of the English merchants there
Would sell their woollens at a lower rate
Than the just laws allow, and have entreated
The Signory to hear them.

                   Is this well?
Should merchant be to merchant as a wolf?
And should the stranger living in our land
Seek by enforced privilege or craft
To rob us of our profits?

GUIDO.

                What should I do
With merchants or their profits? Shall I go
And wrangle with the Signory on your count?
And wear the gown in which you buy from fools,
Or sell to sillier bidders? Honest Simone,
Wool-selling or wool-gathering is for you.
My wits have other quarries.

BIANCA.

Noble Lord,

I pray you pardon my good husband here,
His soul stands ever in the market-place,
And his heart beats but at the price of wool.
Yet he is honest in his common way.

[*To* SIMONE]

And you, have you no shame? A gracious Prince
Comes to our house, and you must weary him
With most misplaced assurance. Ask his pardon.

SIMONE.

I ask it humbly. We will talk to-night
Of other things. I hear the Holy Father
Has sent a letter to the King of France
Bidding him cross that shield of snow, the Alps,
And make a peace in Italy, which will be
Worse than war of brothers, and more bloody
Than civil rapine or intestine feuds.

GUIDO.

Oh! we are weary of that King of France,
Who never comes, but ever talks of coming.
What are these things to me? There are other things
Closer, and of more import, good Simone.

BIANCA. [*To* SIMONE]

I think you tire our most gracious guest.
What is the King of France to us? As much
As are your English merchants with their wool.

.   .   .   .   .

SIMONE.

Is it so then? Is all this mighty world
Narrowed into the confines of this room
With but three souls for poor inhabitants?
Ay! there are times when the great universe,
Like cloth in some unskilful dyer's vat,
Shrivels into a handsbreadth, and perchance
That time is now! Well! let that time be now.

Let this mean room be as that mighty stage
Whereon kings die, and our ignoble lives
Become the stakes God plays for.
                              I do not know
Why I speak thus. My ride has wearied me.
And my horse stumbled thrice, which is an omen
That bodes not good to any.
                              Alas! my lord,
How poor a bargain is this life of man,
And in how mean are market are we sold!
When we are born our mothers weep, but when
We die there is none weep for us. No, not one.
                    [*Passes to back of stage.*]

BIANCA.

How like a common chapman does he speak!
I hate him, soul and body. Cowardice
Has set her pale seal on his brow. His hands
Whiter than poplar leaves in windy springs,
Shake with some palsy; and his stammering mouth
Blurts out a foolish froth of empty words
Like water from a conduit.

GUIDO.
                    Sweet Bianca,
He is not worthy of your thought or mine.
The man is but a very honest knave
Full of fine phrases for life's merchandise,
Selling most dear what he must hold most cheap,
A windy brawler in a world of words.
I never met so eloquent a fool.

BIANCA.

Oh, would that Death might take him where he stands!

SIMONE. [*Turning round*]
Who spake of Death? Let no one speak of Death.
What should Death do in such a merry house,
With but a wife, a husband, and a friend
To give it greeting? Let Death go to houses

Where there are vile, adulterous things, chaste wives ˙
Who grow weary of their noble lords
Draw back the curtains of their marriage beds,
And in polluted and dishonoured sheets
Feed some unlawful lust. Ay! 'tis so
Strange, and yet so. *You* do not know the world.
You are too single and too honourable.
I know it well. And would it were not so,
But wisdom comes with winters. My hair grows grey,
And youth has left my body. Enough of that.
Tonight is ripe for pleasure, and indeed,
I would be merry, as beseems a host
Who finds a gracious and unlooked-for guest
Waiting to greet him.   [*Takes up a lute.*]
              But what is this, my lord?
Why, you have brought a lute to play to us.
Oh! play, sweet Prince. And, if I am bold,
Pardon, but play.

GUIDO.

              I will not play tonight.
Some other night, Simone.
[*To* BIANCA] You and I
Together, with no listeners but the stars,
Or the more jealous moon.

SIMONE.

                    Nay, but my lord!
Nay, but I do beseech you. For I have heard
That by the simple fingering of a string,
Or delicate breath breathed along hollowed reeds,
Or blown into cold mouths of cunning bronze,
Those who are curious in this art can draw
Poor souls from prison-houses. I have heard also
How such strange magic lurks within these shells
And innocence puts vine-leaves in her hair,
And wantons like a maenad. Let that pass.
Your lute I know is chaste. And therefore play:
Ravish my ears with some sweet melody;
My soul is in a prison-house, and needs

Music to cure its madness. Good Bianca,
Entreat our guest to play.

BIANCA.

                Be not afraid,
Our well-loved guest will choose his place and moment:
That moment is not now. You weary him
With your uncouth insistence.

GUIDO.

             Honest Simone,
Some other night. To-night I am content
With the low music of Bianca's voice,
Who, when she speaks, charms the too amorous air,
And makes the reeling earth stand still, or fix
His cycle round her beauty.

SIMONE.

             You flatter her.
She has virtues as most women have,
But beauty is a gem she may not wear.
It is better so, perchance.

             Well, my dear lord,
If you will not draw melodies from your lute
To charm my moody and o'er-troubled soul
You'll drink with me at least? [*Sees table.*]
             Your place is laid.
Fetch me a stool, Bianca. Close the shutters.
Set the great bar across. I would not have
The curious world with its small prying eyes
To peer upon our pleasure.

            Now, my lord,
Give us a toast from a full brimming cup. [*Starts back.*]
What is this stain upon the cloth? It looks
As purple as a wound upon Christ's side.
Wine merely is it? I have heard it said
When wine is spilt blood is spilt also,
But that's a foolish tale.

            My lord, I trust
My grape is to your liking? The wine of Naples

Is fiery like its mountains. Our Tuscan vineyards
Yield a more wholesome juice.

GUIDO.

I like it well,
Honest Simone; and, with your good leave,
Will toast the fair Bianca when her lips
Have like red rose-leaves floated on this cup
And left its vintage sweeter. Taste, Bianca. [BIANCA *drinks.*]
Oh, all the honey of Hyblean bees,
Matched with this draught were bitter!

Good Simone,
You do not share the feast.

SIMONE.

It is strange, my lord,
I cannot eat or drink with you, to-night.
Some humour, or some fever in my blood,
At other seasons temperate, or some thought
That like an adder creeps from point to point,
That like a madman crawls from cell to cell,
Poisons my palate and makes appetite
A loathing, not a longing.   [*Goes aside.*]

GUIDO.

Sweet Bianca,
This common chapman wearies me with words.
I must go hence. To-morrow I will come.
Tell me the hour.

BIANCA.

Come with the youngest dawn!
Until I see you all my life is vain.

GUIDO.

Ah! loose the falling midnight of your hair,
And in those stars, your eyes, let me behold
Mine image, as in mirrors. Dear Bianca,
Though it be but a shadow, keep me there,
Nor gaze at anything that does not show

Some symbol of my semblance. I am jealous
Of what your vision feasts on.

BIANCA.

                    Oh! be sure
Your image will be with me always. Dear,
Love can translate the very meanest thing
Into a sign of sweet remembrances.
But come before the lark with its shrill song
Has waked a world of dreamers. I will stand
Upon the balcony,

GUIDO.

                    And by a ladder
Wrought out of scarlet silk and sewn with pearls
Will come to meet me. White foot after foot,
Like snow upon a rose-tree.

BIANCA.

                    As you will.
You know I am yours for love or Death.

GUIDO.
Simone, I must go to mine house.

SIMONE.
So soon? Why should you? The great Duomo's bell
Has not yet tolled its midnight, and the watchman
Who with their hollow horns mock the pale moon,
Lie drowsy in their towers. Stay awhile.
I fear we may not see you here again,
And that fear saddens my too simple heart.

GUIDO.
Be not afraid, Simone. I will stand
Most constant in my friendship. But to-night
I go to mine own home, and that at once.
To-morrow, sweet Bianca.

SIMONE.

                  Well, well, so be it.
I would have wished for fuller converse with you,
My new friend, my honourable guest,
But that it seems may not be.

                 And besides
I do not doubt you father waits for you,
Wearying for voice or footstep. You, I think,
Are his one child? He has no other child.
You are the gracious pillar of his house,
The flower of a garden full of weeds.
Your father's nephews do not love him well.
So run folk's tongues in Florence. I meant but that;
Men say they envy your inheritance
And look upon your vineyard with fierce eyes
As Ahab looked upon Naboth's goodly field.
But that is but the chatter of a town
Where women talk too much.

                 Good night, my lord.
Fetch a pine torch, Bianca. The old staircase
Is full of pitfalls, and the churlish moon
Grows, like a miser, niggard of her beams,
And hides her face behind a muslin mask
As harlots do when they go forth to snare
Some wretched soul in sin. Now, I will get
Your cloak and sword. Nay, pardon, my good Lord,
It is but meet that I should wait on you
Who have so honoured my poor burgher's house,
Drunk of my wine, and broken bread, and made
Yourself a sweet familiar. Oftentimes
My wife and I will talk of this fair night
And its great issues.

             Why, what a sword is this!
Ferrara's temper, pliant as a snake,
And deadlier, I doubt not. With such steel
One need fear nothing in the moil of life.
I never touched so delicate a blade.
I have a sword too, somewhat rusted now.
We men of peace are taught humility,
And to bear many burdens on our backs,

And not to murmur at an unjust world,
And to endure unjust indignities.
We are taught that, and like the patient Jew
Find profit in our pain.
                            Yet I remember
How once upon the road to Padua
A robber sought to take my pack-horse from me,
I slit his throat and left him. I can bear
Dishonour, public insult, many shames,
Shrill scorn, and open contumely, but he
Who filches from me something that is mine,
Ay! though it be the meanest trencher-plate
From which I feed mine appetite—oh! he
Perils his soul and body in the theft
And dies for his small sin. From what strange clay
We men are moulded!

GUIDO.
                    Why do you speak like this?

SIMONE.
I wonder, my Lord Guido, if my sword
Is better tempered than this steel of yours?
Shall we make trial? Or is my state too low
For you to cross your rapier against mine,
In jest, or earnest?

GUIDO.
                    Naught would please me better
Than to stand fronting you with naked blade
In jest, or earnest. Give me mine own sword.
Fetch yours. To-night will settle the great issue
Whether the Prince's or the merchant's steel
Is better tempered. Was not that your word?
Fetch your own sword. Why do you tarry, sir?

SIMONE.
My lord, of all the gracious courtesies
That you have showered upon my barren house
This is the highest.

Bianca, fetch my sword.

Thrust back that stool and table. We must have

An open circle for our match at arms,

And good Bianca here shall hold the torch

Lest what is but a jest grow serious.

BIANCA. [*To* GUIDO]

Oh! kill him, kill him!

SIMONE.

Hold the torch, Bianca.

[*They begin to fight.*]

Have at you! Ah! Ha! would you?

[*He is wounded by* GUIDO.]

A scratch, no more. The torch was in mine eyes.

Do not look sad, Bianca. It is nothing.

Your husband bleeds, 'tis nothing. Take a cloth,

Bind it about mine arm. Nay, not so tight.

More softly, my good wife. And be not sad,

I pray you be not sad. No: take it off.

What matter if I bleed? [*Tears bandage off.*]

Again! again!

[SIMONE *disarms* GUIDO.]

My gentle Lord, you see that I was right.

My sword is better tempered, finer steel,

But let us match our daggers.

BIANCA. [*To* GUIDO]

Kill him! kill him!

SIMONE.

Put out the torch, Bianca.

[BIANCA *puts out the torch.*]

Now, my good Lord,

Now to the death of one, or both of us,

Or all the three it may be.   [*They fight.*]

There and there.

Ah, devil! do I hold thee in my grip?

[SIMONE *overpowers* GUIDO *and throws him down over table.*]

GUIDO.

Fool! Take your strangling fingers from my throat.
I am my father's only son; the State
Has but one heir, and that false enemy France
Waits for the ending of my father's line
To fall upon our city.

SIMONE.

                              Hush! your father
When he is childless will be happier.
As for the State, I think our state of Florence
Needs no adulterous pilot at its helm.
Your life would soil its lilies.

GUIDO.

                            Take off your hands.
Take off your damned hands. Loose me, I say!

SIMONE.

Nay, you are caught in such a cunning vice
That nothing will avail you, and your life
Narrowed into a single point of shame
Ends with that shame and ends most shamefully.

GUIDO.

Oh! let me have a priest before I die!

SIMONE.

What wouldst thou have a priest for? Tell thy sins
To God, whom thou shalt see this very night
And then no more forever. Tell thy sins
To Him who is most just, being pitiless,
Most pitiful being just. As for myself....

GUIDO.

Oh! help me, sweet Bianca! help me, Bianca,
Thou knowest I am innocent of harm.

SIMONE.

What, is there life yet in those lying lips?

Die like a dog with lolling tongue! Die! Die!

And the dumb river shall receive your corse

And wash it all unheeded to the sea.

GUIDO.

Lord Christ receive my wretched soul tonight!

SIMONE.

Amen to that. Now for the other.

[*He dies.* SIMONE *rises and looks at* BIANCA. *She comes towards him as one dazed with wonder and with outstretched arms.*]

BIANCA.

> Why

Did you not tell me you were so strong?

SIMONE.

> Why

Did you not tell me you were beautiful?

> [*He kisses her on the mouth.*]
>
> CURTAIN

La Sainte Courtisane;
Or, The Woman Covered With Jewels

The text is taken from Ross, ed., *Miscellanies* (London: Methuen, 1908), 231–39. The manuscript which Ross almost certainly worked from is in the Clark Library; a transcript of parts of it, indicating the ways in which Ross reordered the material, can be found in Small, *Oscar Wilde Revalued*, 146–48.

> *The scene represents the corner of a valley in the Thebaid. On the right hand of the stage is a cavern. In front of the cavern stands a great crucifix.*
>
> *On the left [sand dunes].*
>
> *The sky is blue like the inside of a cup of lapis lazuli. The hills are of red sand. Here and there on the hills there are clumps of thorns.*

FIRST MAN.

Who is she? She makes me afraid. She has a purple cloak and her hair is like threads of gold. I think she must be the daughter of the Emperor. I have heard the boatmen say that the Emperor has a daughter who wears a cloak of purple.

SECOND MAN.

She has birds' wings upon her sandals, and her tunic is of the colour of green corn. It is like corn in spring when she stands still. It is like young corn troubled by the shadows of hawks when she moves. The pearls on her tunic are like many moons.

FIRST MAN.

They are like the moons one sees in the water when the wind blows from the hills.

SECOND MAN.

I think she is one of the gods. I think she comes from Nubia.

FIRST MAN.

I am sure she is the daughter of the Emperor. Her nails are stained with henna. They are like the petals of a rose. She has come here to weep for Adonis.

SECOND MAN.

She is one of the gods. I do not know why she has left her temple. The gods should not leave their temples. If she speaks to us let us not answer and she will pass by.

FIRST MAN.

She will not speak to us. She is the daughter of the Emperor.

MYRRHINA.

Dwells he not here, the beautiful young hermit, he who will not look on the face of woman?

FIRST MAN.

Of a truth it is here the hermit dwells.

MYRRHINA.

Why will he not look on the face of woman?

SECOND MAN.

We do not know.

MYRRHINA.

Why do ye yourselves not look at me?

FIRST MAN.

You are covered with bright stones, and you dazzle our eyes.

SECOND MAN.

He who looks at the sun becomes blind. You are too bright to look at. It is not wise to look at things that are very bright. Many of the priests in the temples are blind, and have slaves to lead them.

MYRRHINA.

Where does he dwell, the beautiful young hermit who will not look on the face of woman? Has he a house of reeds or a house of burnt clay or does he lie on the hillside? Or does he make his bed in the rushes?

FIRST MAN.

He dwells in that cavern yonder.

MYRRHINA.

What a curious place to dwell in.

FIRST MAN.

Of old a centaur lived there. When the hermit came the centaur gave a shrill cry, wept and lamented, and galloped away.

SECOND MAN.

No. It was a white unicorn who lived in the cave. When it saw the hermit coming the unicorn knelt down and worshipped him. Many people saw it worshipping him.

FIRST MAN.

I have talked with people who saw it.

. . . . .

SECOND MAN.

Some say he was a hewer of wood and worked for hire. But that may not be true.

. . . . .

MYRRHINA.

What gods then do ye worship? Or do ye worship any gods? There are those who have no gods to worship. The philosophers who wear long beards and brown cloaks have no gods to worship. They wrangle with each other in the porticoes. The [   ] laugh at them.

FIRST MAN.

We worship seven gods. We may not tell their names. It is a very dangerous thing to tell the names of the gods. No one should ever tell the name of his god. Even the priests who praise the gods all day long, and eat of their food with them, do not call them by their right names.

MYRRHINA.

Where are these gods ye worship?

FIRST MAN.

We hide them in the folds of our tunics. We do not show them to any one. If we showed them to any one they might leave us.

MYRRHINA.

Where did ye meet with them?

FIRST MAN.

They were given to us by an embalmer of the dead who had found them in a tomb. We served him for seven years.

MYRRHINA.

The dead are terrible. I am afraid of Death.

FIRST MAN.

Death is not a god. He is only the servant of the gods.

MYRRHINA.

He is the only god I am afraid of. Ye have seen many of the gods?

FIRST MAN.

We have seen many of them. One sees them chiefly at night time. They pass one by very swiftly. Once we saw some of the gods at daybreak. They were walking across a plain.

MYRRHINA.

Once as I was passing through the market place I heard a sophist from Cilicia say that there is only one God. He said it before many people.

FIRST MAN.

That cannot be true. We have ourselves seen many, though we are but common men and of no account. When I saw them I hid myself in a bush. They did me no harm.

.   .   .   .   .

MYRRHINA.

Tell me more about the beautiful young hermit. Talk to me about the beautiful young hermit who will not look on the face of woman. What is the story of his days? What mode of life has he?

FIRST MAN.

We do not understand you.

MYRRHINA.

What does he do, the beautiful young hermit? Does he sow or reap? Does he plant a garden or catch fish in a net? Does he weave linen on a loom? Does he set his hand to the wooden plough and walk behind the oxen?

SECOND MAN.

He being a very holy man does nothing. We are common men and of no account. We toil all day long in the sun. Sometimes the ground is very hard.

MYRRHINA.

Do the birds of the air feed him? Do the jackals share their booty with him?

FIRST MAN.

Every evening we bring him food. We do not think that the birds of the air feed him.

MYRRHINA.

Why do ye feed him? What profit have ye in so doing?

SECOND MAN.

He is a very holy man. One of the gods whom he has offended has made him mad. We think he has offended the moon.

MYRRHINA.

Go and tell him that one who has come from Alexandria desires to speak with him.

FIRST MAN.

We dare not tell him. This hour he is praying to his God. We pray thee to pardon us for not doing thy bidding.

MYRRHINA.

Are ye afraid of him?

FIRST MAN.

We are afraid of him.

MYRRHINA.

Why are ye afraid of him?

FIRST MAN.
We do not know.

MYRRHINA.
What is his name?

FIRST MAN.
The voice that speaks to him at night time in the cavern calls to him by the name of Honorius. It was also by the name of Honorius that the three lepers who passed by once called to him. We think that his name is Honorius.

MYRRHINA.
Why did the three lepers call to him?

FIRST MAN.
That he might heal them.

MYRRHINA.
Did he heal them?

SECOND MAN.
No. They had committed some sin: it was for that reason they were lepers. Their hands and faces were like salt. One of them wore a mask of linen. He was a king's son.

MYRRHINA.
What is the voice that speaks to him at night time in his cave?

FIRST MAN.
We do not know whose voice it is. We think it is the voice of his God. For we have seen no man enter his cavern nor any come forth from it.

.   .   .   .   .

MYRRHINA.
Honorius.

HONORIUS (*from within*).
Who calls Honorius?

MYRRHINA.
Come forth, Honorius.

.   .   .   .   .

My chamber is ceiled with cedar and odorous with myrrh. The pillars of my bed are of cedar and the hangings are of purple. My bed is strewn with purple and the steps are of silver. The hangings are sewn with silver pomegranates and the steps that are of silver are strewn with saffron and with myrrh. My lovers hang garlands round the pillars of my house. At night time they come with the flute players and the players of the harp. They woo me with apples and on the pavement of my courtyard they write my name with wine.

From the uttermost parts of the world my lovers come to me. The kings of the earth come to me and bring me presents.

When the Emperor of Byzantium heard of me he left his porphyry chamber and set sail in his galleys. His slaves bare no torches that none might know of his coming. When the King of Cyprus heard of me he sent me ambassadors. The two Kings of Libya who are brothers brought me gifts of amber.

I took the minion of Cæsar from Cæsar and made him my playfellow. He came to me at night in a litter. He was pale as a narcissus, and his body was like honey.

The son of the Præfect slew himself in my honour, and the Tetrarch of Cilicia scourged himself for my pleasure before my slaves.

The King of Hierapolis who is a priest and a robber set carpets for me to walk on.

Sometimes I sit in the circus and the gladiators fight beneath me. Once a Thracian who was my lover was caught in the net. I gave the signal for him to die and the whole theatre applauded. Sometimes I pass through the gymnasium and watch the young men wrestling or in the race. Their bodies are bright with oil and their brows are wreathed with willow sprays and with myrtle. They stamp their feet on the sand when they wrestle and when they run the sand follows them like a little cloud. He at whom I smile leaves his companions and follows me to my home. At other times I go down to the harbour and watch the merchants unloading their vessels. Those that come from Tyre have cloaks of silk and earrings of emerald. Those that come from Massilia have cloaks of fine wool and earrings of brass. When they see me coming they stand on the prows of their ships and call to me, but I do not answer them. I go to the little taverns where the sailors lie all day long drinking black wine and playing with dice and I sit down with them.

I made the Prince my slave, and his slave who was a Tyrian I made my Lord for the space of a moon.

I put a figured ring on his finger and brought him to my house. I have wonderful things in my house.

The dust of the desert lies on your hair and your feet are scratched with thorns and your body is scorched by the sun. Come with me, Honorius, and I will clothe you in a tunic of silk. I will smear your body with myrrh and pour spikenard on your hair. I will clothe you in hyacinth and put honey in your mouth. Love—

HONORIUS.

There is no love but the love of God.

MYRRHINA.

Who is He whose love is greater than that of mortal men?

HONORIUS.

It is He whom thou seest on the cross, Myrrhina. He is the Son of God and was born of a virgin. Three wise men who were kings brought Him offerings, and the shepherds who were lying on the hills were wakened by a great light.

The Sibyls knew of His coming. The groves and the oracles spake of Him. David and the prophets announced Him. There is no love like the love of God nor any love that can be compared to it.

The body is vile, Myrrhina. God will raise thee up with a new body which will not know corruption, and thou wilt dwell in the Courts of the Lord and see Him whose hair is like fine wool and whose feet are of brass.

MYRRHINA.

The beauty ...

HONORIUS.

The beauty of the soul increases till it can see God. Therefore, Myrrhina, repent of thy sins. The robber who was crucified beside Him He brought into Paradise.   [*Exit.*]

MYRRHINA.

How strangely he spake to me. And with what scorn did he regard me. I wonder why he spake to me so strangely.

· · · · ·

HONORIUS.

Myrrhina, the scales have fallen from my eyes and I see now clearly what I did not see before. Take me to Alexandria and let me taste of the seven sins.

MYRRHINA.

Do not mock me, Honorius, nor speak to me with such bitter words. For I have repent-ed of my sins and I am seeking a cavern in this desert where I too may dwell so that my soul may become worthy to see God.

HONORIUS.

The sun is setting, Myrrhina. Come with me to Alexandria.

MYRRHINA.
I will not go to Alexandria.

HONORIUS.
Farewell, Myrrhina.

MYRRHINA.
Honorius, farewell. No, no, do not go.

.   .   .   .   .

I have cursed my beauty for what it has done, and cursed the wonder of my body for the evil that it has brought upon you.

Lord, this man brought me to Thy feet. He told me of Thy coming upon earth, and of the wonder of Thy birth, and the great wonder of Thy death also. By him, O Lord, Thou was revealed to me.

HONORIUS.
You talk as a child, Myrrhina, and without knowledge. Loosen your hands. Why didst thou come to this valley in thy beauty?

MYRRHINA.
The God whom thou worshippest led me here that I might repent of my iniquities and know Him as the Lord.

HONORIUS.
Why didst thou tempt me with words?

MYRRHINA.
That thou shouldst see Sin in its painted mask and look on Death in its robe of Shame.

Index

A

Ackroyd, Peter 6
Adey, More 54–55, 58
Adorno, Theodor 9, 79
Aeschylus 97
Aldrovandi, Ulisse 88–89, 96
Alexander, Bill 123
Alexander, George 17, 119–21, 134, 136
Allen, Grant 4
Andersen, Hans Christian 178
Antinoüs 185
Antoninus, Marcus Aurelius 106–107
Apuleius 94
Archaicistes 103
Aristippus 97
Aristotle 97
Arnold, Matthew
    Essays in Criticism 72
Augustine 62
Austin, Alfred 101

B

Bacon, Sir Francis 21
Backhouse, Trelawny 27
Ballad of Reading Gaol, The 7, 42, 82
Barbizon school 103
Bartlett, Neil 6
Barthes, Roland 79
Bateson, F. W. 121–22
Baudelaire, Charles 18, 22, 94, 165
Baylen, Joseph 25
Beardsley, Aubrey
    The Story of Venus and Tannhäuser 188
Beckson, Karl 31, 147, 155
Belford, Barbara 15
Benjamin, Walter 9, 79
Berggren, Ruth 135
Bible 60, 74, 175
"Birthday of the Infanta, The" 185, 189–90
Bloxam, John Francis 34
Boehme, Jacob 92, 95–96
Borges, Jorge Luis 79
Boroughs, Rod 109
Boswell, James 89–90
    Life of Johnson 88

Bowers, Fredson 52
Bresdin, Rodolphe 103
Bristow, Joseph 40
Brontë, Charlotte 33
Brown, Julia Prewitt 49, 79–80, 83, 87
Brown, Terence 119, 148
Buchanan, Robert 186
Buckle, Henry 78
    History of Civilization in England 84
Burton, Richard
    Arabian Nights 110
Byron 57

C

"Canterville Ghost, The" 170
Cardinal of Avignon, The 10–11, 143, 147–51, 158–60,
    178, 184, 190
Carey, John 110
Carlyle, Thomas
    The French Revolution 89
Carrington, Charles 22
Carson, Edward 11, 32–38, 43, 128–30, 134, 141
Casanova 88–89
Cave, Richard Allen 148, 150, 153
Cellini, Benvenuto 88–89
Chameleon 32–44
Charcot, Jean-Martin 19
Chatterton, Thomas 72–73
Chopin 62
Christ / Christian 56–57, 60, 175–76, 183–84, 187–88
Chuang Tzû 78
Church, A. H.
    Precious Stones Considered 166
Cicero 88–89, 91
Clark, Sir Charles 34–36
Cocks, H. G. 40
Cohen, Ed 22, 31
Cole, Alan S. 165
Coleridge 49, 93
Collini, Stefan 1–2
Collins, John Churton 86
Commonplace Book 72
Comte, Auguste 78
Conrad, Joseph 7, 21, 77
    Heart of Darkness 108
Cook, Matt 40–41
Corot 102–103
Craft, Christopher 6
"Critic as Artist, The" 91–102, 107

Cross, John 33
Cuffe, Hon. Hamilton 24–25
Custance, Olive 13

D

Danney, Philip 68
Dante 60, 62
Darwin, Charles 78
Daubigny 102–103
Daudet, Alphonse 18–19
"Decay of Lying, The" 55, 88–92, 102
Defoe, Daniel 89
    History of the Plague 88
de Goncourt, Edmond
    La Faustin 165
de la Tourette, Georges Gilles 19
de Musset, Alfred 155
De Profundis 7, 9, 44, 47–74, 79–80, 87, 99, 114, 127–28,
    134–35, 138, 140, 143, 146, 158, 160, 170, 179, 183
Dickens, Charles 33, 127
Dionysus 96
Dodgson, Campbell 143
Donohue, Joseph 116, 124, 128, 135–36
Douglas, Lord Alfred 7–8, 13–14, 21–22, 24–29, 32,
    47–51, 54–71, 114, 128, 134–36, 141, 143, 146
    Autobiography 132
Dowling, Linda 78, 95
Duchess of Padua, The 146–47, 151

E

Eckhart, Johannes (Meister) 92–93, 95–96
Eliot, George 33
Eliot, T. S. 4–5, 81, 105
    The Waste Land 108–10
Eliot, Valerie 108
Ellis, Henry Havelock 152
Ellmann, Richard 3, 14–15, 18–31, 37, 43, 49, 57, 168
Eltis, Sos 116, 119
Emerson, Ralph Waldo 78
"English Renaissance of Art, The" 100
Euripides 97
    Heracles 98

F

"Fisherman and His Soul, The" 177–84, 189
Florentine Tragedy, A 10–11, 146–48, 150–60, 189–90
Ford, Ford Madox 165

Forster, John 33
Foucault, Michel 40
France, Anatole 110
Froissart 88
Fronto, Cornelius 96, 105–107

G

Gagnier, Regenia 155–57
Gaskell, Elizabeth 33, 127
Gautier, Théophile 166, 181, 184
    Emaux et camées 171–78
Gide, André 26–28
Gilbert, Brian 8
Gilbert, W. S.
    Engaged 115
Gill, Charles 24–25
Gissing, George 127
Genet, Jean 79
Goethe 60, 62
Gosse, Edmund 152
Grainger, Walter 143
Grant, Duncan 142
Gray, John 29
Greg, W. W. 52
Grote, John
    History of Greece 83

H

Hanno
    Periplus 88
"Happy Prince, The" 11, 21, 170–73, 181, 185, 187–89
Happy Prince and Other Tales, The 169
Harris, Frank 13–14, 18–19, 147
Hart-Davis, Rupert 3, 14, 16, 50, 71
Hazlitt, W. Carew 111
    Essays and Criticisms by Thomas Griffiths Wainewright
    73, 91
Hegel, Friedrich 78, 87
    Lectures on the Philosophy of History 83
Helfand, Michael S. 78, 83, 86–87
Henley, W. E. 32, 39
Herodotus 84, 88–89
    Histories 90–91
Heron-Allen, Edward
    Ashes of the Future 165
Hichens, Robert
    The Green Carnation 95
Hoggart, Richard 5

Holland, Merlin 6, 16, 19–20, 24, 148, 150, 153

Holland, Vyvyan 13–14

Hope, Adrian 29

House of Pomegranates, A 169, 174, 178, 185

Housman, A. E. 20

Housman, Laurence 28

Huysmans, J.-K.
  A Rebours 103, 110, 165, 181

Hyde, H. Montgomery 14, 16, 21, 24

Hypnerotomachia 94

I

Ideal Husband, An 55, 114–16, 120, 123, 126, 131, 133, 137, 142–46, 160, 167

Importance of Being Earnest, The 6, 17, 21, 26, 39, 53, 55, 98–99, 114–16, 120, 124–37, 140, 147, 156, 164, 167

Impressionism 103–104

Intentions 9, 55, 62, 66, 72–73, 77–112, 165, 167, 169, 171, 174

Ives, George 41

J

Jackson, Russell 138–40

James, Henry 7, 24, 77, 104, 159

Jones, Henry Arthur 21, 82, 115, 139
  The Case of Rebellious Susan 133

Jones, William
  History and Mystery of Precious Stones 165

Jopling, Louise 31

Jowett, Benjamin 111
  Dialogues of Plato 101

Joyce, James 4, 165

K

Kant 9, 79
  Critique of Pure Reason 80

Kaplan, Joel 119–20

Keats 66

Kelly, Walter K. 111

Kiberd, Declan 79

Kierkegaard, Søren 79

Knox, Melissa 15, 19, 24–25

Kott, Jan 122

Kronenberger, Louis 14

Kropotkin, Prince Peter 78

L

Lady Windermere's Fan 72, 95, 99, 114–16, 120, 123, 132, 140, 145, 146–47, 158, 168

Lambart, Alfred 68

Lane, John 30

Lawrence, D. H. 34

Leavis, F. R. 5, 121–22

Lee, Sir Sydney 33

Lefébure, Ernest
  Embroidery and Lace 166

Le Gallienne, Richard 30–31, 95

Lewis, Sir George 65, 69

Livy 105

Lloyd, Fabian 22

Lodge, David 4

Longinus 96

"Lord Arthur Savile's Crime" 128, 170, 191–93

Lord Arthur Savile's Crime and Other Stories 169, 190

Lorrain, Jean 110

Louÿs, Pierre 110

Lucian 96

Lycosthenes, Conrad 89, 96
  Prodigiorum et Ostentorum Chronicon 88

M

Mackail, J. W. 85

Macmillan 167, 184

Magnus, Olaus 88–89, 96

Mallock, W. H.
  The New Republic 93–94

Malory, Sir Thomas 88–89

Marvell, Andrew
  "To His Coy Mistress" 110

Mason, Stuart 80–82
  Bibliography of Oscar Wilde 15, 85, 149

Masson, David 73

Matthiessen, F. O. 4

Maturin, Charles
  Melmoth the Wanderer 165

Mavor, Sidney 132

McBath, Robert L. 25

McKenna, Neil 2, 6, 8, 11, 15, 23, 25–31, 36–37, 41–44, 93, 140–41, 161, 193

Meinhold, Wilhelm
  Sidonia the Sorceress 165

Mercure de France, 55, 60, 64, 66–68

modernism / modernist 6, 81

Mommsen, Theodor
  History of Rome 84, 86

Monet 102–103

Moore, Thomas Sturge 148, 150, 152, 155–56

Moreau, Gustave 103

Morley, John 186

Morley, Sheridan 14

Morris, William 171
    "The Hill of Venus" 187

Mount-Temple, Lady 143

Mr. and Mrs. Daventry 147

Murray, Isobel, 48, 78–79

N

Napoleon 88–89

Narcissus 186

Nelson, Major 59

Nietzsche, Friedrich 9, 77, 79

Noel, Roden 152

O

Orwell, George 5

Osbourne, Lloyd, 48

Oscariana 3

Ovid 105

P

Palimieri, Matteo 101

Parker, Charles 129–30

Pater, Walter 7, 24, 33, 77, 81, 83, 92–97, 100–101, 104–11, 184
    Appreciations 92
    Imaginary Portraits 72–73, 95
    Marius the Epicurean 94–96, 105–109, 165
    The Renaissance 93–95, 105, 165, 188
    "Style" 95

Pausanias 96

Pearce, Joseph 15

"Pen, Pencil, and Poison" 73, 90–91, 94, 97–8, 111, 138, 177

"Phrases and Philosophies for the Use of the Young" 33–34, 73

Philo Judaeus 92–93, 95

Picture of Dorian Gray, The 7, 11, 20–21, 29, 31–39, 72, 77, 82, 98, 109, 110, 116, 138, 140, 145, 150, 153, 158, 164–93
    Preface to 63, 66, 171

Pine, Richard 79

Pinero, Arthur Wing 21, 82

Pissarro 103

Plato 92–93, 95, 97, 100–101, 105

Pliny 89, 96, 105
    Natural History 88

Poe, Edgar Allan
    "The Oval Portrait" 165

Poems 151

Polo, Marco 88–89

Polybius 84, 99
    Histories 100

"Portrait of Mr. W. H., The" 39, 169–70

postmodernism / postmodernist 77, 81, 112, 116

Poulet-Malassis, Auguste 18

Pound, Ezra 4, 108–109
    Hugh Selwyn Mauberley 175

Proudhon, Pierre-Joseph 78

Prowse, Philip 122–23

Q

Queensberry, Lady 60, 68

Queensberry, Marquess of 32, 36, 65
    Queensberry libel trial 11, 16, 32–36, 39, 65, 73, 128–29, 132, 134, 143

Quintillian 96

R

Raby, Peter 17

Raffalovich, André 29–30
    Uranisme et Unisexualité 110

Ransome, Arthur 18–19, 50–51

Redon, Odilion 103

Renan, Ernest
    Vie de Jésus 56

Rhys, Ernest 152

"Rise of Historical Criticism, The" 80–81, 83–87, 98–99

Robins, Elizabeth 21

Rodd, Rennell 30

Rogers, Charles
    Boswelliana: The Commomplace Book of James Boswell 90

Rosebery, Lord 22, 25

Ross, Robert 7, 15, 17, 18–19, 26–27, 29, 47, 49–51, 55–56, 58–64, 69, 71, 84–85
    Collected Edition 17, 53, 81, 148, 150–51

Rossetti, Dante Gabriel 33, 73

Rubinstein, Anton 126

Ruskin, John
    Praeterita 33

S

Sainte Courtisane, La 10–11, 146–48, 159–60, 178, 182, 184, 189–90

Sallust
  Bellum Catilinae 91

Salome 10, 95, 146–47, 159, 167, 181, 184, 190

Satyricon 22, 108–11, 173

Schiller, Friedrich 9, 79

Schmidgall, Gary 15, 23–25

Schwob, Marcel 110

Schroeder, Horst 39

Scott, Clement 120

"Selfish Giant, The" 21, 170

Shakespeare 16, 21, 33, 39, 53, 62, 122, 157
  As You Like It 152
  Hamlet 56, 60, 152
  Henry IV 152
  Twelfth Night 152

Shaw, George Bernard 116

Shelley
  The Cenci 150, 152

Sherard, Robert Harborough 13–14, 21, 66–68

Shewan, Rodney 147

Showalter, Elaine 41

Sinfield, Alan 21, 23, 40, 132, 142

Smith, Philip E., II 78, 83, 86–87

Smithers, Leonard 42–43, 115, 135

"Soul of Man Under Socialism, The" 15, 78

Spencer, Herbert 84

Spenser, Edmund
  Prothalamion 110

Sphinx, The 31, 151, 171, 184, 185

"Sphinx without a Secret, The" 191

Spinoza, 72–73, 171

Stephens, Sir Leslie 33

Stevenson, Robert Louis
  Dr. Jekyll and Mr. Hyde 37–38, 48, 165
  Treasure Island 39

Stoddart, James 178

Stowell, Sheila 119

Strachey, Lytton 142, 145

Suetonius 88
  Lives of the Caesars 165

Sutherland, John 4

Swedenborg 92, 95
  De Coelo et ejus mirabilibus 96

Swinburne, Algernon Charles 33, 111, 152
  "Laus Veneris" 187
  Notes on Poems and Reviews 176, 186
  Poems and Ballads 176, 186–87
  Songs before Sunrise 186

Under the Microscope 186

Symonds, John Addington 28
  Many Moods: A Volume of Verses 185
  Studies of the Greek Poets 83
  The Renaissance in Italy 166

Symons, Arthur 152

syphilis 18–19

T

Tacitus 88–89
  Annals 91

Tannhäuser 187–88

Taylor, Alfred 129–30, 132

Teleny 23

Tennyson
  In Memoriam 61

Thucydides 84, 99

Tóibín, Colm 6

Tree, Herbert Beerbolm 119–20, 142

Turner, Reginald 18–19

Tylor, Edward 78

U

Ulrichs, Karl Heinrich 110

V

Vera; Or, the Nihilists 146–47

Virgil 105

Vizetelly, Henry 32, 36

W

Wagner, Richard (see also *Tannhäuser*) 187

Wainewright, Thomas Griffiths 73, 90–91, 94, 177

Ward, Lock & Co. 36, 168

White, Gleeson 30

Wife's Tragedy, A 147

Wilde, Constance 3, 140, 143

Wilde, Oscar
  bankruptcy 15
  plagiarism 5, 6, 116
  nationality 121
  (homo)sexuality, sexual life 2, 8, 15, 18–43, 78, 129–34, 140–46, 168, 173
  trials (see also Queensberry) 7, 16, 21, 24, 29, 40, 65, 134

Willard, Edward Smith 150–51, 153

Williams, Raymond 5

Wilson, Daniel 73

Woman of No Importance, A 34, 39, 70, 72, 98, 114–16, 120, 123, 137, 141–46, 158, 191

Woodcock, George 78–79

Woolf, Virginia 165

Wordsworth 62, 88–89
    Lyrical Ballads 90

Wortham, Briscoe 69

Wyndham, Charles 139

Y

Yeats, W. B. 79

"Young King, The" 11, 185–89

Z

Zola, Emile 32